The COMPLETE IDIOT'S GUIDE TO

Excel for Windows® 95

by LauraMaery Gold and Dan Post

A Division of Macmillan Publishing
A Prentice Hall Macmillan Company
201 W.103rd Street, Indianapolis, IN 46290

International Standard Book Number: 0-7897-0640-7
Library of Congress Catalog Card Number: 94-73410

97 96 95 8 7 6 5 4 3 2 1

Interpretation of the printing code: the rightmost number of the first series of numbers is the year of the book's printing; the rightmost number of the second series of numbers is the number of the book's printing. For example, a printing code of 95-1 shows that the first printing of the book occurred in 1995.

Screen reproductions in this book were created by means of the program Collage Complete from Inner Media, Inc., Hollis, NH.

Printed in the United States of America

Publisher
Roland Elgey

Vice President and Publisher
Marie Butler-Knight

Editorial Services Director
Elizabeth Keaffaber

Publishing Manager
Barry Pruett

Managing Editor
Michael Cunningham

Development Editor
Melanie Palaisa

Technical Editor
Herb Feltner

Production Editor
Mark Enochs

Copy Editor
Audra Gable

Cover Designer
Dan Armstrong
Barbara Kordesh

Book Designer
Kim Scott

Illustrations
Judd Winick

Technical Specialist
Cari Skaggs

Indexer
Kathy Venable

Production Team
Steve Adams, Chad Dressler, Terri Edwards, Joan Evan, DiMonique Ford, John Hulse, Damon Jordan, Beth Lewis, Gina Rexrode, Michael Thomas, Jody York

Contents at a Glance

Contents

Part 2: Build Your Own Spreadsheet 53

6 Enter Here: Entering Data in a Worksheet 55

7 Shake, Copy, and Move: Filling Blocks of Cells 69

8 The Editing Test: Change the Contents of Your Spreadsheet 79

Introduction

Welcome to *The Complete Idiot's Guide to Excel for Windows 95*, a book about getting started now. If you want to become the office computer guru, consider another approach (three years in a seminary should do). But if what you really want to do is dig right in and get down to the business of working with your spreadsheet, then, buddy, you're in the right place 'cuz that's what we're here to do. This book is for people like you who, while cognizant of the status computers have gained in their lives, still prefer to have no more than a professional relationship with their machines.

In this book, you won't find yourself buried under mountains of techno-jargon, tossed in simply to please the computerazzi. And we won't wax poetic about how computers are more dependable than a mate. (You already know that, so what would be the point?) We took great care to assemble a book that is both informative and caffeinated.

So sit back and make yourself comfortable. We prefer the leaning-back/feet-on-desk/straddling-the-monitor work position—so you will ring the doorbell before you walk in on us that way, won't you?

How Do I Use This Book?

This is a guide book, and it's best absorbed in smaller bits and pieces. Consider Chapter 1 essential, and take it anywhere you want from there.

You'll find that most of your work can be done using just the basic spreadsheet features, which are covered in Parts 1 and 2 of this book. But keep us around for those times when you have to dig around for information on unusual tasks such as generating a database list, importing a chart, or adding a song to your spreadsheet. These skills are covered in Parts 3 and 4. In Part 5, you'll find all sorts of groovy appendices, including a list of every Excel function in the world and a complete listing of Excel keystrokes for people who hate to use the mouse.

We've used a few conventions in this book to help... well, really, to help ourselves find our place in the book, but we expect these conventions will help you, too. For example, if you need to select, press, or type something, we made it **bold**. Elements within Excel's dialog boxes (which you'll learn about in Chapter 3) appear in a different type to make them easier to distinguish. And we *italicized* words that have earned a place in "Speak Like a Geek: The Complete Archive," a comprehensive glossary found at the back of the book.

In addition, we added some helpful hints in shaded boxes like the ones shown here.

Techno Nerd Teaches

You'll see Techno Nerd Teaches boxes fairly often in this book. In these boxes, we've placed definitions and tables that, although perhaps not 100 percent essential to the operation being described, are absolutely essential for joining in the conversation at International Geek Fest.

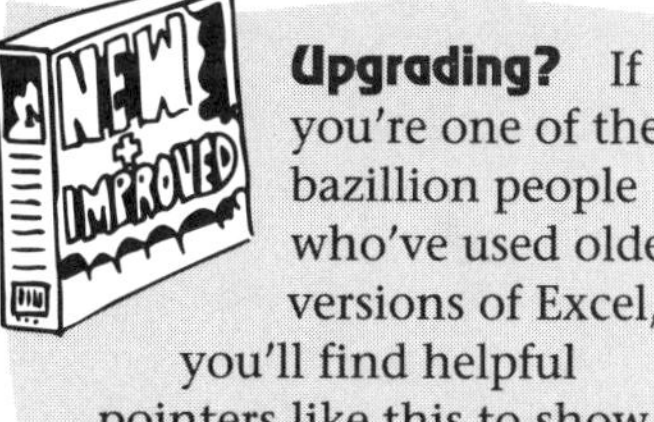

Upgrading? If you're one of the 200 bazillion people who've used older versions of Excel, you'll find helpful pointers like this to show you how it's changed in this, version 7.

Check This Out...

Check This Out When we've got a really cool secret tip or shortcut, we've placed it in a box like this. When you've finished reading the tip, tear it out of the book and eat it.

Acknowledgments

Thanks to Martha O'Sullivan and Melanie Palaisa for their guidance, for their help when things went crash, and for keeping us awake.

Thanks to Stan Zielinski, friend, dad, and countryman, for some solicited advice.

Hugs and kisses to our friends and neighbors for not commenting on the unwashed, unkempt look we've tried to make fashionable the last month or so.

Sye-Sye to Dean Bottorff, for years of making at least one of us smart about computers.

And thanks, most of all, to our kiddos, who spent most of a summer on tiptoe. Pack up the car, kids! It's time for Disneyland!

Trademarks

We used lots of words in this book. Many of them are probably copyrighted, trademarked, double-crossed, tick-marked, pock-marked and hexed. The following words, for example, are trademarks and proper nouns, not to be messed with by amateurs:

CorelDRAW

dBase

Lotus 1-2-3

Macintosh

Microsoft Excel

Microsoft Query

Paradox

Taco Bell

Donald Trump

Terms suspected of being trademarks or service marks have been appropriately capitalized. Que cannot attest to the accuracy of this information. Use of a term in this book should not be regarded as affecting the validity of any trademark or service mark.

Part 1
Just Enough to Be Dangerous

You've got to start somewhere! But if this is the only section you read, we prefer that you continue to work strictly on your own machine.

In this section, you'll get started by learning how to open an existing spreadsheet (A.K.A., a template), move the cursor around, enter data, print, and close. This section also covers differences between Excel 5.0 and Excel for Windows 95.

Chapter 1

The Top 10 Things You Need to Know

What? Are you serious? You really thought you could learn Excel in 10 easy steps?

There's a good reason this book weighs more than a quarter pound (before cooking): Excel is more complicated than Woody Allen's love life.

Nevertheless, this chapter is going to take its best shot at giving you Excel in Ten Easy Pieces. No fancy-pants techno-jargon to make the gang at Denny's think you've gone smart on them. No-sirree. Just enough so you can sit back in your chair with a self-satisfied smirk and declare, "Look, Ma, I'm crunching numbers!"

1. Getting Started

You can't impress people with a screen full of nothing but screen saver—unless, of course, you've got the *Sports Illustrated* swimsuit edition screen saver (which, by the way, we found to be extremely distasteful and exploiting on both our 13- and 21-inch monitors).

Power up your PC, and you'll find yourself staring in bewilderment at the standard Windows 95 interface.

If you're really, really fortunate, you may find a picture—or *icon*—labelled "Excel" or "Microsoft Excel" right there on your opening screen. It could be floating forlornly by itself in the middle of the screen, or it could be part of a collection of icons—called a *toolbar*—for the Microsoft Office suite of applications.

If you see the icon, click on it, quick! ("Click on it" is geek-speak for using your mouse to move the arrow-shaped *pointer* to the Start button and then pressing the left-hand mouse button. Using the word "click" all the time gets annoying, so we occasionally swap in new words like "select" or "choose" or "pick" or "activate" or "highlight.")

If you don't immediately see the Excel icon, don't give up hope. We'll get you started anyway.

In the lower left corner is a button labeled Start. Click on it with your mouse. When you click on the Start button, the Start menu appears (see the following figure).

Getting started with Windows 95.

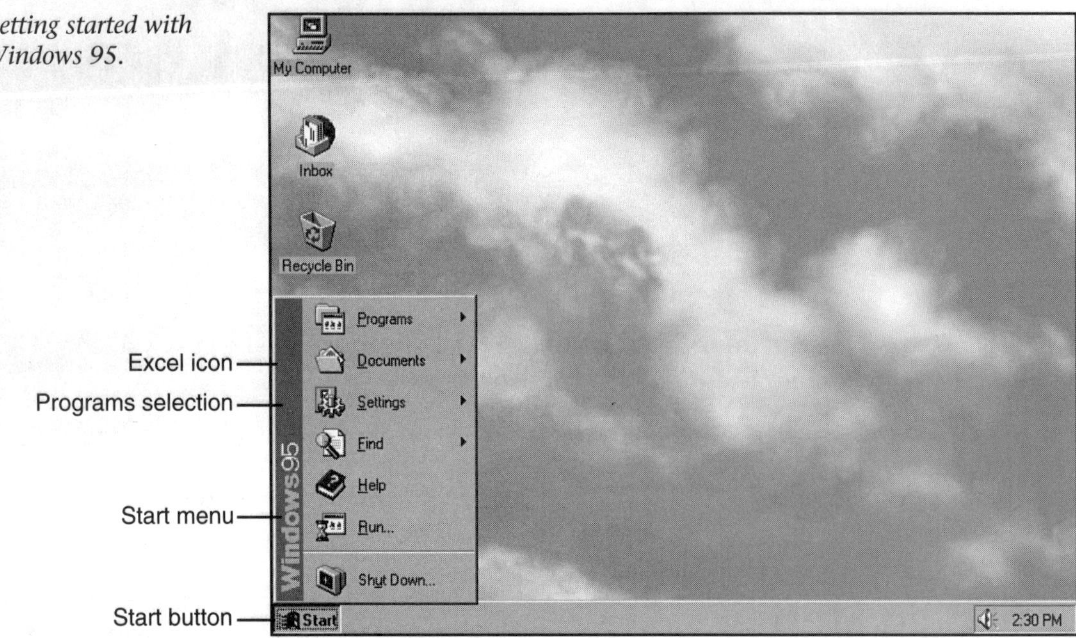

You may see the Excel icon near the top of your Start menu. If not, you'll have to dig deeper. Move your pointer to the **Programs** selection. When the Programs menu appears, find the Excel icon. Depending on your set-up, you may need to dig through a menu called Microsoft Office to find the Excel icon. Once you find it, move your pointer over to the **Excel** listing and give it a click.

Take this opportunity to engage in witty chat with your friends. Excel is loading. Then turn to Chapter 2, "Know Before You Go," to find out what to do next.

2. What It Is

This is not something you really need to know to get things started, but if you're going to go around yelling things like, "Look, Ma, I'm crunching numbers," you need to be prepared to answer a few questions.

Cells are little rectangles that hold your spreadsheet data, and they are organized in rows and columns. Each spreadsheet full of cells—blank or otherwise—is called a *worksheet*. Excel gathers up a handful of worksheets and combines them in a single *workbook*. If somebody (your employer, for example) wants to know more than that, direct her to Chapter 2, "Know Before You Go."

3. What's New

This item presumes that you are actually a grizzly old Excel vet—the kind who grew up thinking Backspace was a pencil eraser and Ctrl+Alt+Del was when you crumpled up a sheet of paper and tossed it in the can. That's you? Welcome to the '90s. And if you hear anyone say Excel was better in the old days, take them on a tour of Chapter 2, where we explain what's changed since version 5.

4. Pre-Existing Spreadsheets

One way to look good fast is to load up someone else's work and treat it as your own. There's an ugly word for that in the book business, but in Excel it's called using templates, and you can't go to jail for it.

But instead of giving away the whole store, we'll just recommend Chapter 3, "Getting to Know You," for your reading enjoyment.

5. Printing

No operation is complete without proof, and what better proof than a printout? Okay, a letter with the raised seal of a notary public might provide better proof, but if you do that, your friends won't be impressed with how well you know Excel. They'll just think you're nuts!

Check out the printing facts in Chapter 4.

6. Call for Help

Don't know what a particular button is for? Hold the mouse over it long enough, and an explanation appears.

Excel excels at providing on-screen information. Click the **Help** button and move the new question-mark pointer over any item you have a question about. Excel may provide an answer. (Of course, sometimes it may not, which is why you absolutely must have this book.) Read more about the Help button and other Help features in Chapter 5, "Help, Help."

7. Write It Down

Excel expects that you'll enter data correctly, but if you don't, the program can adjust a bit with its automatic correction features. For example, Excel corrects your spelling for you. Go ahead and mistype the word "teh," followed by a space, in a cell. Did you see what happened?

Unfortunately, it can't check your numbers for you, which won't help much as far as impressing your friends goes. But you can learn about all of Excel's data entry rules and tricks in Chapters 6 through 9.

8. Calculating Formulas

We can give you one here, but that's all.

=SUM(A1+B1)

There. That's all you get, for now.

Overall, Excel can handle more than 300 functions, more than 4,000 cell locations per worksheet, up to 255 worksheets per workbook, and as many workbooks as your system can hold. That makes for a lot of formula possibilities. To learn more, check out Chapters 10, 11, and 12.

9. Juggling in Excel

Sometimes you find you just have too many things going on at the same time to be neat and organized. You should learn, right from the start, to keep a clean hard disk with plain, easy-to-remember folder and file names. We show you lots of other tips and tricks for keeping things clean, managing multiple files, and prettying them all up in Chapters 13 through 16.

10a. Graphing

Graphing earns an entire section in this book, but if you just want a sneak peak at what's possible, find the ChartWizard button and give it a click. It's easy to find. It's the one near the top right corner of your screen that says ChartWizard when you rest the pointer on it.

Of course, you'll only scratch the surface with that hint. You can display data in 2-D, 3-D, or splattered across a map of the United States of America. So we think everyone will understand when you opt for the orderly and logical approach of checking out Chapter 17, "Graphics Workshop," first and then moving on to Chapter 18, "Top of the Charts," and Chapter 19, "Mapping Your Future."

10b. Data Manipulation

See? We told you you couldn't learn it in 10 steps.

Data manipulation is the heart and soul of spreadsheeting: the endless playing of what-if games. Create and chart scenarios and possibilities. Show your boss what would happen if he gave you that raise. "See," you'll be able to say, "The company doesn't go down in flames." For superior data manipulation techniques, check out Part 4 called, appropriately enough "Data Manipulation." For an extra special treat and a real display of power, take a close look at Chapter 22, "PivotTables." You'll be moving items around so quickly you'll have your '60s friends thinking—flashbacks!

There they are: ten items, more or less, that you need to know to get started. Oh sure there's more. That's why there's a book attached to the back of this page.

So make yourself comfortable, back up your good files, and get ready to go. Feel free to play around with Excel as you go through this book. And don't worry. As long as you don't remove the back cover of your monitor and drool on the live components, you're perfectly safe fiddling around.

Chapter 2

Know Before You Go

In This Chapter

- Spreadsheets then and now
- What's in the big (13-inch) picture
- Getting started
- The old vs. new
- Always allowed: An almanac of all-purpose advice

In the beginning, there were accountants. Regular people just didn't have time to deal with numbers. They had other, more important matters to deal with—learning to shave with stones, for example. It was a time when fast food referred to the speed of the chosen prey.

The tools of ancient accountants were roughly similar to those in use by American rioters today, consisting generally of a rock, a chisel, and a basket of apples pilfered from Eve. This period produced some of the most profound mathematical puzzles of all time: if Johnny had six apples and split them evenly among his four friends, how many apples would Johnny have?

Many an apoplectic seizure occurred when an uninitiated layman questioned his accountant about the figures on the stone tablet and asked, "What if we changed...?"

Spreadsheet Primer: An Introduction to Spreadsheets

The notion of an accounting spreadsheet didn't change much until the 1970s, when the personal computer came onto the scene. Only a few visionaries and a handful of enthusiasts seemed to realize at the time that a revolution was beginning (although there is always someone who will claim that Nostradamus first predicted Excel for Windows 95 way back in 1555). To the less visionary among us, personal computers seemed to be the thing that would forever protect us against the embarrassment of writing another bad check.

If you've used other software—word processors or databases, for example—you'll recognize some vague similarities between those programs and the Excel spreadsheet. The Excel spreadsheet looks something like a word processor, as viewed through the bars of a prison cell.

Cell. That's a word you'll see frequently throughout this text. A spreadsheet is a collection of *cells* arranged in columns and rows. Cells can hold numbers, text, or formulas. Each cell has an *address*, the point where the row and the column intersect. Figure out how to speak in spreadsheet cryptics, and you'll soon find yourself talking to your supervisor in condescending tones, like this: "It's simple, sir. Cell B3 starts at column B as labeled across the top of the spreadsheet grid and continues down until it intersects with row 3, as labeled on the left side of the grid. That internal cell reference you see on the right is a trace to cell D5."

Ask What It Can Do for You

Once you start using a spreadsheet, you can put away your abacus for good. A spreadsheet automates all the recalculating that has to be done each time you change a value. Remember that battered piece of scratch paper you used for algebra class in high school? You had to erase and change every problem on it at least twice, and every change meant you had to completely recalculate from top to bottom. At the time it seemed as though your entire junior prom night might be spent running through the calculations "one more time."

A spreadsheet enables you to do what you wish you could have done with that piece of paper (and your prom date): play around all evening and never make a permanent commitment. It does all the recalculating automatically without ever causing a bit of trouble. Let's stop the analogy here, before someone turns on the cold water. In a spreadsheet, you write complicated formulas only once, and to make that job even easier, software manufacturers have tried to anticipate your needs by creating a number of *templates*, spreadsheets that are already made up, tested, and ready to go. Okay, that's quite enough of that.

Excel's spreadsheets, or *worksheets*, are something like those battered sheets of paper from algebra class. Now imagine a folder with 16 of those battered pieces of paper. That folder is what Excel calls a *workbook*.

Let's look now at a real spreadsheet. There's no time like the present. (Actually, there are probably seven or eight times like the present, but never mind.)

Getting Started

If you've run other software under Windows 95 then, yes, there has definitely been a time like the present. You grizzly old vets of other Win 95 applications can skip this section and use the time to reflect on the past or settle in for an afternoon nap.

Get to Know Your Mouse

Elephants hate mice. You, on the other hand, can develop a close personal relationship with yours. Most everything you do in Windows 95 and its applications, you can do with a mouse.

Your computer mouse has a ball on the bottom and two or three buttons on top. You use the mouse to control the *mouse pointer*, the little cursor on your screen that's usually shaped like an arrow. You move the mouse on your desk in the direction you want to move the mouse pointer on the screen.

The left mouse button is the "do it" button: it tells Windows to execute whatever command the mouse pointer indicates. Throughout this text, we tell you to *click* on certain things. That means you position your mouse pointer on the specified item and click the left button.

Sometimes you'll be instructed to *double-click* on an object. That means you point at the object and press the left mouse button twice quickly. See? This isn't rocket science.

When you see an instruction to *drag* something (usually the frame of a window), you point at that thing, press and hold down the left mouse button, and move the mouse to a new position.

Occasionally, we tell you to *right-click* (click on the right mouse button), which gives you access to various shortcut menus. Never, ever do we tell you to use the middle button—which should delight the owners of two-button mice.

In the Beginning...

In the beginning, you see the Windows 95 screen, a few significant icons on the left, and the all-important taskbar at the bottom. On the left end of the taskbar is the Start button, your access point for almost anything you want to do with Windows 95. Click on the **Start** button, and the Start menu pops up.

Move the pointer up the Start menu and position it over the **Programs** selection. The Programs menu appears to the right. Move through your folders until you locate the Excel folder. You may find Excel located in the Microsoft Office folder if you purchased it as part of that package. See the installation guide (Appendix A) for details on Excel installations. Once you find the right folder, click on the **Excel** icon and make yourself comfortable while Windows 95 loads Excel.

What's on the Big (13-Inch) Screen

Let's try a quick run-through of what first appears on the main Excel screen. To help make it interesting, try getting through the next paragraph without taking a breath.

From top to bottom, the Excel screen features the Title bar, Main menu, Standard toolbar, Formatting toolbar, Formula bar, and worksheet area. Across the bottom you find file-folder-like tabs for the worksheet pages, as well as the horizontal scroll bar and a status bar. At the far right of the screen is the vertical scroll bar.

Whew! Now the details. Holding your breath through this section is for iron-lunged readers only.

Judging a (Work) Book by Its Title (Bar)

The trend today in computing is to make software as simple as possible. Okay, not simple, actually. More like identical. Little Stepford software that give you the eerie feeling of viewing an Andy Warhol print gone bad. To help you get your bearings, Windows 95 displays a Title bar across the top of every program window you open. The *Title bar* tells you the name of the program you're running—Excel, we hope—as well as the name of the file you're working on.

To the far right are three small display buttons:

The Minimize button reduces the program to a button on the Windows taskbar at the bottom of your screen. Reopen the minimized window by clicking on it from the taskbar.

The Maximize button toggles between full-screen and window view.

The Close button closes the application.

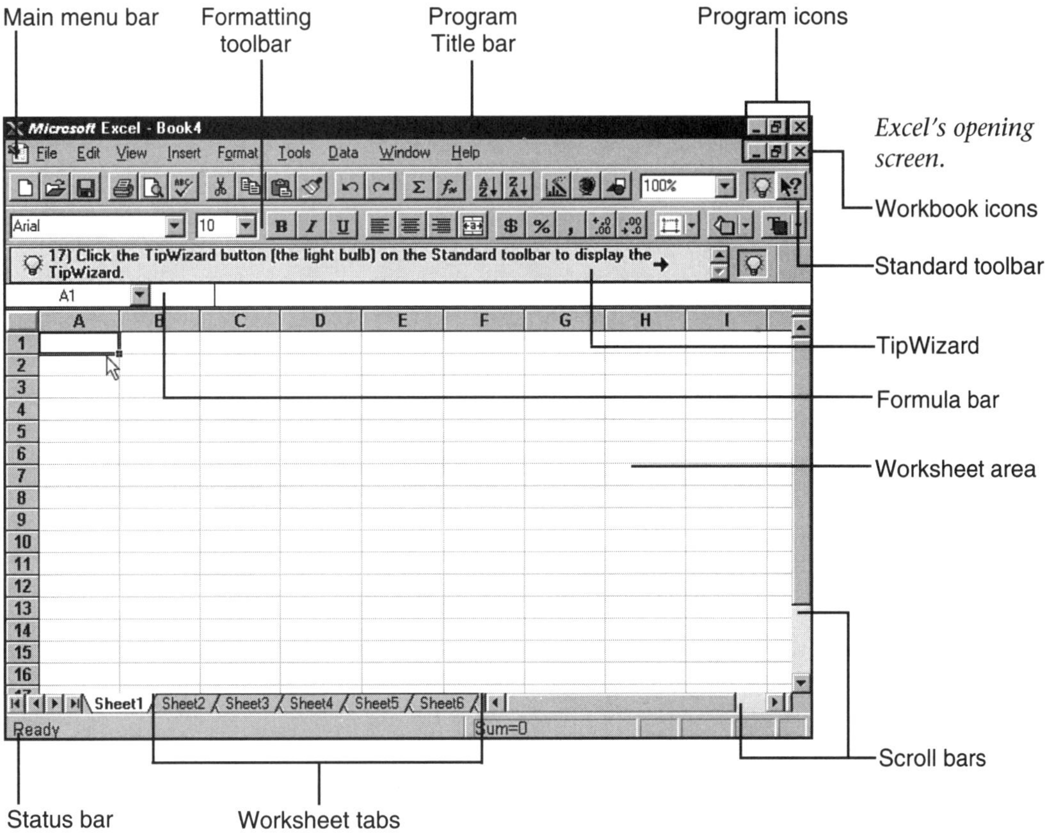
Main menu bar
Formatting toolbar
Program Title bar
Program icons
Workbook icons
Standard toolbar
TipWizard
Formula bar
Worksheet area
Scroll bars
Status bar
Worksheet tabs
Microsoft Excel - Book4
File Edit View Insert Format Tools Data Window Help
17) Click the TipWizard button (the light bulb) on the Standard toolbar to display the TipWizard.
Sheet1 Sheet2 Sheet3 Sheet4 Sheet5 Sheet6
Ready
Sum=0

Excel's opening screen.

Check This Out...

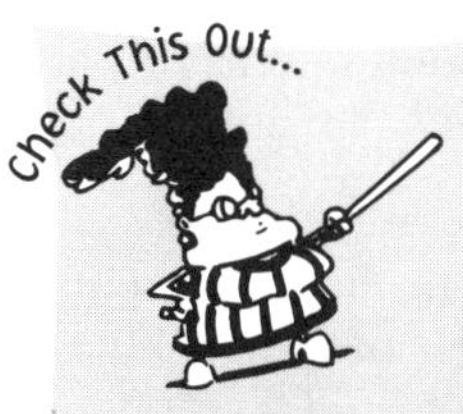

Your Screen Doesn't Look Like This?

When you first open Excel, you may see an extra toolbar called the WorkGroup toolbar. This toolbar includes buttons that enable you to perform tasks in a networked environment. For example, you can use these buttons to send and receive e-mail, write-protect your workbook so others on the network can look at it but can't change it, update a read-only workbook (assuming someone on the network or work group makes changes you want to save), find a file, or add a routing slip to the current workbook. To remove this toolbar from view, click on **View** in the Main Menu bar and click on **Toolbars**. In the Toolbars dialog box, click on the **WorkGroup** check box to remove the check. Click **OK** and the toolbar disappears.

Menu, Please

Directly below the Title bar is Excel's *Main menu bar*, which breaks out Excel commands into groups of related functions. The commands on the menu bar are grouped under File, Edit, View, Insert, Format, Tools, Data, Window, and Help. To the right are three more display buttons. The first reduces the workbook (not the entire program) to an icon within the Excel window. The second toggles between full Excel screen and Excel window view. The third button closes the current workbook.

About That Toolbar in the Window (The One with the Waggily Icon)

Excel displays several *toolbars*: ribbons of buttons and controls that are designed to simplify your work. Some of the icons have obvious meaning; others, however, are mysteries that rival the Sphinx puzzle. Fortunately, no matter how mysterious, toolbar buttons generally duplicate commands that you can access via the menus. That means you've almost always got at least two ways to do something.

Check This Out...

What Does This One Do? Confused by all the toolbar buttons on your screen? To find out what one does, position your mouse pointer over a button on the Standard toolbar. The room around you grows dark, thunder sounds in the distant plains, and an explanation appears on-screen. Fear not. The explanation disappears when you move the pointer.

Excel has multiple toolbars, all of which are basically alike: a logical grouping of shortcut buttons. For now, we concern ourselves only with the two that appear on the opening screen.

- **Standard toolbar** The Standard toolbar features shortcut icons for the most common commands you use in Excel; using these toolbar buttons saves you from having to search through the menu items (if you can figure out what they all mean).
- **Formatting toolbar** Next up (or down, as the case may be) is the Formatting toolbar. The Formatting toolbar bundles those commands that have to do with the appearance of your text: font type, size, alignment, and other options. Turn to Chapter 16 for a discussion of these functions.

The TipWizard

The TipWizard is a toolbar that suggests more efficient ways to perform an Excel task. You'll find a complete explanation of TipWizard and other Help features in Chapter 5. Click the **TipWizard** button on the Standard toolbar to hide or unhide the TipWizard. We've hidden it for the screens shown in this book.

A Winning Formula

In the fifth position (below the Formatting toolbar), is the Formula bar. The *Formula bar* gives you information about the active cell. You can enter and edit formulas in the Formula bar. Chapter 8 explains editing in general, and Chapter 11 explains how to use formulas.

The Work Area

And now, the reason we are here: the worksheet. This collection of cells, very cleverly laid out in columns and rows, is where you do all of the real "spreadsheet" work. Your labels (the titles you put at the tops of columns and the left of rows), values, formulas, or whatever else you might choose to slap down on a sheet of paper all come to life here. The following figure shows the elements of a worksheet.

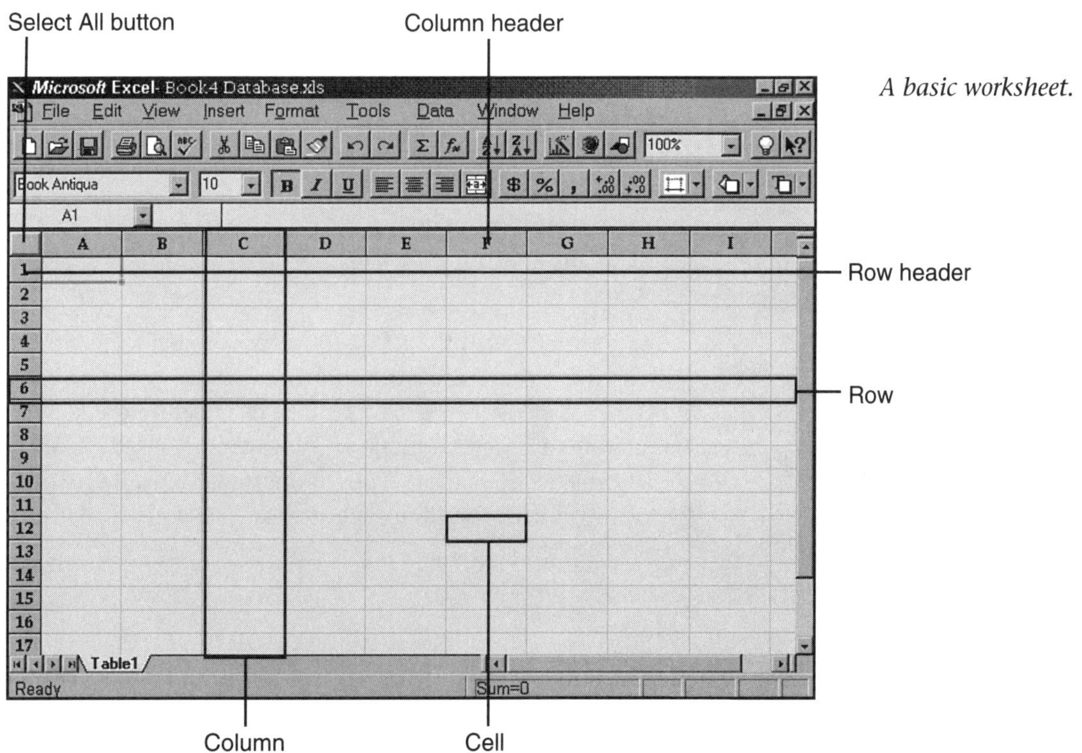

A basic worksheet.

Highlighting, or selecting, cells is a life skill as fundamental as walking, balancing your checkbook, or riding an escalator. Here are some different ways you can do the job:

Do I Know You? When you want to know what a menu command or a toolbar button does, look for an explanation in the Status bar.

- To select a single cell, just double-click on it.
- To select a range, click at one corner of the block and drag your mouse diagonally across the rectangle of cells.
- To select an entire row or column, click on its header (the grayed-in number or letter at the left or at the top of the worksheet).
- To select using the mouse, just move the cursor to the edge of a range, column, or row, press and hold the **Shift** key, and use the arrow keys to move to the other edge.

Navigational Tools

Below and to the right of the worksheet area, you see an assortment of scroll bars, arrows, and tabs. You use these tools to navigate around your workbook. Click on a tab (or the arrows to the left of the tabs) to move to another worksheet in the same workbook. Use the scroll bars to move around the spreadsheet in great gallumphing strides.

All Your Tabs Aren't Showing? If you want to see more tabs and less scroll bar, position your pointer just to the left of the left scroll bar arrow. When the pointer changes shape, you can resize the scroll bar and make room for additional tabs.

Experiment with the navigation tools to get a feel for moving around the workbook. As you do, you'll notice that the *mouse pointer* is a kind of changeling that assumes a different shape and meaning depending on its on-screen location. The following table shows the various forms the mouse pointer can take on.

The Shapes of Excel's Changing Mouse Pointer

Shape	Pointer Type	Description
	Regular mouse pointer	The standard mouse pointer appears when you point at command functions. Use it to select commands from the Main menu or the toolbars.
	Shaded cross pointer	The shaded cross pointer appears in the cell area of the workbook. Use it to select a range of cells you want to work with.
	I-beam pointer	The I-beam pointer appears in the Formula bar or in any area of the screen where you can enter data. Point to the Formula bar or double-click on a selected cell to get this pointer.
	Two-arrow beam	The two-arrow beam resizes grayed-in areas of the worksheet. Place the pointer next to grayed-in arrows, column headers, or row headers and drag them to a new size.
	Double-headed arrow	The double-headed arrow resizes graphic elements: imported pictures, charts, maps and drawings.

What's Your Status?

At the bottom of the main Excel screen is the *Status bar*. It displays information about your document and the currently selected (active) cell. (The Status bar also displays the results of the AutoSum function, described in Chapter 9.)

What's Changed from Earlier Versions

If you've used Excel before, you'll find lots to learn in version 7.0. Now don't go running to the mirror to check for whiskers: you're not Rip Van Winkle, and you didn't sleep through version 6.0. Just consider software version numbering one of those great cosmic mysteries, and go with it. There are plenty of changes in this upgraded package. The following sections outline the most important upgrades.

Add-Ins

Microsoft added these new commands and functions to make Excel even more powerful:

- **AccessLink** If you use the Microsoft Access database, you'll be happy to discover that Excel now uses Access forms and reports and that you can even export data to Access. Chapter 21 describes data retrieval and consolidation.
- **Update Add-In Links** This is obscure, but if you need it, it's helpful. With version 7.0, you can now use an add-in to update links to Microsoft Excel version 4.0 add-ins. Turn to Appendix A for instructions on installing add-ins.

New Automated Functions

If you thought you were fast when you worked in previous versions, you can now consider yourself turbocharged. You'll wonder how you ever lived without these functions:

- **AutoComplete** It'll make you crazy at first, but once you grow accustomed to having Excel think faster than you do, you'll love the automatic word completion feature. Another AutoComplete function enables you to pick a correct entry from a list that Excel creates based on your previous entries. It's all explained in Chapter 6.
- **AutoCorrect** Yeah, we sometimes spell it "teh," too. That's okay. Excel for Windows 95 knows what you mean and corrects it before you know you've done it. You'll find a great tip for using AutoCorrect as a form of shorthand in Chapter 8.
- **AutoFilter** You saw the filter function in version 5.0. In this upgrade, Microsoft added an option for picking out the top ten items from a list. You can also pick the bottom ten items or change the number of items it finds. Chapter 9 explains how.
- **AutoSum** Excel now has the capability to automatically sum, average, or count the items in any highlighted range. Turn to Chapter 9 for information on using this function.

Editing Made Easy

These new features give you Perry White-like powers over everything you edit:

- **Drag-and-drop editing** Now you can drag cells and ranges to another worksheet or even to a completely different workbook.
- **Improved number formatting** Why didn't someone think of this years ago? Telephone numbers, social security numbers, and ZIP codes have their own formats now, and right-button formatting simplifies the task. Learn all about it in Chapter 6.
- **CellTips** You've always known you really ought to document those obscure formulas and references. Now you've got no excuse because Excel enables you to attach notes. Chapter 13 explains how you can finally do it right.

- **Scroll tips** Navigation just got easier. As you use the scroll bars to get around a spreadsheet, a pop-up tip box tells you which row or column you're on. This, and other navigation information, is explained in Chapter 6.
- **Templates** You may never build a spreadsheet again after you check out Excel's pre-built templates. Chapter 3 explains how to use templates.

Data Manipulation

Excel developers have found new ways to display and use data.

- **Data Map** One of the most exciting new features of Excel is the Data Map function. Excel graphically depicts the distribution of data over a geographic map. See Chapter 19 for mapping information.
- **List sharing** Networked users now have the option of sharing files. To make that easier, Excel allows multi-user editing, maintains a status sheet, and records a conflict history. Chapter 15 has the details.

Document Handling

The power of Windows 95 extends to Excel, giving you new ways of handling the documents you deal with every day.

- **Document retrieval** The new preview function gives you a sneak peak at the file before you open it, and content-based document searches provide a powerful way to track your files. Learn more in Chapter 13.
- **Improved document management** The Open dialog box (which you access from the File, Open command) has new options that will change the way you manage your documents. You can now click the right mouse button to call up a menu of file management options, a collection of buttons changes the way your files are displayed, and the Find Fast document indexing function speeds searches. We discuss all these improvements in Chapter 15.

Wizards

Excel for Windows 95 adds new *Wizards* to the stew. A wizard is a series of dialog boxes that lead you step by step through a procedure. The AutoTemplate Wizard is a five-step procedure for creating template links to databases (see Chapter 20). The Answer Wizard changes the way you interact with the Help system. It contains sections for solving specific problems, explaining with visual examples, and providing key word references for software programmers. You'll find the details in Chapter 5.

The Least You Need to Know

In this chapter you learned the basics of Excel for Windows 95. You opened Excel and memorized the jargon words describing all the stuff on the screen. When you wake up in the morning, here's what you should remember:

- Spreadsheets are, essentially, nothing more than tablecloth-sized scratch paper.
- When you start Excel for Windows 95, you see a blank spreadsheet and a screen full of tools.
- The toolbar buttons only duplicate menu commands. There's nothing new there.
- Even if you've used Excel in the past, there are enough new features in Excel for Windows 95 to fill a book. In fact, that's exactly what we've done: filled a book.

Chapter 3

Getting to Know You

In This Chapter

- A sheet with a view
- Learn this!
- Where templates roam
- Fill dirt
- Adding that personal touch
- Tempting Template Tips

There are two ways to have a barbecue. One is to head out into the wilderness, gather firewood, slaughter an unsuspecting cow, shove chunks of raw meat on sticks, and cook them over an open flame. Then you have a rip-roaring good time playing with that cow bell you saved as a souvenir. The other method is to toss fresh soybean patties on the grill, lie back on a lawn chair with a cold beer, and enjoy the fruits of your labor.

People who prefer the first method probably wouldn't appreciate templates: the computing equivalent of prepackaged food. Templates come already assembled. You just load one up and start punching in the numbers. All of the figuring and formulas have already been done for you, so you can sit back in your favorite easy chair and let the program do the number crunching. Cold beer is optional.

If you're new to Excel, or even if you've had some previous experience using Excel, you may want to use a template instead of creating a spreadsheet from scratch simply because a lot of the design and organization for your numbers and information is already done. That's why we're starting with templates: to get you up and running quickly.

Cracking the (Work) Books

Whoa! Is it that late already? Let's move right along. In this chapter, you'll get right to work. In minutes, you'll have friends and neighbors ooh-ing and ah-ing and throwing charcoal briquettes as you customize an existing workbook.

Templates in 100 Words (More or Less)

A *template* is a blank workbook that someone else turned into a useful document for a specific application. When you need to create a new workbook, you can start with a template and adapt it to fit your needs. You may find templates so useful that you decide you never need another spreadsheet.

Templates come preformatted with labels and formulas. Think of them as being like generic business forms you buy from an office supply store. The big difference here is that an Excel template also does the math for you. (Of course, you might get a clerk in an office supply store to do your math for you, too, but then you'd have to say "please" and "thank you" and "are you sure?" and, really, who has the time?) Invoices, purchase orders, and amortization schedules are often available in template form. Less often available are secret documents from the CIA and Bill Gates' 1987 income tax return.

Excel comes equipped with a number of templates. Find one that suits your needs, and use the time you save to round up some stray cattle for that barbecue—guilt free.

Menus for Beginners

Before we launch into Excel, there are a couple of things you'll need to understand: Excel's menus and dialog boxes.

The Main Menu

The Main menu at the top of your Excel screen lists the major groups of Excel commands: File, Edit, View, Insert, Format, Tools, Data, Window, and Help. These are the names of Excel's pull-down menus.

There are two ways to get to an Excel menu. Use your mouse pointer to click on the menu name, or hold down the **Alt** key on your keyboard and press the underlined letter in the name of the menu you want to open. For example, to see the Edit menu, you could click on the word **Edit**, or you could press **Alt+E** because E is the underlined letter in "Edit."

When you select a menu name, a menu drops down to display the commands for that feature. For example, under the Edit menu, you see the commands Undo Font, Repeat Font, Cut, Copy, and Paste and a few others. By default, the selection bar highlights the first command on the menu. You can issue any of the commands by clicking on it, or by using your arrow keys to highlight the command with the selection bar and pressing the **Enter** key on your keyboard.

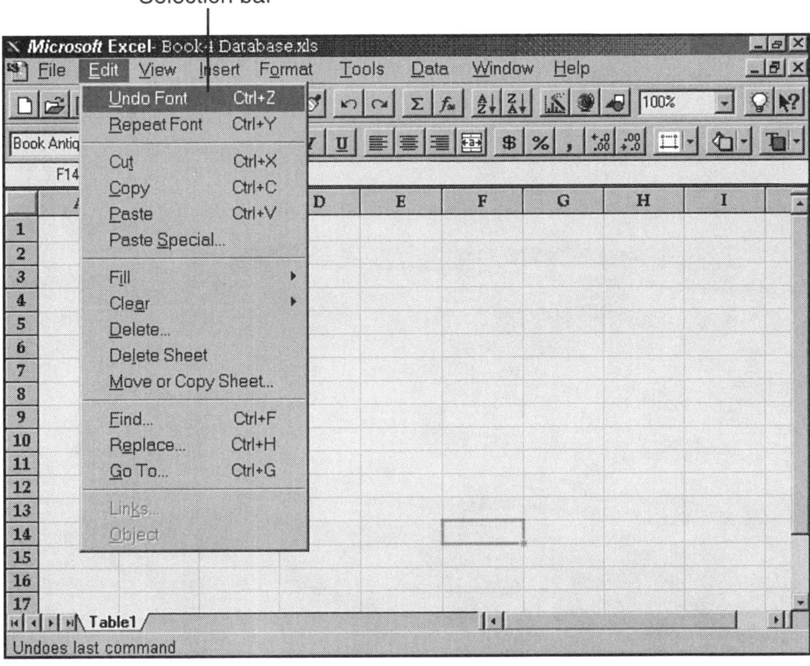

The Edit menu contains commands you use to edit your worksheets.

Next to the command, you may see any of the following things:

➤ **Ctrl+*letter*** This is called a shortcut key combination, and it means that you can execute the command by pressing the **Ctrl** key and the specified letter at the same time. As you can see in the figure above, the Ctrl+Z shortcut key combination executes the Undo Font command.

➤ **An ellipsis** Three dots (...) after a command means that when you click on the command, a dialog box will appear. (You learn more about dialog boxes in the next section.) In the previous figure, the Paste Special command is followed by an ellipsis. Clicking on Paste Special brings up a dialog box.

- **An arrow head** When you select a command with an arrow head beside it, Excel displays a submenu with new commands. In the previous figure, the Fill command calls up a submenu.
- **Grayed-out commands** When a particular command cannot be executed at the present moment, the command appears in a different—usually lighter—color. In the previous figure, the Links command is grayed out.
- **No symbol** When you select a command that does not have any of the above indicators (such as the Delete Sheet command in the previous figure), Excel executes the command immediately.

Dialog Boxes

Certain menu commands call up *dialog boxes*, windows in which Excel gives you several choices for how you want the command to operate. Most dialog boxes are far less complicated than the one in this figure:

A dialog box gives you control over the operation.

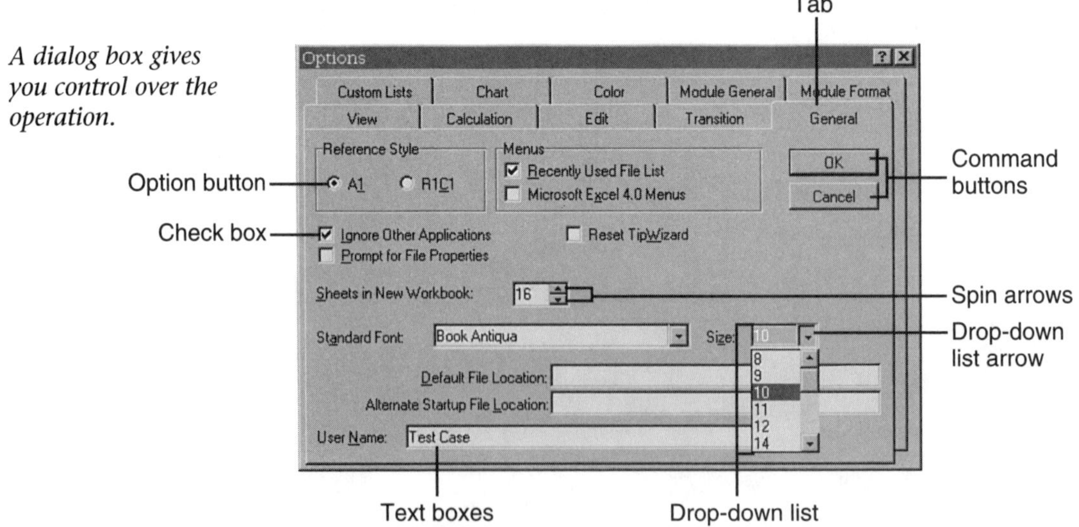

To select an option button, a check box, tab, spin arrow, or command button, simply click on the button or box to choose it. To make a selection from a drop-down list, click on the drop-down list arrow and click on your selection. A text box indicates that you need to enter the information being requested. Just click on the text box and enter your choice.

Okay. Menus, commands, dialog boxes. We've covered 'em. Now you know everything you need to know to get started with templates.

Finding the Right Template

To access a template, click on **File** on the Excel Main menu bar. Lights flash, sirens sound, and a pull-down menu appears. Select **New** to bring up—what else—the New dialog box. Click on the tab called **Spreadsheet Solutions**. The Spreadsheet Solutions options appear.

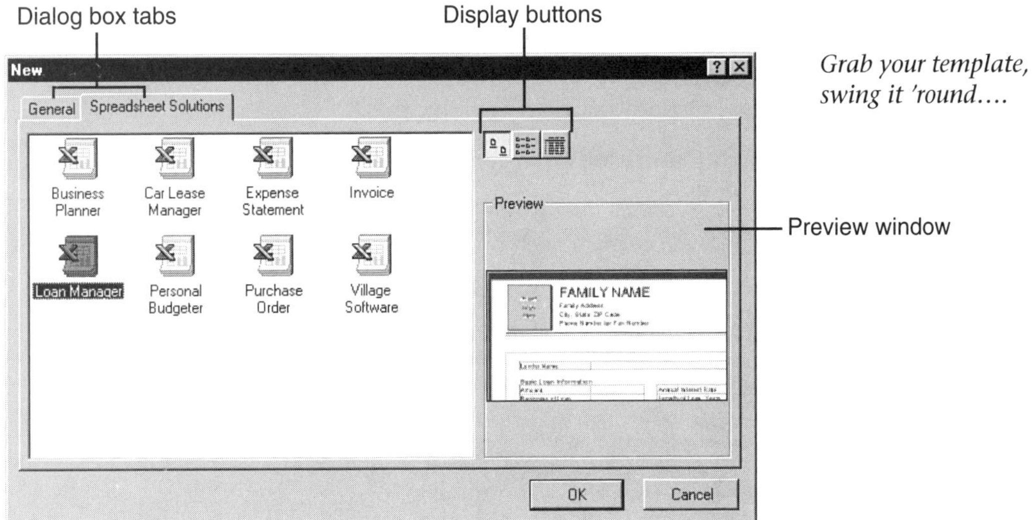

Grab your template, swing it 'round....

The Spreadsheet Solutions tab displays icons for the available templates. Click on the icon that seems most likely to meet your needs, and the Preview window shows you enough of the template to determine whether or not it's worth a closer look.

Above the Preview box on the Spreadsheet Solutions tab are three Display icons. These icons enable you to modify the way the icons appear on your screen. You can choose from large icons, an icon list, a detail list, and a partridge-in-a-pear-tree list.

Excel contains the following templates:

Business Planner A complex accounting system that contains areas for compiling a balance sheet, asset chart, income statement, income chart, or cash flow planner.

Car Lease Manager This lets you play "what-if" games with various interest rates and payment terms. Sets up a payment table and compares results of various scenarios that you create.

Change Request A quality control tracker and version manager to track changes made to a project. Assigns test conditions, outlines available resources, and tracks status of changes.

Expense Statement A form for tracking business-related expenses: accommodations, transportation, meals, entertainment, and other categories. Performs all related calculations.

Invoice A basic invoice form.

Loan Manager You input loan factors (interest rate, payments, principle) and let Excel calculate the loan. Includes a loan amortization table.

Personal Budgeter Sets up a family budget. Tracks income, utilities, insurance, living expenses, entertainment, and credit cards.

Purchase Order A purchase order form with vendor name, shipping information, and payment details.

Sales Quote Quotation form with quantity and item details.

Timecard Clocks straight time and overtime to generate a standard timecard. Tracks employee information and calculates employee productivity.

Village Software An information request form for direct mailings.

Using Templates: A Walking Tour

In this part of the show, we walk you through using a template. You open one of the templates that came with your copy of Excel and make a few simple entries. You also learn how to add some personality to the template, in the form of your name and phone number.

Template Navigation You move around the template using the same methods to navigate any other spreadsheet. That means you use your mouse or the Tab key to move from box to box, and then enter sample data.

Fear not; this stuff is easy. You'll get involved just enough to get a feel for templates. (Surgeon General's Warning: We have a friend who swears spreadsheets are the most fun you can have with your clothes on. So if you find yourself waking up in the middle of the night for a template fix, well, don't say you weren't warned.)

If you're not in the New dialog box, open Excel, click on the **File** menu, and select **New**. In the New dialog box, click on the **Spreadsheet Solutions** tab, and then double click on **Invoice**. Within a few seconds (or hours if you have a machine purchased during the Bush administration), an invoice template appears on your screen.

What's This Thing?

When the template appears on-screen, you may see a pop-up box, called a *toolbar*, near the center of your screen. You'll recognize the toolbar by the X button in its upper right corner. You don't want that thing in the middle of your worksheet, do you? To get it out of your way, click on any blank area of the toolbar, hold down your left mouse button, and drag it to the bottom of your screen. The toolbar changes shape and stays out of harm's way while you do your work. You'll learn more about pop-up toolbars near the end of this chapter.

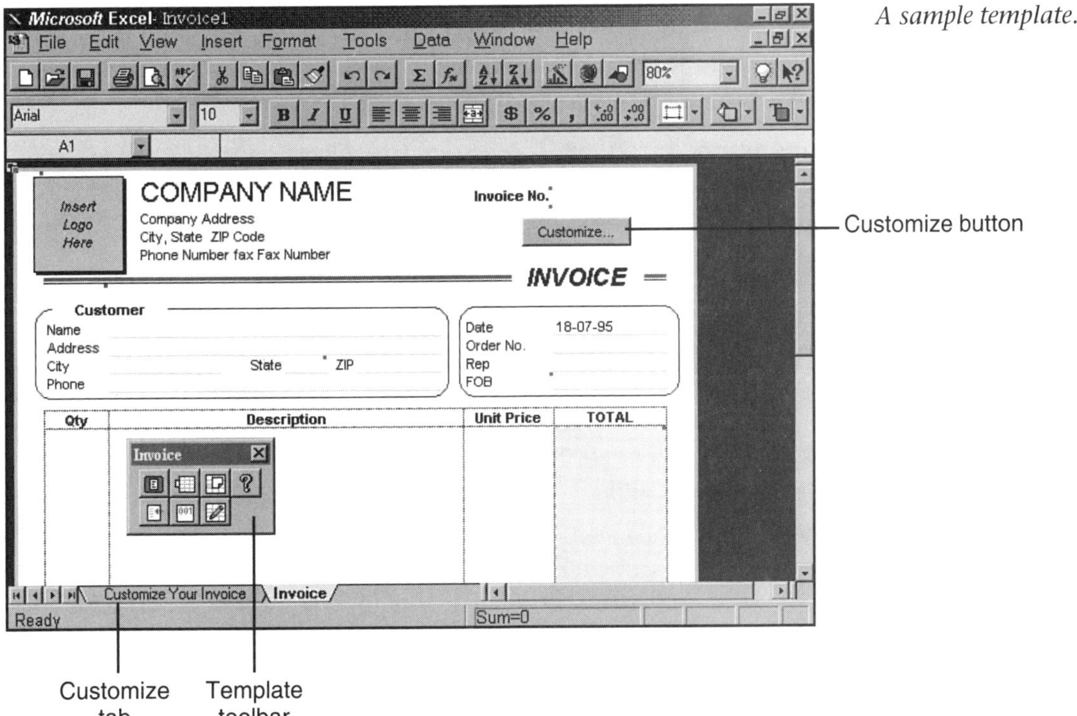

A sample template.

In this template, you find the Template toolbar, described in the next section, as well as the Customize button and Customize tab. The same three items appear on most of the Excel templates.

Move the pointer to the first cell in the Qty column. When the pointer changes to the shaded cross, click the left mouse button to select the cell, and then type an entry in the cell. We entered the number 9. There is nothing special about the number 9; we chose it at random. If you want to choose another number, feel free. We promise not to be offended. This is not some cheesy parlor card game. At no time does the hand leave the wrist.

Next, make an entry in the Description column. This step has no real value in demonstrating how the template will function, but it does add an air of authenticity to the final product. So go ahead and make an entry. But please show some imagination. No "widgets" under description, if you please.

Now click on the first cell of the Unit Price column, and make a dollars and cents entry there. We entered $9.98, based on the understanding that there is a cosmic rule stating that if the price is an even dollar amount, nobody will buy the goods. Press **Enter** to record the number.

If you used the same numbers we did, the amount in the Total column should now read $89.82. If you used a different number, you're on your own. If you want to check Excel's math skills, you'll have to figure it out yourself.

You can make as many entries as you like, but first press the **Page Down** key on your keyboard to move to the bottom of the form. There you see that in the default condition, Excel added $7.00 to the cost for shipping and handling. Looks like Microsoft thought of everything when they created these Excel templates. Go ahead and change this or ignore it.

Using the Buttons on the Template Toolbar

When your template first opened, a toolbar appeared near the center of the screen. That pop-up toolbar contains a handful of icons dedicated to simplifying tasks related to your template.

> Check This Out...
>
> **What Does It Do?** To determine the function of a button on a toolbar, position the mouse pointer on the button. After a moment, Excel displays a pop-up explanation of that button's function.

To get the pop-up toolbar out of your work space, you can click a blank spot on the toolbar and drag it to a space off the worksheet, or you can click on the **X** on the toolbar to close it altogether. You can reopen the toolbar at any time by opening the **View** menu, selecting **Toolbars**, and choosing the **Invoice** toolbar (or any other one you might want) from the list of available toolbars in the dialog box.

When it comes to template toolbars, no two toolbars are necessarily alike. A button (such as a calculator button) that represents an important function in one template, may not be useful in another template. Don't be surprised, then, that pop-up toolbars vary from template to template.

You use the template toolbar in the same way you use any other toolbar in Excel: simply click on the desired button.

If you need information about a particular button and how to use it, click on the **Help** toolbar button at the far right end of the Standard toolbar, and then click on the toolbar button in question. Amazing, isn't it? You're now linked directly into the Help system. Chapter 5 explains how to use Excel's complicated help features.

Almost Perfect: Customizing Your Template

Unless you really do live in Anytown, USA, you'd better read this section to learn how to customize your new template worksheet. If you've followed along this far with your own template, scroll back up to the top of the form with your arrow keys or the Page Up key, and we'll make some other changes.

Click on the **Customize** button or click on the **Customize** tab at the bottom of your workbook. This takes you to a new sheet in the same workbook. The following figure shows the Customize worksheet for the Invoice template; however, it is different for each template.

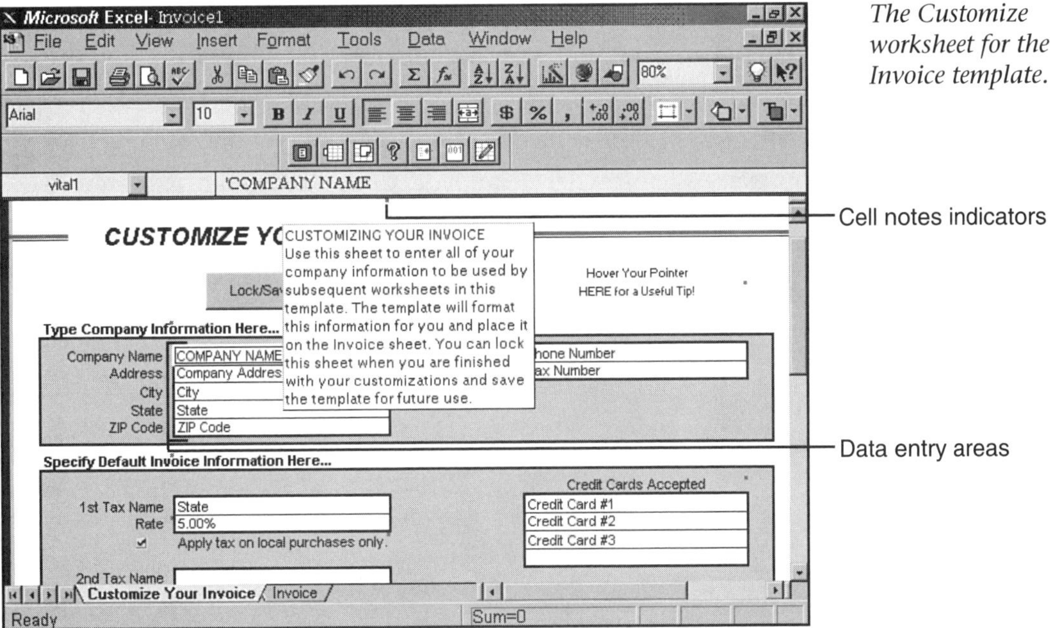

The Customize worksheet for the Invoice template.

In the Customize worksheet, you can insert the information you want in your template. Enter any information that never changes, such as your name, address, tax rates, shipping charges, and U.S. senator. The information you enter here remains in your template, and Excel carries it over into the appropriate areas of other sheets in the template. For example, if your phone number appears on other worksheets, Excel fills it in with the phone number you enter here.

All of the template's fields are clearly labeled in the Customize sheet, which makes it a breeze to navigate. Use your mouse or press the **Tab** key to move to the data entry field you want to update. Then simply enter the data. Excel automatically updates that information in other sheets in the template.

Now that you've entered your data in the Customize worksheet, you're almost done with the template. Save your changes by clicking the **Lock/Save Sheet** button near the top of the template. A simple dialog box appears, giving you the choice of locking in your changes for this session only, or locking them and making them permanent. Make your choice, and then click the **Invoice** tab to return to the Invoice template.

When you finish customizing your template, it's time to get cleaned up for dinner. Let's move along to Chapter 4 to finish up this thing.

The Least You Need to Know

Congratulations. If you got through this chapter, you've taken your first shot at real-life spreadsheeting. Here's what you'll want to tell the boss:

- Using templates can make you look smart. If you can find the template that suits your needs, you can be up and running and doing real work faster than you can say 1-2-3. Excel provides a collection of ready-made templates to suit most occasions.
- To open a template, choose **File**, **New**.
- You can customize any Microsoft Excel template. Click the **Customize** button to access the sheet in which you enter unique data such as telephone numbers and company logos.
- Avoid making more than minor changes to the template itself. You might mess up some of the underlying formulas and render the template useless.

Chapter 4

Saving and Closing Documents

In This Chapter

- Naming a workbook
- Saving a workbook
- Printing controls
- Closing a workbook

A few decades ago a revolution swept across the great American plains. After almost 100 years of adhering to mindless rules, the American people emerged from under the iron hoops of Queen Victoria's gown and declared themselves liberated. No longer would they bow to the convention that forced parents to name their children Tom, Dick, Harry, and Tina. No, the names of new American children would represent the heart and soul of their new Yankee parents. Thus were born names such as Buttercup, MoonBeam, and SocketWrench.

Once you've played a bit with your Excel template, you'll want to name, save, and print your work and then close down the operation. This chapter shows you how to do all those things.

Saving the Document

When you save a document, you must do three things: name it, indicate where you want it stored, and execute the save. The following sections give you the details on how to perform each of those steps.

What's in a Name?

Bet you wouldn't ask this question if your name were Chastity Sue. Names have but one purpose: to help distinguish one person, place, or thing from another. Somewhere back in the middle ages, someone thought it would be a good idea if a name also gave an idea of what a person did (Brewer, Farmer, Cartwright, Walmart). The name fit the function.

Until now, MS-DOS computer users have followed a similar naming convention when naming files; they tried to make the names unique yet descriptive. The big difference was that they were limited to using no more than eight characters followed by a three-character extension for a file name.

For years, this hasn't seemed to be a bad method. Give or take several thousand possibilities, there are approximately 3.51E+12 legitimate names a person could use under the *filename.ext* naming system. Problems arose, however, when people discovered that there were fewer than six ways to name a file in a way that would make logical sense several months later. Using JOHNFILE.001 might have been a clever way of naming your first few files, but by the time you got to the file named JOHNFILE.099 and you wanted to know what JOHNFILE.054 was, you were wishing you had used a better naming method.

With the introduction of Windows 95, the PC-compatible family of computers enters a new age in file-naming conventions. What you used to have to say in eight or fewer characters you can now stretch out across 255 letters and numbers.

Here are the requirements for choosing a Windows 95 file name:

➤ The complete path to the file (including the drive letter, the server name, the folder, and the file name) can contain no more than 255 characters.

➤ File names cannot include any of the following characters:

    / \ > < * ? " | : ;

  And you can only use this character if you can pronounce it:

    (♀)

However, there is one catch to this new-found freedom. If you do any work in DOS mode, or if you exchange files with people who haven't yet upgraded to Windows 95, your long file names are changed to fit the old file naming conventions. For example, a file named

JOHNSFILE 001 EXCEL EXPENSES 1995 becomes JOHNSF~1.XLS when you view it from the DOS prompt or open it in a previous version of Excel. But don't let that stop you from using long file names if it helps your productivity.

So what's in a name? There is still much to be said for the KISS! (Keep It Simple, Stupid!) principle. Even though you now have more than enough characters to play with, a file with a name like "all that money stuff from before" will be much harder to locate than "expenses 1995 excel."

Save That Workbook

To save a file for the first time, click on the **File** menu and select **Save As**. Alternatively, you can press the **F12** key on your keyboard. Either way, the Save As dialog box appears.

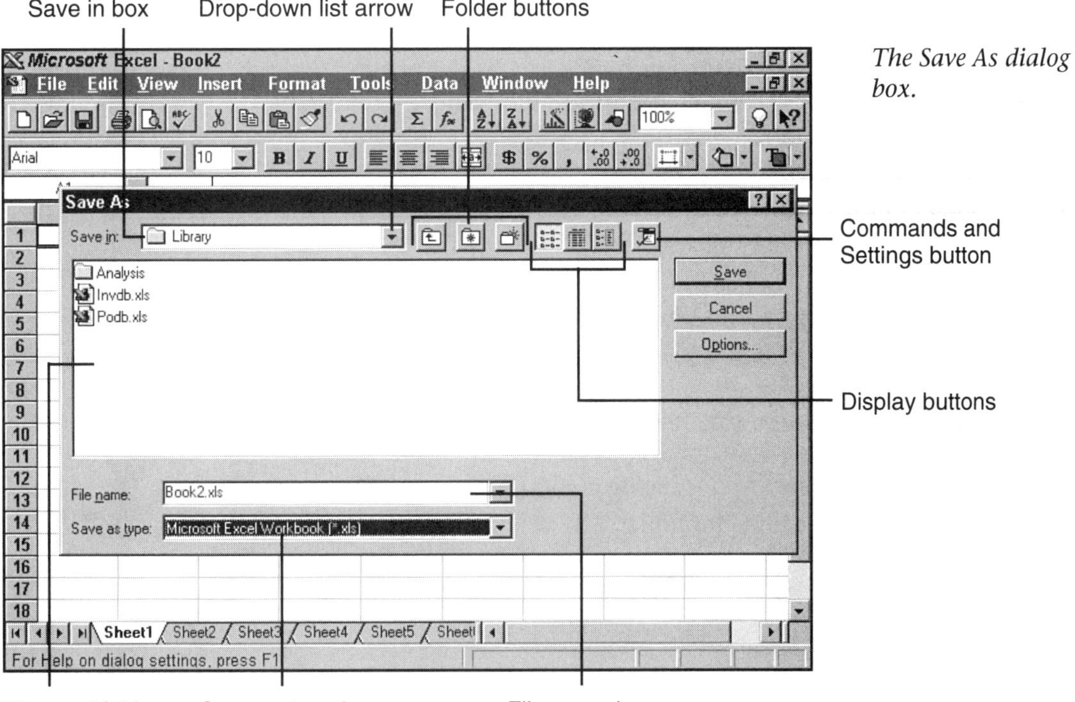

The Save As dialog box.

In the Save As dialog box, you see several options. The Save in box names the current or most recently used folder or subfolder. Unless you change this folder or drive, this is where Excel will save your new workbook.

Folder vs. Directory
In older versions of Excel, you saved your files in directories and subdirectories. Now you save them in *folders* and *subfolders*. Nothing's changed but the name.

To change to another folder or drive in which you want to save your workbook, click on the down arrow to the right of the Save in box. A drop-down list appears, from which you can select the folder you want.

Next to the Save in box is a row of buttons. The first three are folder buttons. Click on these buttons to move up one folder level, go straight to a folder named "Favorites," or create a new folder (from left to right, respectively). The three display buttons control how Excel displays your files in the files and folders display area. Click on these buttons to have Excel list your files and folders by name in columns, by name with detailed information, or by name in a list format (again, from left to right, respectively). The final button, Commands and Settings, accesses a menu in which you have the following choices:

- Properties If you have highlighted a file name, select the **Properties** option to see a box with detailed background information about that Excel file. The resulting dialog box contains tabs for General information (such as file creation dates), Summary information about file ownership, Statistical information about who accessed it, Content information, and Customize information that you can define yourself. See Chapter 20 for an extended discussion of multiple users.
- Sorting This option enables you to sort the file display by file name, file size, file type, or date you last viewed the files. (It's rumored that some versions of Excel contain an option that sorts files according to the pants size and weight of the file originator.)
- Map Network Drive If your computer is part of a network, use this option to add the network location to the map of disk drives in your Save in box (described above).

The largest area in the Save As dialog box is the files and folders display area. There you see the names of the files and folders that already exist in the folder that's selected in the Save in box. That's a hint, you know: don't give your new file a name you've already used. Don't worry, though. If you ever do attempt to reuse an existing file name, Excel is courteous enough to ask you if you're sure you want to write over the existing file.

To the right of the screen are three command buttons: Save, Cancel, and Options. Click on Save only when you're sure all the information (the file name and the folder to which it will be saved) is correct. Cancel enables you to back out of the Save As command completely. Clicking the Options button accesses a dialog box you can use to protect and back up your file. If you share files with other users, take advantage of these options to prevent errant file changes (or just use them to annoy and harass other users, if you want).

In the File name box, you find Excel's suggestion for a file name. Be revolutionary. Accept no defaults. Simply type over the suggested name with a clever name like "Why I Deserve a Raise." Excel adds the requisite .XLS extension automatically. (That's how Excel knows, in the future, that this is an Excel file—not a picture of your father's St. Bernard wearing a blonde wig.)

At the very bottom of the dialog box is the Save as type box. By choosing a different option from this list, you can save files in the format of another spreadsheet, word processor, or database program (for example). So if you share spreadsheet data with users who use other versions of Excel, you need to convert your Excel spreadsheets to their backward, ancient, outmoded file formats. (Be sure to remind them of that each time you swap disks.)

When all the information in the dialog box is correct, click on **Save** to save the file and return to your worksheet.

Other Sorts of Saves

Suppose you created a worksheet last week and saved it, and today you opened it and made some changes. You need to save it again with those changes, but you don't need to go through the process of naming the file and telling Excel where to store it. When you want to save existing worksheets or partial worksheets, click on the **Save** button on the Standard toolbar or open the **File** menu and choose **Save** to save the entire existing worksheet. (You can also use the File, Save command to save the same worksheet with a new name.)

If you want to save just the settings of your current workbook, without any of the contents, open the **File** menu and choose **Save Workspace**.

Check This Out...

Simple Save
Instead of choosing the Save or Save As commands from the File menu, try using the Save button on the Standard toolbar each time you save.

Excel determines on its own whether you're saving a new file or an existing file. If you have saved the file under this name before, Excel saves it under this name again; if you have not saved the file under this name before, Excel displays the Save As dialog box.

Print the Light Fantastic

Even though you miss the on-screen pyrotechnics of Excel when you print, there are times when you really want a hard copy of your spreadsheet. This is particularly true if you work for a boss who still believes that if you can't weigh it, it isn't work. This section teaches you everything you need to know to print in Excel.

The Water's Fine

If you want to jump right in and print an open file, hold down the **Ctrl** key and press **P**. When the Print dialog box appears, press **Enter**, and you're printing. This method is quick and painless—and is perfectly viable if you like surprises and have plenty of paper. However, sometimes the printed worksheet is not what you expected.

Although Excel does an adequate job of printing based on its own default settings, you can control a number of printing variables. Take a few moments to play with Excel's print features, and you'll soon be producing eye-popping documents all by yourself.

Let's examine the entire printing process, which begins with setting up a page.

It's a Setup

Before you print, be certain that your page is set up properly with correct margins, scaling, page numbers, and other options. To set up your page, open the **File** menu and choose **Page Setup**. The Page Setup dialog box appears.

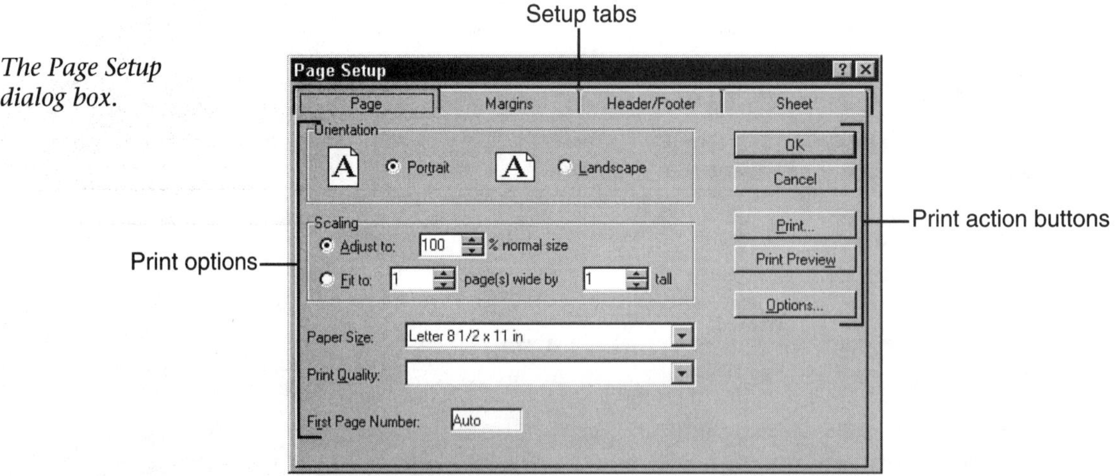

The Page Setup dialog box.

There are four tabs in the Page Setup dialog box:

- **Page** The **Page** tab features settings that enable you to adjust for different paper sizes and change the paper orientation (portrait or landscape). In addition, you can use the **Scaling** feature to have Excel automatically print your spreadsheet on the number of pages you specify.
- **Margins** This tab enables you to set a margin for every occasion. From as wide as you like to as small as your printer allows, set the margins here.

➤ Header/Footer This is where you set page numbers and set up *headers* and *footers* (lines that print at the top or bottom of every page of a spreadsheet). You can select a header or a footer from Excel's preformatted list, which includes lines with your name, your company name, the date, and page numbers in various formats. Or you can click the Custom Header or Custom Footer button to open a dialog box in which you enter your own information (page numbers, date, time, workbook title, the name of your one true love) in the header or footer areas of your document. We explain headers and footers further in Chapter 16.

Name That Name

Your user name and company name were recorded when you installed Excel, and they appear in the list of options for headers and footers. If you don't like the way you recorded your company name, you're stuck: it can't be changed unless you reinstall the software. However, changing the way your user name appears in headers and footers is simple. Open the **Tools** menu and click on **Options**. In the Options dialog box, click on the **General** tab and reenter your user name.

➤ Sheet This tab enables you to control whether or not Excel prints gridlines and column/row labels. You'll find a collection of check boxes for changing the things that appear on your printed document. This page also sets up your sheet order when your spreadsheet is too large for the paper.

The Page Setup dialog box also contains a set of print action buttons. The following table describes the function of each of those buttons.

Print Command Buttons in the Page Setup Dialog Box

Button	Description
Options	Accesses the dialog box for your own printer. Although this dialog box varies depending on which printer you use, a typical printer dialog box contains options for print quality, page orientation, and page size.
Print Preview	Shows you a preview of your file before you print. You can also access this feature by selecting the **File**, **Print Preview** command. (Print Preview is described in detail in the next section.)
Print	Opens the Print dialog box, described later in this chapter.

continues

Print Command Buttons in the Page Setup Dialog Box Continued

Button	Description
Cancel	Returns you to the main screen without printing and without recording any changes you made in the Setup box.
OK	Records the changes you made in the Setup box and returns you to the main screen without printing.

If you choose the Options button and Excel displays information for the wrong printer, you can change it. Select **File**, **Print**. In the Print dialog box, open the **Printer** drop-down list and select a different printer.

Look Before You Print

After you've set up your page, use the Print Preview feature to see how it will look before you commit it to paper. To preview a worksheet, click on the **Print Preview** button in the Page Setup dialog box or open the **File** menu and select **Print Preview**.

Print Preview shows you exactly how your page will look when printed.

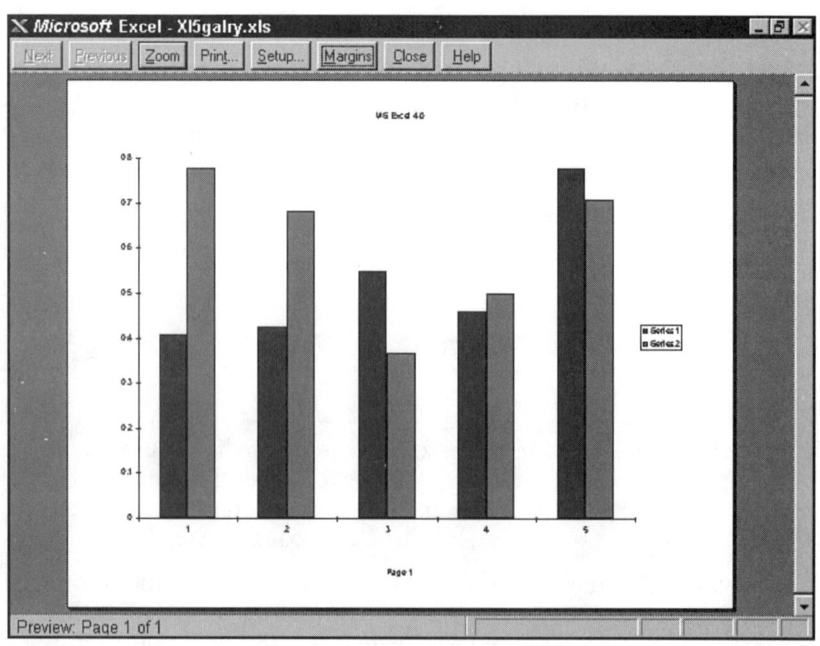

Across the top of the Print Preview screen, you see a number of buttons. Next and Previous show additional pages of a multi-page document. Zoom enables you to examine smaller areas of the print-out in finer detail. The Print button sends the current document straight to the printer. Setup returns you to the Page Setup dialog box. Margins enables you to adjust the margins. Close closes the Print Preview screen and returns you to the main screen. Help displays an overhead hologram of the Beatles live, in concert, Shea Stadium, 1965 (if you have the special Rubber Soul edition of Excel, that is). You'll learn more about Help in Chapter 5.

Color or Black and White If you use a color printer, Excel displays the graphics in the Print Preview screen in color. Otherwise, it displays the preview in black and white.

Time to Print

When you're happy with your page (as shown in Print Preview), click on the **Print** button in the Print Preview screen or the Page Setup dialog box, or open the **File** menu and choose **Print**. The Print dialog box appears.

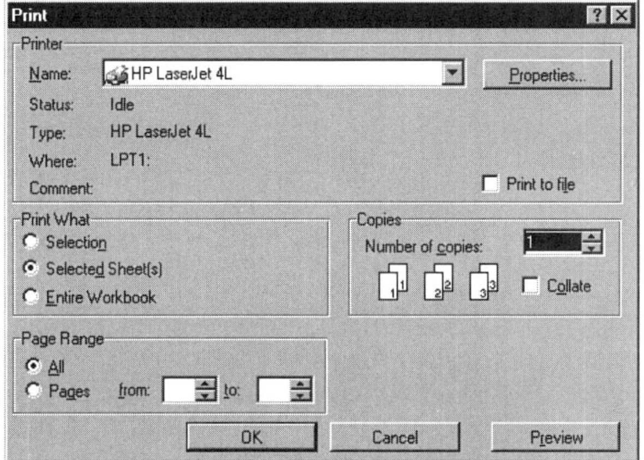

The Print dialog box.

In the Print dialog box, you give Excel all the instructions it needs to print your file. The Printer option lists all the printers you have installed under Windows 95. (If you've installed a fax option with other software, that appears here as an additional printer.) Select the printer you want to print to, if necessary. The Properties button accesses a dialog box of options for the selected printer.

Print to File

If you select the Print to file check box in the Print dialog box, Excel saves your document as a file with a .PRN extension. The theory is that your .PRN file can then be printed from any program. Unfortunately, early releases of Excel aren't able to reopen .PRN files for printing. Go figure. The best alternative? If you want to save the text of your worksheet, select **File**, **Save As** and choose the **Text (Tab delimited)(*.txt)** option in the Save as type box. Excel saves your text as a .TXT file.

If you want to save a graphic (a chart or a graph), press the **Print Screen** button on your keyboard to copy your entire screen to the Windows Clipboard. Then open a graphics program such as Windows Paint and press **Ctrl+V** to paste the graphic. Save your graphic as a .BMP file, and you can easily distribute it to non-Excel users.

Other Print dialog box options enable you to choose how much of your workbook or worksheet you want to print and how many copies your printer should spit out. Make the appropriate selections and press **OK** to start printing.

If you decide, instead, that you would like to make additional changes to your worksheet, click on the **Cancel** button to return to the main screen.

Free to Choose: Printing an Area

There may be times when you don't want to print all of the cells in a worksheet. Here's how you limit your printout to a few chosen cells.

1. Use your mouse to highlight a rectangular block of cells you want to print. (Start at one corner of the print area, press and hold down the left mouse button, and drag your mouse to the opposite corner.)
2. Open the **File** menu, select **Print Area**, and select **Set Print Area**. You can make sure the selected area is correct by using Print Preview (see the earlier section "Look Before You Print").
3. When you are satisfied with your preview, click on **Print** to print the page or pages in the usual way.
4. To clear your selection, open the **File** menu, select **Print Area**, and select **Clear Print Area**.

Closing a Workbook

It's déjà vu. Closing a workbook is (not surprisingly) similar to saving a workbook. Excel automatically saves and closes your workbooks when you exit the program. However, if you want to continue working in Excel, you can simply close the current workbook and open another.

To close a workbook, open the **File** menu and choose **Close**. (If that's too slow for you, use your mouse to click on the **X** button in the corner of your workbook.) If you have not made any changes since the last time you saved, the workbook disappears immediately. If you have made changes since your last save, a dialog box appears, asking if you want to save your changes or cancel the close operation. Select **Yes** to have Excel save and close the workbook. Select **No** to have Excel close the workbook without saving the changes. (Make sure you don't need any changes you've made to the file because once you select No, all your unsaved work is gone for good.)

Closing Excel

Ah, the easiest step of all. Click on that **X** button in the upper-right corner, and Excel shuts itself down. (You can also choose the **File**, **Exit** command.) If you've got workbooks open, Excel closes them one by one and asks you about saving any changes you may have made since the last save. Keep answering questions until Excel completely disappears from your screen.

There. You've done it. Your first Excel session was a complete success.

The Least You Need to Know

This chapter taught you how to name, save, and print an Excel document and how to shut down Excel itself. These are the things you mustn't forget:

- To save a file, choose the **File**, **Save** command.
- To save a new workbook or give a new name to an old workbook, choose the **File**, **Save As** command.
- Preview your work with the Print Preview feature (select **File**, **Print Preview**) before you print. Print Preview gives you easy access to most of your print options.
- To print, choose the **File**, **Print** command.
- To print a select group of cells, highlight the group with the mouse and choose the **File**, **Print Area** command.
- To close a workbook, select **File**, **Close**.

Chapter 5

Help, Help

In This Chapter

- Help me if you can
- And help me if you can't
- Deliriously delightful DOs and DON'Ts

When we invited friends out on our 14-foot fiberglass boat we took great pains to mask our ignorance. After all, is there any reason to let people who must trust your judgment discover you're ten cents short of a dime when it comes to knowing how to operate your vessel? To maintain an illusion of competence, one of us used to conceal laminated 3 × 5 help cards in strategic areas of our little ship. For instance, the cards on the underside of those large orange things lying on the front seats said, "It's a life jacket, dummy. Wear it!"

It was a great system until one wild and wet afternoon. The winds had kicked up a little more than expected, and we were taking on water. While we frantically searched through our collection of help cards, a passenger and former friend decided to take matters into his own hands. He grabbed the flare gun and fired. Fortunately for us, the flare shot low over the horizon where it was intercepted by the Coast Guard.

Later, from the deck of the Coast Guard ship, we sadly watched as our "Queen Merry" disappeared below the waves. The captain of the Coast Guard listened to our sorry tale and offered his condolences. It was a good idea, he said, to have helpful guides pasted in strategic locations on our boat. It was just too bad that we didn't know where the right card was at the critical time. At that, he handed us a card of his own, suggesting we never let it out of sight. It read, "High water, little boat; fills with water, doesn't float."

We can still hear that sick laughter.

Navigating the Sea of Help

Getting help used to mean you'd lean over to the next desk and ask "Hey, how do you print from this thing?" Well, welcome to the '90s, where you need help figuring out how to get Help.

It's the artificial intelligence what done it. Artificial intelligence is a "Yeah, you wish!" term meaning that software is a heck of a lot more complicated than it used to be. In theory, it means that when you ask for help, the software should be smart enough to see not only what you're doing and where you're doing it, but why you can't figure out how to do it right.

What it means, in reality, is that Microsoft figured out a way to keep you from calling its technical support line with common questions. Because 2.3 billion people complained they couldn't figure out how to move the cursor to the end of the line, Microsoft set up Windows 95 so that any time you press the right arrow key and click the **Help** button, a window pops up to tell you "Use the Control key, Dummy!"

As is the case with many new programs, Excel's Help function has become so complex that learning how to use it is like learning a completely new program. In this chapter, you learn how to manipulate the Excel Help system to find the things you probably would have figured out on your own given time, interest, and a helpful coworker one desk over.

Excel has many forms of Help. We'll start by examining the main Help files, which you access by opening the **Help** menu and clicking on **Microsoft Excel Help Topics**. (If that's too much trouble, just press the **F1** key.)

Excel Help appears as a large dialog box with four tabs at the top for various ways of getting your information. We'll start with the newest Help function, the Answer Wizard.

Help Me, Mr. Answer Wizard!

When you enter the Help command (via the Help menu or the F1 key), the Answer Wizard appears. If you see a different screen displayed when you start Help, click on the **Answer Wizard** tab on the screen to call it up.

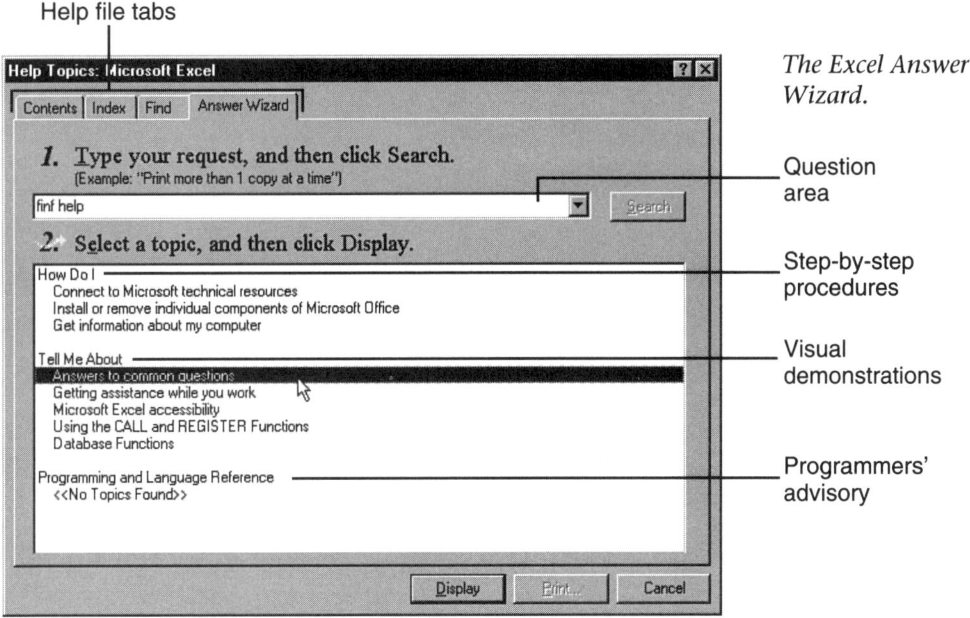

The Excel Answer Wizard.

Answer Wizard uses Microsoft's own artificial intelligence technology, called *IntelliSense*, which enables you to ask regular English-language questions and get appropriate responses. This technology is *context-sensitive*, which means that Excel gives you an explanation that's related to the task you're working on. Go ahead. Ask it how to add up a column of numbers. Inquire about printing a page. Seek information about the nature of God. Excel knows everything!

When you finish typing a question (be sure you spell the nouns and adjectives correctly), click on the **Search** button to get a list of responses. The responses in Answer Wizard are grouped into three sections:

➤ How Do I These answers walk you step by step through a procedure. Some of the How Do I? answers lead directly to an option that helps you complete the procedure.

As an example of how step-by-step procedures work, open a test worksheet, ask Answer Wizard how to find a subtotal (type **how do I find a subtotal?**), choose **Remove automatic subtotals** from the list of procedures that appears, and click on **Display**. Then click on **Next** as necessary, and watch as Excel attempts to complete this procedure for you.

Answer Wizard demonstrates complex procedures.

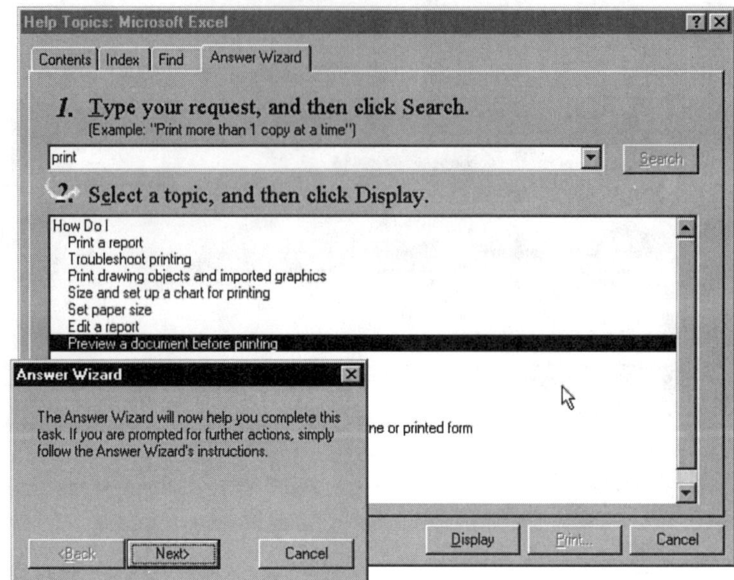

- ➤ Tell Me About This section provides visual explanations of a particular function and demonstrates the sorts of documents you can produce in Excel.
- ➤ Programming and Language Reference This section is a help for software programmers. (In other words, if you didn't already know what it meant, you probably don't want to look at this section.)

When viewing a Help file, you may see underlined words and words written in green letters. These words are called *Hypertext links*. Click on a Hypertext link, and Excel jumps to a related topic or displays a definition of the specified word.

Excel's Hypertext help links also appear as icons or as toolbar buttons with double arrows. Click on any of these devices to get help on related topics.

To leave Answer Wizard, click on the **Cancel** button at the bottom of the screen. If you don't find the answer you seek in Answer Wizard, don't give up. The Help Topics dialog box also contains the Contents, Index, and Find tabs, which are explained in the following sections.

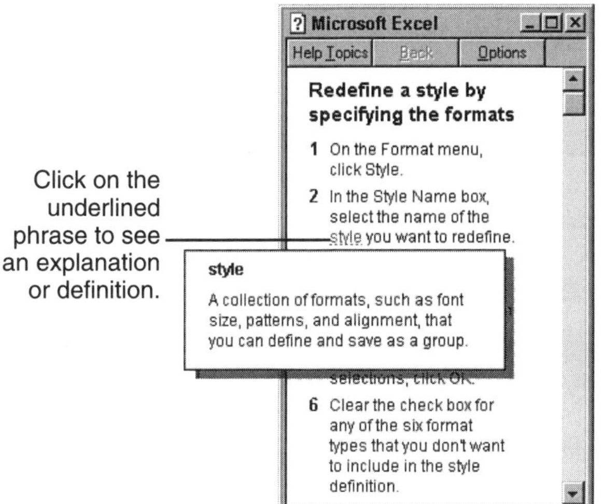

Click on a Hypertext link to get more information on Help topics.

Contents Tab

You use the Contents tab when you want a general overview of a topic. To use Contents, click on the **Contents** tab of the Help Topics dialog box. In the Contents screen, the Help topics are categorized into "books." Select the book that appears to contain the information you need. For example, double-click on the book **Working with Charts and Maps** for information on adding data to a chart. That book opens to display Help chapters or topics. Continue to select chapters or topics as necessary until you find the help you need.

Index Tab

Use the Index tab when you know the name of the topic you're looking for and want to see specific related subtopics. The Index tab brings up a page that looks a great deal like the index in the back of that printed User's Guide you wish you could find. Help topics are categorized alphabetically and are detailed by subcategories.

Find Tab

The first time you open the Find tab, Excel attempts to index all of its Help files. Let 'er rip, because once the indexing is finished, you have a handy index of every word in the Help files (including all the "the's" and "and's" and "nevermore's").

Find works much like Index. To use it, just start typing a word or phrase in box 1, and watch while box 2 begins narrowing the list. For example, in box 1, type fun and pause. In box 2, you see Function, function_num, and several other variations on that theme.

Here's where Find gets fun. Press the **Spacebar** on your keyboard and type **datab**. The Find feature narrows down your options to all topics containing both "fun" and "datab," the initial letters of the words function and database. In box 3, Excel displays a list of all topics that contain both terms. You can view the list in box 3 by clicking on any topic in the list and using the arrow keys to scroll up or down through the list. Select the topic that you need help on and press **Enter** to display it.

The Options button in the Find window gives you access to the Find Options dialog box, in which you can change the way Find searches for Help topics. The following figure shows the Find Options dialog box.

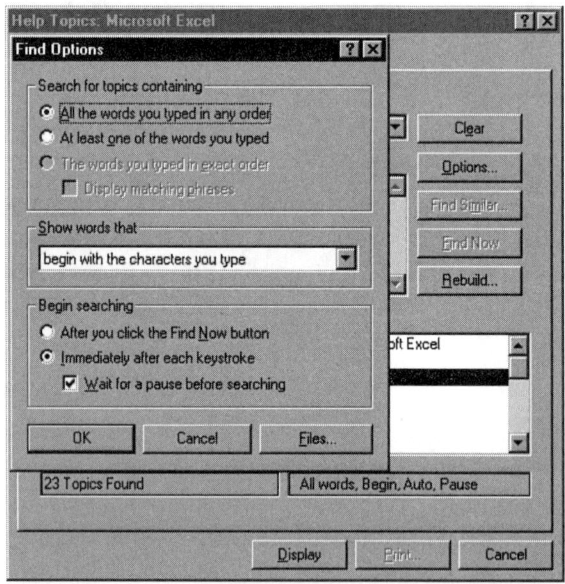

The Find Options dialog box enables you to control Find.

Indicate whether you want Find to search for all the words you type or to expand the search to include any of the words you type. Then tell Find whether to show words that begin with the letters you type, simply *contain* the letters you type, end with those letters, or exactly match the letters. And, finally, select an option to tell Find when to start searching.

The Files button at the bottom of the dialog box enables you to add or subtract Excel Help files from the list of files indexed for the Find feature. Select all files to maximize your search capabilities. If you change the number of Help files, you need to click the **Rebuild** button in the main Find window to change the actual index.

When you finish setting the Find options, click **OK** to return to the main Find window. Let Find run the search, and when it finishes, select the topic you need help on.

Find can lead you on wild chicken chases, of course, because any given word can be used so many different ways. However, it proves to be a good last resort when you don't know the official jargon for the thing you want to do.

Other Help Sources

Excel provides many kinds of help besides the context-sensitive Help files you access by pressing F1. The most useful of those resources are the TipWizard, Screen Tips, and About Microsoft Excel features.

The TipWizard

The TipWizard is a toolbar that suggests more efficient ways to perform an Excel task. Each time you open Excel, TipWizard produces a free, no-strings-attached random tip.

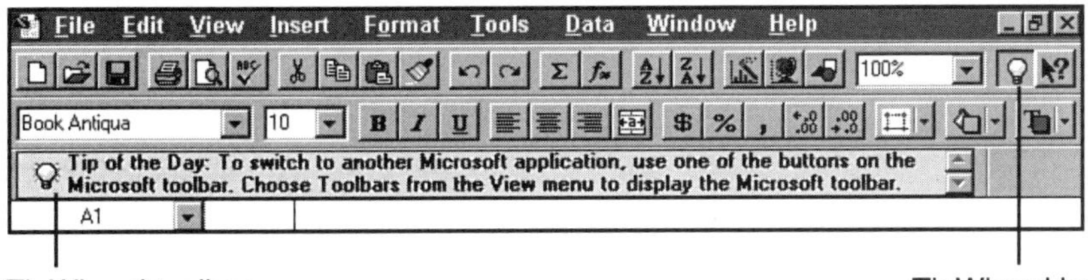

The Excel TipWizard.

Unfortunately, other tips aren't quite so forthcoming. To get additional tips, you have to at least try your hand at the task you want to perform. Once TipWizard figures out that you're doing something new, it displays the related tip.

To call up TipWizard, click on the **TipWizard** icon. Each time Excel displays a new tip, the light bulb icon on the Formatting toolbar turns from white to yellow. Get it? White to yellow. Clever, eh?

Once TipWizard appears on-screen, you can scroll through the existing TipWizard tips by clicking on the up and down arrows. Hide the TipWizard by clicking again on the **TipWizard** light bulb icon.

Screen Tips

Excel's Help system provides easily accessible definitions and explanations about virtually any item that appears on-screen. The nice thing about screen tips is that you don't have to go into the Help system and wade through a lot of topics to find the information you need. The following list tells you how to find explanations and definitions for certain types of screen elements.

Standard screen items For explanations of items you see on-screen or on a menu, click the **Help** button on the Standard toolbar, and then click on that screen or menu item. An explanation of that item appears on-screen in a pop-up window. Press any key or click anywhere on your screen to make the pop-up window disappear.

Dialog boxes Click on the question mark button in the upper right corner of any dialog box, and then click on the item in question to see an explanation. Again, press any key or click anywhere in the dialog box to make the explanation disappear.

Toolbars For an explanation of a toolbar button, position your pointer over the button, and a definition of that button appears on-screen.

Information About My Computer

Here's dubious help, at best. If your computer hardware or software isn't working properly, your best move is probably to bribe your favorite computer geek with a box of Ding Dongs. However, if you've already expended this month's entire pastry allowance, you might be forced to examine the hardware and software settings yourself. Before you do, you can use the Help system to learn more about your particular computer system.

To see listings of important information about the hardware and software your system uses, open the **Help** menu and select **About Microsoft Excel**. In the dialog box that appears, choose **System Info**. Excel displays critical system information that includes complex data about memory and hardware usage (ugly numbers that might keep you lying awake nights worrying). Remember, you're probably better off not knowing this.

This dialog box does have one thing that might come in handy though. Excel provides a button that gives you access to a list of Microsoft technical support services.

Don't Close Help To move back and forth between the Help file and Excel without closing the Help file, hold down the **Alt** key and press **Tab**. This enables you to page through all your open applications, including the Help file and Excel.

The Least You Need to Know

If there is such a thing as an ultimate "The Least You Need to Know" list, this is it. Learn to navigate the Help files, and you can find out everything you ever wanted to know about Excel but didn't know who to ask.

- Excel's help files are context-sensitive. That means, in theory, that when you ask for help, you shouldn't have to dig around too much.
- F1 is the magic button for context-sensitive Help.
- The TipWizard toolbar gives additional context-sensitive help.
- To get help with screen or menu items, click the **Help** button on the Standard toolbar, and then click on the screen or menu item in question.

Part 2

Build Your Own Spreadsheet

All the good stuff is hidden in this section. You'll learn to build your own spreadsheet, write your own formulas, audit for errors, manage multiple documents, make it all pretty, and leap tall buildings in a single bound.

Chapter 6

Enter Here: Entering Data in a Worksheet

In This Chapter

- Surfin' the sheet
- Starting the build
- Text case
- Got your number
- Hit the formats
- Time and date
- Excellent, educated entering

There are two good reasons for tossing coins in a fountain: the romantically optimistic hope that your wish will come true, and the positive impression it can make on your girlfriend. On an evening when everything else has gone bust, this may be your last chance for your wish to come true.

If you can suspend disbelief for a moment, entering data in a worksheet is a little like tossing coins in a fountain. You throw numbers on it in hopes that your dreams can come true. Juggle enough numbers, and you might find enough spare change in the food budget for that Porsche you've always dreamed of. Drive that by the girl who dumped you at the fountain!

I Get Around

When you first start Excel it opens to Sheet 1 of an empty workbook. You learned in Chapter 2 that workbooks are made up of a collection of worksheets, and that worksheets are made up of rows and columns. We call the intersection of each row and column a cell. To find cell C5, you start at the top of column C and go down until it intersects with row 5.

Data In

You can enter data into the *active cell area* only. A heavy border indicates which cell or group of cells is active. To change the active cell, move the pointer (the shaded cross) to another cell and click, or use your arrow keys to move the active cell indicator. This chapter concentrates on working with single active cells. Chapter 7 goes into greater detail about handling blocks of cells.

Moving About

Make It Active When you move to another area of the worksheet using the scroll bars or any of the keyboard shortcuts, your active cell doesn't change. When you reach your destination, you must activate a cell by clicking on it before you can enter or edit its contents.

Navigating a spreadsheet can be cumbersome, especially if the thing is larger than your desk. From baby steps to giant steps, here's how you move around in an Excel worksheet:

- Use the arrow keys to move the active cell indicator to a new location.
- Click on a cell to make it active.
- Use the horizontal and vertical scroll bars (the bars at the right side and bottom of your worksheet) to move a screen at a time.
- Use keyboard shortcuts to move longer distances. The following table lists keyboard shortcuts that help you move quickly around the spreadsheet.

Keyboard Navigation Shortcuts

Press	To Move To
Ctrl+any arrow key	Edge of text block (in the direction of the arrow)
Ctrl+End	End of sheet
Ctrl+Home	Home cell (A1)
PgDn	Page down
PgUp	Page up
Alt+PgDn	Page right
Alt+PgUp	Page left
Ctrl+Shift+F6	Next workbook

In addition, you can use the Go To command to move to a specific cell or group of cells within your worksheet. If, for example, you know that you need to go to cell N30 of your 1994 Expenses spreadsheet to find out what your gross income was (and see if you really *did* get that 10% raise they promised), you use the Go To command to jump directly to the specified cell.

You can issue the Go To command in any of three ways: open the **Edit** menu and choose **Go To**, press **F5**, or press **Ctrl+G**. To repeat the Go To command, press **Shift+F4**. When you do, the Go To dialog box (shown in the following figure) appears.

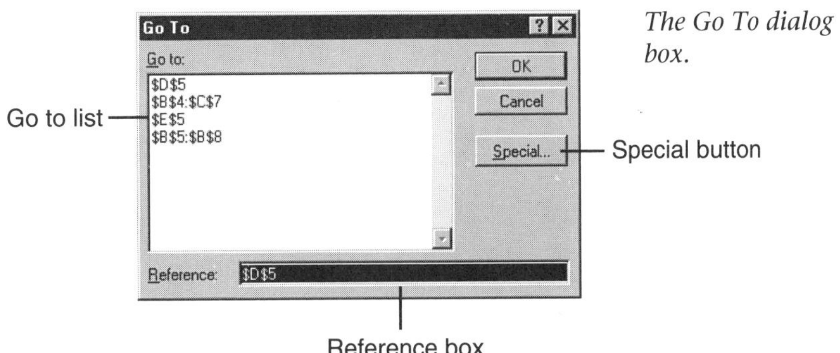

The Go To dialog box.

When the Go To dialog box appears, select the destination cell from the Go to list, or enter a cell address (the intersecting point of the row and the column) in the Reference

Scroll Tips As you use the scroll bars to get around a spreadsheet, a pop-up tip box tells you which row or column you're on.

box. You can also click the **Special** button to select from a long list of other locations, including blank cells, formulas, last cell, and objects. Click on **OK** to execute the Go To command.

Use the range name box (the box at the left end of the Formula bar) to go directly to a named range. See Chapter 10 for more information on ranges.

Par Example

Remember that old saying "You learn by doing"? Well, that's the approach we're going to take in this chapter. Feel free to follow along as we build a sample worksheet that you can use as you learn the basics of entering data.

To start, click on cell **B2**, type **Employees**, and press **Enter**. Your screen should look like the one here. Pretty simple, huh?

The text you type appears in the active cell.

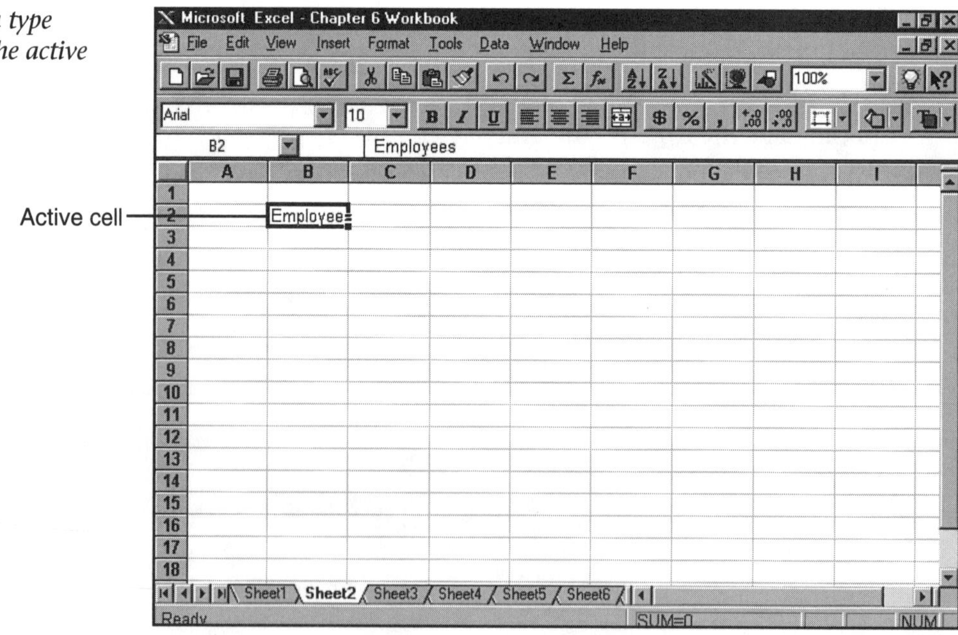

If you make a mistake, use your mouse or the arrow keys to return to cell B2, and then retype your text. The following table shows you some shortcut keys you can use to speed up the process of entering and editing data. For additional editing tips, see Chapter 8.

Shortcut Keys for Entering Data

Press This	To Do This
Data Entry Shortcuts	
Enter	Complete the cell entry and move down to the next cell
Shift+Enter	Complete the cell entry and move up to the next cell
Tab	Complete the cell entry and move right to the next cell
Shift+Tab	Complete the cell entry and move left to the next cell
Arrow keys	Complete the cell entry and move to the next cell in the direction of the arrow
Other Shortcut Keys	
Esc	Cancel your entry
Backspace	Delete contents of the cell
Delete	Delete the contents of the cell

Because you must follow different data entry rules when entering text and entering numbers, we'll look at each subject separately.

Entering Text

Text. Without it, we'd be lost in a sea of numbers and formulas. Labeling worksheets, columns, rows, and cells guarantees that if you turn away from your spreadsheet for 15 minutes, it will still make sense upon your return.

Text as Text, Nothing More, Nothing Less

To continue entering text, simply move the pointer to a new cell, click on the cell, and type. For example, let's move to cell A1. (Put down that steak knife; A1 is simply a logical starting point.) Click the left mouse button to make cell A1, also called the *home cell*, active. There is, of course, a natural law that the word "widget" must be incorporated in all examples. Therefore, we name our company "Widget Inc."

For no reason other than aesthetic considerations, move to cell B3 and begin listing the names of your employees. Enter a name and press **Enter**, and the next cell in the column becomes the active cell. Feel free to use any names you choose, but be sure to include the name "Hillary Clinton" in your list. There. Doesn't that make your chest swell with pride? List as many or as few as you like. Based on the normal default setting, all entries align at the left edge of the column.

Let's look at a few of the simpler changes you can make to the text. First, move the pointer to the first cell containing a name (cell B3 on our sample worksheet). Then, press and hold the left mouse button and drag to the bottom of your list of names. The names appear highlighted. Right-click anywhere in the middle of the highlighted area, and a shortcut menu appears, displaying options related to the current function. Select **Format Cells.** In the Format Cells dialog box, click on the **Alignment** tab. The Alignment tab (shown in the following figure) contains options for horizontal and vertical alignment and text orientation. For the sample worksheet, click on the **Right** alignment button.

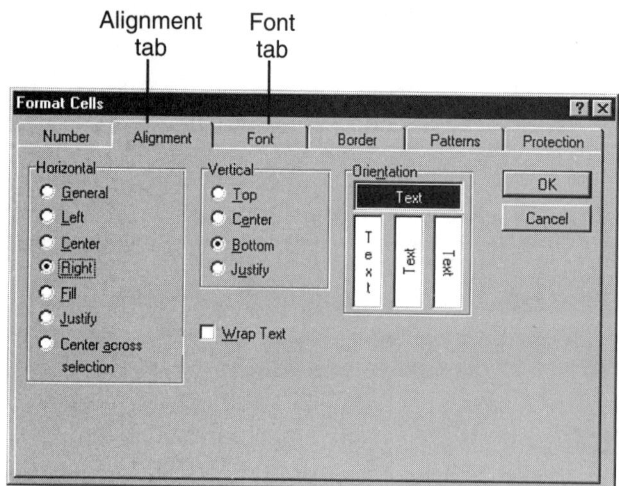

The Format Cells dialog box.

Now click on the **Font** tab. On the Font tab, you can choose from the available fonts, font styles, font sizes, and other special features such as underline, color, superscript, subscript, and strikethrough (all of which are discussed in more detail in Chapter 16). Right now, let's keep it simple. For the sample worksheet, click on **Bold** to change the font style from regular to bold.

When 6 Means Six

Just as Excel has certain data entry rules for numbers and others for text, it also has different formatting options for figures and text. Because of this, Excel assumes that when you enter a number, you're going to use it in a calculation. But what if you want to enter a number as text, following regular text rules? Say, for example, you want to compare a class of third graders to a class of fourth graders, and you want to label the first column "3" and the second column "4."

Have no fear. Excel makes an exception for those times when you want a number to be a label and not a value. But it's up to you to distinguish whether you want Excel to treat the 6 you type as 6 (a number) or six (text).

The simplest way to indicate that Excel should treat a number as text is to type an apostrophe before the number. Take a minute to go back to the sample worksheet and add another entry to the employee list in column B. Type the name of an employee who works in division 2, and enter an apostrophe in front of the number. (Use the number 2 because, as most trivia buffs know, there is no number 1.)

Alternatively, you can enter the number 2 in the usual way, select the cell, right-click on it, and select **Format Cells** from the shortcut menu. In the Format Cells dialog box, click on the **Number** tab and choose **Text** to reformat the number as text.

The AutoComplete Function

Like a significant other who won't ever let you... ahem... complete your sentences, AutoComplete works by matching the characters you type with existing text entries. Just as soon as it thinks it knows what you intend, Wham! It fills in the remaining text for you.

Here's how it works. In the sample worksheet, you typed the name Hillary Clinton in the employee list in column B. Move to the bottom of that list now and type **H**. You should see the entire name appear in the box.

If AutoComplete doesn't work on your first try, try these tricks:

1. Continue typing. If your column contains multiple entries with the same beginning letters, AutoComplete doesn't fill in the entry until you type enough characters to make it unique. For example, if your column lists Martha and Mary, and you type Mar, Excel is clueless as to what to do. The next letter should solve the problem.
2. Pick and choose. If you really like AutoComplete, press **Alt+down arrow** after you start typing your entry. A list of all the possible entries (such as Martha and Mary) appears. Click on the desired entry, or use the arrow keys to highlight it and then press **Enter**.
3. Make sure AutoComplete is turned on. To turn on AutoComplete, open the **Tools** menu and click on **Options**. In the Options dialog box, click on the **Edit** tab. In the Settings box, click on **AutoComplete** to place a check in the box. (An empty box means that the feature is not turned on.) Click **OK** after you make your selection. To turn AutoComplete off, repeat the steps and remove the check from the box.

There is a limitation to this incalculably significant feature. Excel chooses its AutoCompletions from your existing entries in the current column *only*. Items in column B, for example, will not AutoComplete in column A.

We can't say AutoComplete will actually save you time or effort, but it may provide hours of unique fun.

Entering Numbers

Excel is good with numbers. Unless your intention was to purchase a word processor, you're probably delighted to hear that. In this section, you'll add a few numbers to the simple sample spreadsheet you've been building. You have been following along, right?

Pick a Number, Any Number

Numbers are what Excel does best, and entering a number is every bit as easy as you would expect. Select a cell and type a number. Simple. Done.

Of course, life isn't always that simple. Sometimes those numbers should have several decimal places behind them or dollar signs in front of them. They could be negative numbers. Stay with us here. Excel accommodates them all.

The default number format (how Excel displays numbers by default) is the General number format: unstructured numbers with floating decimal points and no commas. If you're dealing with other kinds of numbers, though, that format doesn't work out very well.

If you're from the old school of spreadsheets, you remember a time when every number had to be entered in painstakingly correct form. Spreadsheet writers had to be careful to properly format every cell. Of course, you're still free to do everything the proper way: plan things out and select the format before you make your data entries. Or you can just wing it. You can enter a number in a valid format (numbers, commas, and decimals in place), and Excel recognizes the format and changes the cell accordingly.

Try it on the sample spreadsheet. Enter some dollar amounts in column C. Assume that you're the boss and these are hourly wages, and adjust your generosity accordingly.

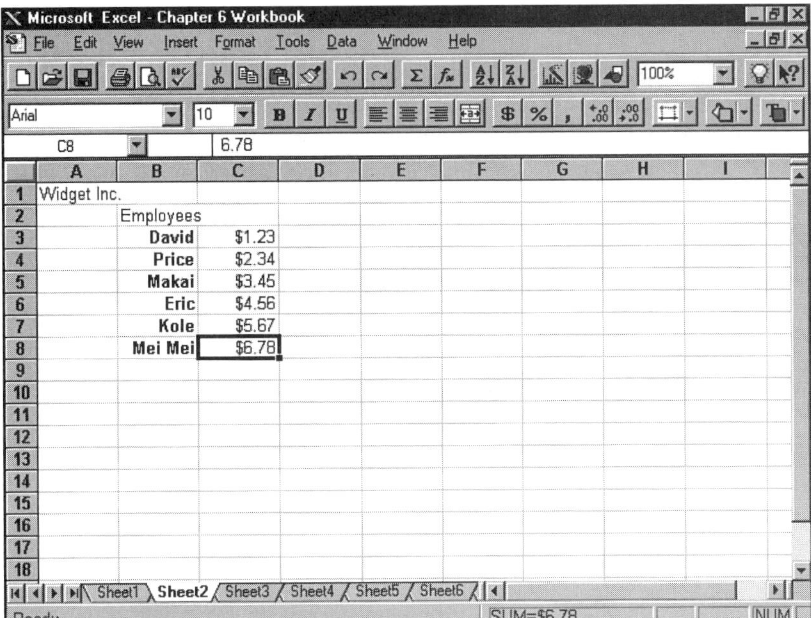

The sample spreadsheet with numbers.

Formats, Get Your Formats Here

Cells can be defined by the type of data they contain: numbers, text, or a mix of the two. The cell's contents determines the format. Although Excel now permits you to format individual cells as you enter the information, you'll probably find that it's easier to just type away and reformat after the fact. This is especially true if you're entering lots of numeric information and don't want to be bothered with the commas, dollar signs, or parentheses as you work.

You know, of course, that all great experiments require some preparation. We'd never have known about Benjamin Franklin's great lightning experiment if he hadn't first arranged for someone else to hold the kite string. To see a slightly-less-than-Franklinesqe experiment in number formatting, enter the number **456** into cell D3.

The simplest way to change a format is to select the cell or group of cells you want to change, right-click to display the shortcut menu, and choose **Format Cells**. The Format Cells dialog box appears. Click on the **Number** tab, and then choose your format from the Category list.

Format numbers with the options on the Number tab of the Format Cells dialog box.

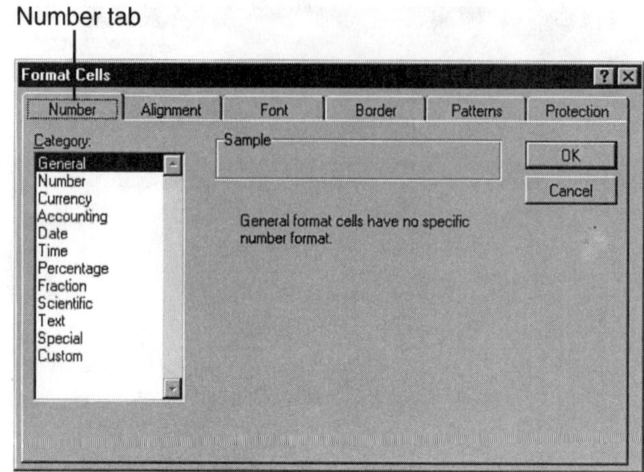

The following table explains each of the formats in the Category list.

Excel's Number Formats

Format	Description
General	This format has no commas and a floating number of decimal places. (It is the default choice.)
Number	Number has an optional thousands separator (generally, a comma), an optional number of decimal places, and four options for displaying negative numbers.
Currency	Currency features that all-important currency sign (a $ in the U.S.), an optional number of decimal places, and four options for displaying negative numbers.
Accounting	This is the same as the Currency format except that the decimal places and currency symbols line up.
Dates	Even if it's another Saturday night and you ain't got nobody, at least you have a date... cell. You have 11 choices for displaying the date, two of which include the time. (See "Does Anybody Know What Time or Day It Is?" later in this chapter.)
Time	Excel provides eight ways to display time, two of which include the date. (See "Does Anybody Know What Time or Day It Is?" later in this chapter.)

Format	Description
Percentage	This displays your entry as a percentage. Decimal places are optional.
Fractions	This format displays the cell value in one of nine formats (your choice). Why so many? Excel gives you the option of rounding fractions clear down to halves.
Scientific	Choose this format to have Excel display all values in scientific notation. The number 1223 becomes 1.22E+03.
Text	This tells Excel to treat anything you enter, including numbers, as text.
Special	These are the formats so special that they require their own categories: ZIP Codes, ZIP Codes+4, Social Security Numbers, and Telephone Numbers.
Custom	This option gives you a list of 38 starting points from which to create your own format. (Only people who read this book merely for amusement will use this category.)

Play around with a few formats. As you do, notice that the **Sample** box displays how the data in your cell will appear with the selected format. When you are satisfied with your selections, click **OK**.

In the sample worksheet, change cell D3 to the Currency format. Click on **Currency**, and then click **OK** to save the change and return to the worksheet.

Check This Out...

It's Not What You Think

Sometimes formatting can hide the true value of a cell. A cell formatted to display only two decimal places may actually contain a number with two or more decimal places. In a cell formatted for two decimal places, Excel rounds the visible number 1.345 to 1.35, but continues to perform its calculations on the 1.345 figure.

Formatting Shortcuts

We'd hate to go through the trouble of creating a fine chapter detailing all of the proper ways to format a cell and then offer you a cheat list, but we know how much you'll appreciate it. (Please, no gifts. Your eternal gratitude is more than enough.) The following table gives you some shortcuts for formatting cells.

Cell Formatting Shortcuts

Format	Shortcut Keys
Text	
Bold	Ctrl+2
Italics	Ctrl+3
Underline	Ctrl+4
Strikethrough	Ctrl+5
Numbers	
Format Cells dialog box	Ctrl+1
General	Ctrl+Shift+~
Currency	Ctrl+Shift+$
Dates (dd-mmm-yy)	Ctrl+Shift+#
Time (hh:mm pm)	Ctrl+Shift+@
Percentage (no decimal places)	Ctrl+Shift+%
Scientific (two decimal places)	Ctrl+Shift+^
Fixed number (two decimal places)	Ctrl+Shift+!

Always press and hold the **Ctrl** key before you press the additional key or keys. And for key combinations with numbers, use the numbers above the alphabetic keys; the numbers on the numeric keypad don't work with the Ctrl key.

Does Anybody Know What Time or Day It Is?

In the World according to Excel, dates are numbers, and times are decimal fractions. But where we come from, time is money, and the day is late. So let's get right to it.

Excel is smart. If you enter the time or date in an acceptable format, Excel modifies the cell format for you. However, if you enter time in an unrecognized format, Excel converts it to text.

Since nobody anywhere ever remembers the correct formats, though, it's best to do a little planning and format the cells you plan to use for date or time before you enter the data. To do so, select the cells, click the right mouse button, and choose **Format Cells** from the shortcut menu. Click on the **Number** tab to bring it to the front. Select **Time** from the Category list, and the Type list appears, showing you all the ways you can display time.

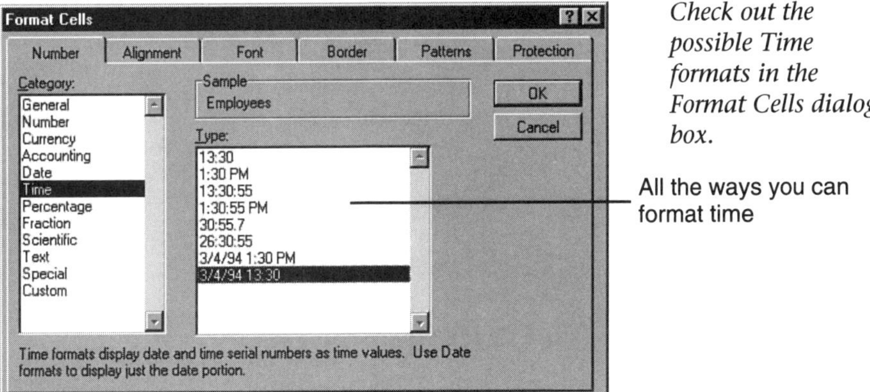

Check out the possible Time formats in the Format Cells dialog box.

Time Bandit

Excel interprets time using a 24-hour clock. As a result, anytime you enter 12:00, Excel interprets it as high noon—and never the witching hour. To get around this, always include am or pm. And as a shortcut, you can actually save one whole keystroke by typing just a or p instead of am and pm (now that's a timesaver).

A Day Unlike Any Other

Here's an interesting piece of trivia about dates: they're not just for breakfast anymore. Nah. Here's a more interesting piece of trivia: Excel uses what it calls the 1900 date system, where all days in the century are assigned a serial number, and January 1, 1900 is number 1. A spreadsheet date is calculated by the number of days that have elapsed since the turn of the century. You'll find this to be useful information at some point in time. Trust us.

What a Difference a Day Makes

Just as it does with time entries, Excel automatically changes a cell's format if you enter the date in a format it recognizes. And Excel treats any date that does not conform to a recognized format as text. Have a go if you will. The following figure shows the Format Cells dialog box with the list of acceptable date formats displayed.

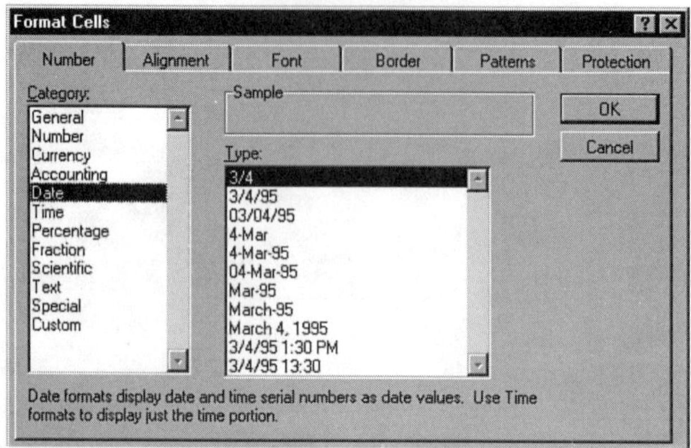

Excel's Date format possibilities appear on the Number tab of the Format Cells dialog box.

The Least You Need to Know

There is just no doubt about it: if you've gotten this far, you can confidently give Excel a place on your resumé (maybe not a large place, but certainly above that line about the high school debate team). This is what you now know about entering data in a spreadsheet:

- You can enter data in an active cell only. The bold border indicates the active cell.
- Different types of data require different cell formats. If you format dates and times incorrectly, Excel misinterprets them as text.
- You can easily format cells by accessing the Format Cells dialog box. The simplest way to do that is to right-click on a cell and choose **Format Cells**.

Chapter 7

Shake, Copy, and Move: Filling Blocks of Cells

In This Chapter

- Fills good!
- Pack 'em up, move 'em out
- Well filled out
- Fine filling factoids

Blocks were invented for the movers and shakers of the world. Blocks appeal to people who run fast and don't lose their gum. They also appeal to mere mortals like you and me who want only to get a bit of work done between blocks of sleep.

Fill 'Er Up: An Introduction to Filling Blocks

Sure you could type the same word hundreds of times across your spreadsheet. But eventually, you'd get to the point where the word didn't look like a word anymore and you were cross-eyed from trying to read the unreadable. Rest your eyes, because Excel's block-filling functions make that a thing of the past. The copy, move, and AutoFill commands automate repetitive tasks and save you hours (okay, maybe minutes) of time.

Let's take a look first at Excel's simplest block functions: copying and moving.

To Move or To Copy, That Is the Question

Just when you thought it was safe to show off your masterpiece spreadsheet, it hits you: everything would be so much clearer if that column on the left was moved to the right. And you could drag this stuff from up top and place it towards the bottom. And instead of using column B as your reference list, maybe you should use D. No problem. You just copy a column... or do you move it?

Excel users tend to lose their hair for two reasons: one is male pattern baldness, and the other is from pulling it out after they copy a group of cells they meant to move. Moving and copying are similar functions in Excel. And because they can wipe out existing information, both are fraught with danger if you perform them without carefully surveying the terrain first.

So, with hair firmly in place, let's... relocate some cells.

Oh What a Drag: The Copy Function

The simplest way to copy cells a short distance on a worksheet is to drag them across the screen with the mouse. To copy a cell or a group of cells, follow these steps:

1. Select the area you want to copy by clicking on one corner of the group, holding down the left mouse button, and dragging to the opposite corner. The area becomes highlighted.

Prefer the Keyboard?

If you love your keyboard and hate that injury-inducing mouse, you can select cells without ever leaving home. Use the arrow keys to move the active cell indicator (the black square that shows where you are on the spreadsheet) to any corner of the cell group you want to select. Press and hold the **Shift** key and continue to use the arrow keys to move the active cell indicator to the opposite corner of the group. Your cell block appears highlighted, and you are free to copy it, move it, or flat out delete it.

2. Position the mouse pointer over the highlighted border. Don't land on that tiny block in the lower right corner, though. That little block does something completely different. Don't ask! (Okay, you can ask. But we won't answer until you get to the AutoFill section, later in this chapter.)
3. Press and hold the **Ctrl** key.

4. Press and hold the left mouse button.
5. Drag the cell(s) to the new location.
6. Release the mouse button and the Ctrl key. Excel now displays your data in both the original location and the new location.

Check This Out...

A Word of Caution If you copy data over cells that already contain data, you lose whatever information was stored there.

Moving Day

The procedure for moving a cell or group of cells is very much the same as that for copying a cell. Follow these steps:

1. Select the area you want to copy by dragging over it with the mouse or by pressing **Shift** and using the arrow keys.
2. Position the mouse pointer over the highlighted border.
3. Press and hold the left mouse button.
4. Drag the cell(s) to the new location.
5. Release the mouse button. Excel removes the data from its original location and places it in the new location.

Techno Talk

Great References

Copying a cell or a group of cells has the obvious consequence of doubling what you had originally. It has some other consequences, as well.

If you move a block of text, all *cell references* (addresses that describe the location of another cell) within that block remain the same. For instance, if a cell contains the formula =A1+B1 before you move it, it still contains the same formula after you move it. (And it no longer appears in its original location.)

If you copy a block, all cell references in the new block become relative, meaning that they change accordingly. For example, if a cell contains a reference to cell A1, and you copy it to a new location one column to the right, the formula in the new location refers to cell B1 (the relative position of the new cell).

Keyboard Cuts and Pastes

You can also accomplish moving and copying tasks using the Cut, Copy, and Paste commands on the Edit menu. This may be useful if you have spreadsheets the size of tablecloths, or if you simply refuse to deal with a mouse.

To copy or move using the keyboard, first select (highlight) the cells you want to work with. To copy, open the **Edit** menu and choose **Copy** (or press **Ctrl+C**). Your original stays in place. To move the selected cells, open the **Edit** menu and choose **Cut** (or press **Ctrl+X**). The box surrounding your selection changes to a moving dotted line.

To paste your cells in the new location, place your cursor in the upper left corner of the new location. Then do it! Open the **Edit** menu and choose **Paste** (or press **Ctrl+V**), and Excel moves or copies your selection to its new location.

AutoFill

One of the best timesavers you'll find in Excel is the AutoFill function. AutoFill is a sort of glorified Copy command. But AutoFill is better than simple copying because it looks at a series of numbers or words, and—in its own Carmack-the-Magician way—figures out where the series is going.

Suppose you wanted to list the numbers 1 through 50 in a column. You could type each number individually, or you could use AutoFill to do all the grunt work for you.

Boring? Hold on a moment. It gets better. Suppose you're creating a worksheet showing quarterly earnings over a 10-year period, and that your fiscal year starts in May. Instead of entering May 1980, Aug 1980, Nov 1980, *ad nauseam*, you can just tell Excel the first two entries in the series and allow AutoFill to figure out the rest. There. Just like that you can save yourself the effort of typing 40 nearly identical column labels.

Using AutoFill is simple. In the next few sections, we'll walk you through the basic process, show you what sorts of data you can AutoFill, and teach you the rules for AutoFilling.

Quick AutoFill Practice

To start the basic AutoFill process, enter the number **10** in a blank cell. Then move one column to the right and enter the number **20**. You have now defined the series: numbers in increments of 10.

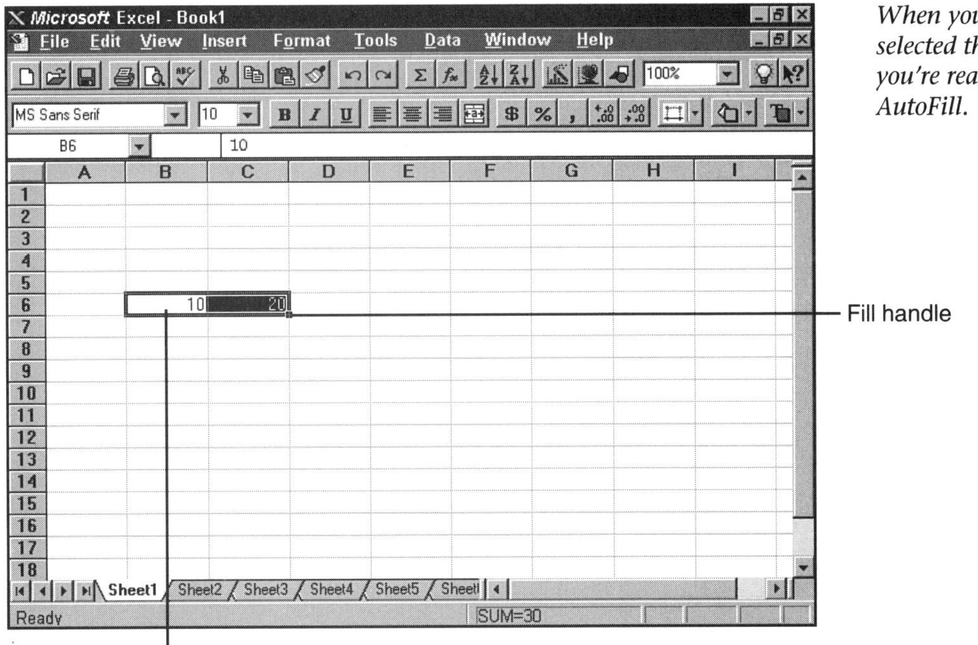

When you have selected the cells, you're ready to AutoFill.

Selection box

To perform the actual AutoFill, select the two cells you just entered. A dark line appears around the selected cells, and all but the first cell become highlighted. With the cells selected, position your pointer over the *fill handle*, the small black square at the bottom right corner of the selection box (see the following figure). The mouse pointer changes to a black cross.

> Check This Out...
>
> **One-Cell Show**
> AutoFill has more than one use. Suppose your "series" is a series of one: you want to repeat the word Total across several columns, for example. Easy enough. Simply select that one cell, and AutoFill as usual. If there is no pattern to follow, AutoFill just copies the cell contents across.

To complete the AutoFill, hold down the left mouse button and drag the right side of the selection box. When you release the mouse button, the newly highlighted cells are AutoFilled with 30, 40, 50, and so on. Well, you did it: your first AutoFill. You can now breathe again and pass out the cigars.

Kinds of Data You Can AutoFill

AutoFill works on the principle that series are logical. This list defines the kinds of series AutoFill recognizes, and the following list shows examples of how AutoFill would complete each series.

- **Numbers** AutoFill recognizes straight consecutive numbers, as well as any series of numbers that changes by increments. Consider the following examples:

If You Type	*AutoFill Completes*
1, 2	3, 4, 5
5, 10	15, 20, 25
2.1, 2.2	2.3, 2.4, 2.5
12, 6	0, –6, –12

- **Calendar entries** AutoFill completes series of times and dates, and can even operate on them as if they were incremental numbers.

If You Type	*AutoFill Completes*
Monday, Tuesday	Wednesday, Thursday, Friday
Mon, Wed	Fri, Sun, Tue
January, July	January, July, January
Feb, Jun	Oct, Feb, Jun
2 am, 5 am	8:00 am, 11:00 am, 2:00 pm
2:00, 12:00	22:00, 8:00, 18:00
Qtr1, Qtr2	Qtr3, Qtr4, Qtr1
Q1, Q3	Q1, Q3, Q1

- **Mixed entries** AutoFill can combine series elements with text and increment or copy each element separately.

If You Type	*AutoFill Completes*
Quarter2, Quarter4	Quarter2, Quarter4, Quarter2
July 7, July 8	July 9, July 10, July 11
Aug 1, Oct 1	Nov 1, Jan 1, Mar 1
1 Sep 94, 3 Oct 96	05-Nov-98, 07-Dec-00, 09-Jan-03

Rules for AutoFill

If you intend to do a lot of AutoFilling, you should know the ground rules.

- **Define the series.** You must define enough elements in your series for Excel to discern the pattern. Two elements are generally sufficient.
- **Add and subtract only.** AutoFill isn't smart enough to discern patterns that involve multiplication, division, algebra, trigonometry, or the preferred provider list from your HMO. Nor does it recognize the names of your childhood pets, your genealogy, or your record of traffic violations. If those series are important to you, investigate the "Creating Custom Lists" section later in this chapter.
- **AutoFill will guess.** If you input the series 5, 7, 11, you won't get a list of prime numbers. Instead, you'll get numbers like 13.6666667, which is Excel's best guess at the trend you've started.

> Check This Out...
>
> **AutoOops** What if you didn't intend to AutoFill? After all, the AutoFill function works a great deal like the copy function described earlier in this chapter. If you find you AutoFilled when you only wanted to copy, there's an easy fix. Just press and hold the **Ctrl** key and repeat the command.

- **Down or out.** AutoFill works across rows or down columns, but cannot do both at once. You can, however, use a single element in two intersecting AutoFills, as long as you perform the AutoFills separately.
- **Cut it out.** If you drag too far, just reselect the cells you originally input and drag back over the offending parts. They'll disappear from the series.
- **Back it up.** AutoFill works backwards as well. Drag your series up a column or to the left in a row to get AutoFill to work in reverse.

Noncontiguous Cells

If you want to AutoFill cells a few rows or columns away, no problem. Just enter the numbers or words for the series you want and select the beginning of the series as usual. Press **Ctrl** and select the destination location, where the rest of the series will appear. (The destination location must be on the same row or column as the original.) Then open the **Edit** menu, select **Fill**, and select **Series**. In the Series dialog box, click on the **AutoFill** option button and click **OK**. AutoFill completes the series in the destination location.

Creating Custom Lists

Suppose you regularly create spreadsheets that list your company's product names. (If you work in a pastry shop, you might list the doughnuts, the pies, or the cupcake flavors.) You can easily create a custom AutoFill list so that the entire list appears each time you start the series.

There are many kinds of custom lists you might want to include: your company's geographic regions, employee names, part numbers, the alphabet, work groups, supervisor names, product categories, or product line divisions. Any way you regularly break out your spreadsheets is a candidate for custom lists.

These steps outline the procedure for creating a custom AutoFill list:

1. Create your list in Excel or a word processor, making sure to use hard returns (press the **Enter** key) after each item on the list.
2. Highlight the list. If it's a non-Excel list, press **Ctrl+C** to copy it to the Windows Clipboard.
3. From Excel's Main menu bar, choose **Tools**, **Options**. In the Options dialog box, click the **Custom Lists** tab.
4. Enter the list using whichever of the following methods is appropriate:

   If you created an Excel list, the cell references appear in the Import box. Click the **Import** button to display the list in the List Entries box.

   If you are bringing in a list from some other application, click in the **List Entries** box and press **Ctrl+V** to paste the list you saved to the Clipboard in step 2.
5. Click **OK** to save the custom list and close the dialog box.

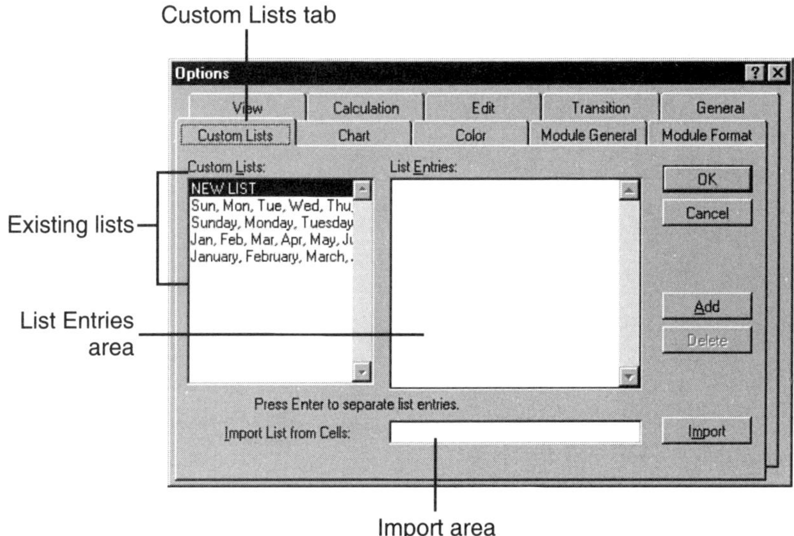

Use the Custom Lists tab of the Options dialog box to create custom AutoFill lists.

You can return to the Custom Lists tab at any time and edit or delete the list. To edit a list, highlight it in the Custom Lists box and make your changes in the List Entries box. Deleting is even simpler. Just highlight the unwanted list and click the **Delete** button. Click **OK** to close the dialog box and save your changes.

Now whenever you enter a word from your new list, Autofill is available to complete the list.

The Least You Need to Know

This chapter taught you the ins and outs of going back and forth. Here's what you should have copied, good buddy:

- Excel enables you to quickly fill a lot of cells at once by copying, moving, or AutoFilling.
- All block operations require you to first select an existing group of cells (a block).
- The simplest way to copy is to hold down the **Ctrl** key and the left mouse button and drag one side of the block to a new location.
- The simplest way to move a block is to drag it to a new location.
- The AutoFill function extends a series or a pattern across several rows or columns.
- You can make custom AutoFill lists for items you use frequently.

Chapter 8

The Editing Test: Change the Contents of Your Spreadsheet

In This Chapter

- Change little things you don't like
- Clean up the errors
- Wipe out the big things you hate

Have you ever wished you could go back and rewrite history—even a little? Come on, admit it. Wouldn't it have been great to have kicked the ladder out from under Adolph Hitler while he was still a paper hanger, to have sold the white polyester suit the week before the disco craze died, or to have been born the favorite nephew of Donald Trump? In a way, that's what editing is all about: changing the past.

It's not important why you edit: changes in the original conditions, forgotten formulas, or out-and-out mistakes. (Did you really intend to charge poor Aunt Mary 150 percent interest on that hearing-aid loan?) Fortunately, Excel was designed for mere mortals. After you've spent hours perfecting that spreadsheet, you can still look at it and say, "Naaa." Then you can reach back, rewrite a bit of history, and move on with your backside covered.

Ch-ch-ch-Changes to Cells

One of the fun things about working in spreadsheets is that you can always find a harder way to do anything. When you made a mistake back in the good ol' days, you turned your pencil over and erased it. But computers offer multiple (more entertaining ways) to complicate the task of changing your data.

Getting Ready to Edit

The first step toward editing your spreadsheet data is to select the cell or cells you want to edit. If you've had your hand surgically attached to a mouse, highlight the cell that contains the bad words or numbers by clicking on it (and dragging if you want to select multiple cells). If your hands don't get out much and would rather stay at home on the keyboard, use those arrow keys to position the *active cell marker* (the bold rectangle that shows where you are on the worksheet).

Going in for the Kill

Now you're ready to change the contents of a cell, and you have several options to choose from. This is the fun part. Use any of these methods to change the data in a cell:

- Press **Backspace** to delete a character to the left of the cursor; press **Delete** to remove a character to the right.
- Double-click on the data and type over it.
- Select all or part of the data in the cell, and then type over it.
- Press and hold the **Shift** key and use the arrows to select the data you want to type over.
- Make your changes in the Formula bar, located above the column headers (see the following figure). To do so, select the cell and press **F2**, the edit key. The active cell's contents appear in the Formula bar, and the blinking cursor in the Formula bar indicates where characters you type will appear. Enter your changes.
- Click on a cell you want to change, type the new data, and then delete the stuff you don't like.

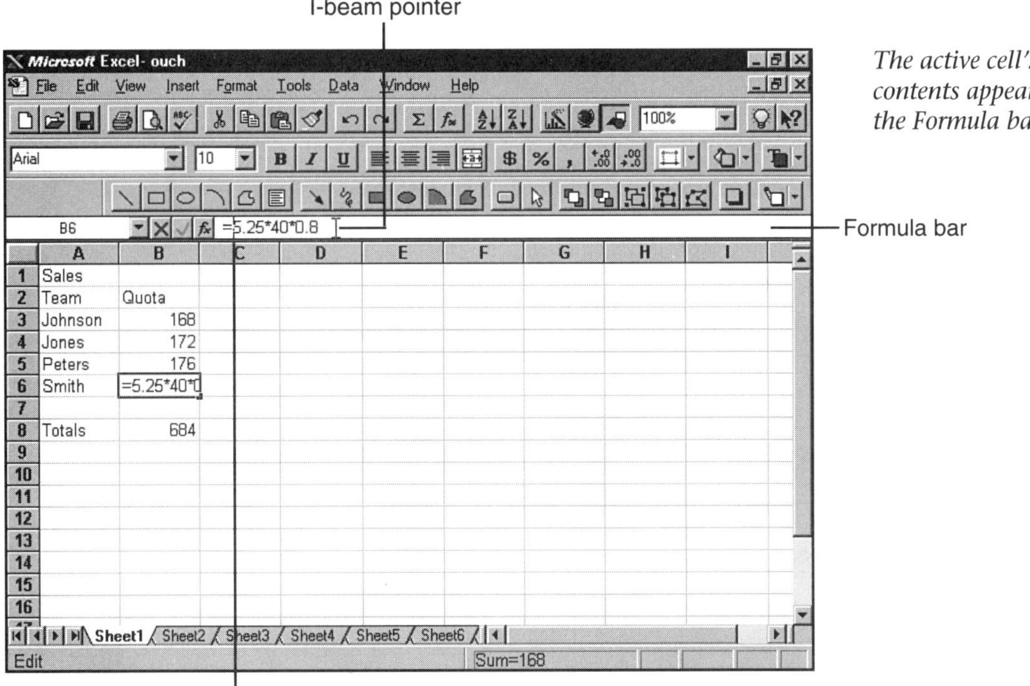

The active cell's contents appear in the Formula bar.

Ending It All

Once you've changed the information in your cell(s), your natural tendency is probably to simply hit the Enter key and get on with things. Go with that feeling. Although Excel provides alternatives, they are nothing but trouble.

See those icons up there in the Formula bar? The ones with the red X and the green check mark? Don't touch them! No! Don't do it! Well, okay, if curiosity is killing you, click on the red X, and all your changes will disappear. (Of course, if that's what you wanted, you could have just as easily pressed the **Esc** key on your keyboard.) Click on the green check mark, and you'll discover a complicated new alternative to the Enter key.

Techno Talk

Lineup Changes
If you've selected a block of cells that involves more than one column, pressing the Enter key works a little differently. After you change the contents of one cell in the block, pressing the Enter key moves you one cell to the right, where you can make your next change. If you haven't selected a block, or if your block is in a single column, pressing the Enter key always moves you down a row.

Cleaning Up Words

Spelling: it's the drudge work of all editors, but Excel can handle it. In this section, learn to check your spelling, prevent spelling errors in the first place, and find and replace words that are misspelled throughout your worksheet.

Spell Check

Excel's spell check feature searches your worksheet for spelling errors and typos. To start a spell check, click on the **Spelling** button on the Standard toolbar. (Alternatively, you can press **F7** or open the **Tools** menu and choose **Spelling**.) Somehow, some way, the road always leads to the Spelling dialog box shown in the following figure.

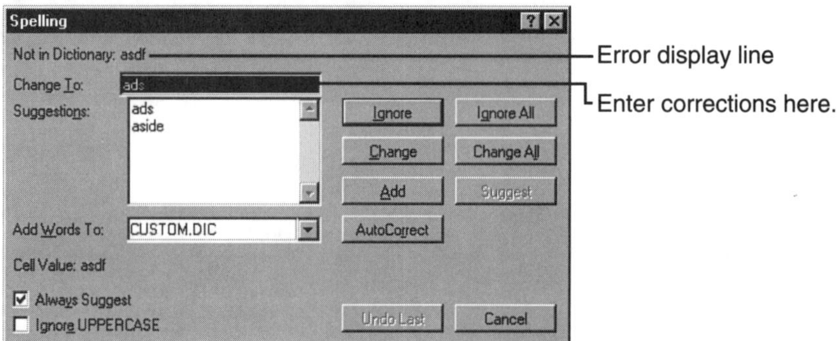

The Spelling dialog box.

The first line of the Spelling dialog box shows the misspelled word, and the Change To box displays Excel's best guess at how the word should be spelled. You can select a different spelling suggestion from the Suggestions box, or you can simply type the correction in the Change To box. Then click **Change** to correct this occurrence of the word or click **Change All** to correct the error throughout your document.

If the word is spelled correctly, you may want to add it to your custom dictionary so Excel won't stop on it during future spelling checks. If so, click on the **Add** button. If you don't want to add the word to your dictionary but you don't want to change it, click **Ignore** to ignore this occurrence of the word or click **Ignore All** to ignore it throughout the document.

The Spelling dialog box also contains options you can select to control whether the spell checker always suggests changes and whether it ignores uppercase/lowercase errors. (A check in these boxes indicates that the feature is turned on.) In addition, Excel provides command buttons with which you can undo your last change or close the spell checker altogether.

The last command button, the AutoCorrect button, enables you to add a change to your AutoCorrect list. Read on to find out the more complicated details of using AutoCorrect.

AutoCorrect

It's numbers you're good at, right? Then why should you be any good at typing? You don't have to be.

Excel understands. That's why it now includes a feature called AutoCorrection that's designed to make you look like an Olympic-calibre typist. Because AutoCorrect is, well, automatic, you don't have to do anything to make it work. Just type away, and Excel corrects your errors as you work. AutoCorrection automatically fixes your typos and spelling mistakes on the fly. Type "adn" followed by a space, for example, and Excel changes it to "and" before you can even enter the next keystroke.

New to Excel 7.0
AutoCorrection is a new feature in Excel 7.0. Watch it fix your mistakes before you realize you've made them!

To enable the AutoCorrect feature, open the **Tools** menu and select **AutoCorrect**. The AutoCorrect dialog box (shown in the following figure) appears.

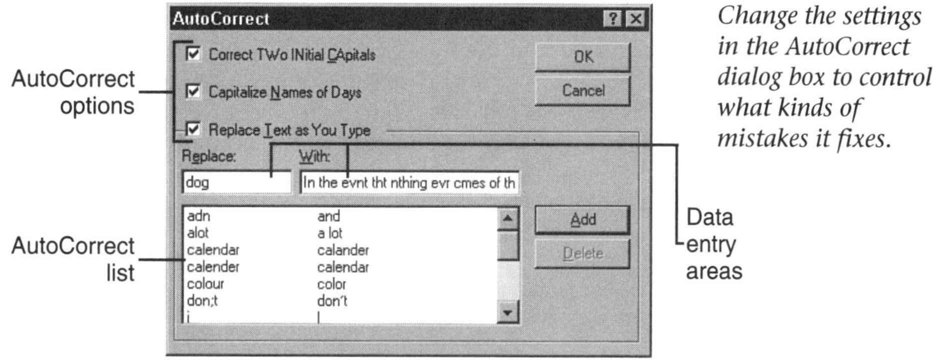

Change the settings in the AutoCorrect dialog box to control what kinds of mistakes it fixes.

Click in the first check box at the top of the dialog box to control whether Excel automatically corrects words with TWo INitial Capitals. (You might not want to use this, of course, if you are from Los Angeles and have employees with names like JEnnEfur.) Click the **Capitalize Names of Days** check box to have Excel correct those errors. And be sure to check the **Replace Text as You Type** box; it turns AutoCorrection on or off. Click **OK** to implement the settings you selected.

AutoCorrection works from a list of common typing and spelling errors. Because the AutoCorrect list starts out short, you will probably amend it from time to time. There are two ways to do this:

- **From the Spelling dialog box** If you find a frequently recurring error, click the **AutoCorrect** button, and Excel adds the change to your AutoCorrect list.
- **From the AutoCorrect dialog box** To add an entry to your AutoCorrect list, type the common error in the Replace text box (for example, type "helo"). Click in or press **Tab** to move to the **With** text box. Input the correct replacement (in this case, "hello"), click the **Add** button, and click **OK** to return to the worksheet. In the future, AutoCorrection will make that correction anytime it occurs.

Really Cool AutoCorrect Tip

AutoCorrect isn't just for typos anymore. Use AutoCorrect as a shorthand tool for completing phrases. For example, instead of typing "First Quarter Earnings" over and over, just tell AutoCorrect to enter that phrase whenever you type 1E.

In a similar way, you can use AutoCorrect to automatically output a long block of text. To do so, create your replacement text block in Excel or a word processor and select the block. Press **Ctrl+C** to copy the text block to the Windows Clipboard. From Excel's Main menu bar, open the **Tools** menu and choose **AutoCorrect**. The AutoCorrect dialog box appears. In the Replace box, type the shorthand term you want Excel to replace. Then move to the With box and press **Ctrl+V** to paste the text block. Click **OK** to save the addition and close the dialog box. Each time you type your shorthand abbreviation in the future, Excel automatically replaces it with the text block.

Find and Replace

There's nothing more frustrating than not knowing where something is—whether that something is your only set of car keys or that Nobel prize-winning formula. Excel's Find and Replace feature may not be of much help with the car keys, but if you're looking for something on your spreadsheet it may be just what you need.

To use either Find or Replace, open the **Edit** menu and select **Find**. (If you prefer, you can avoid all this clicking and dragging by pressing **Ctrl+F**.) Either way, the Find dialog box appears.

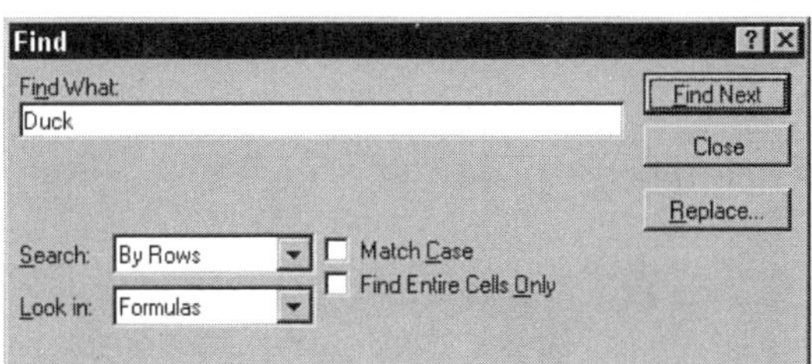

The Find dialog box.

In the Find What text box, type the word or phrase you're looking for. You can enter alphanumeric characters from labels, formulas, dates, times, or values. Click on the appropriate check box if you want to limit your search by matching upper- and lowercase letters or by searching for entire cells that match the search text. In a very large spreadsheet, you might also want to limit your task by searching column by column or row by row. If so, select one of the options in the Search drop-down list.

At this point, the Find path and the Replace path diverge. If you want to replace the word or phrase, click the **Replace** button. The Replace with text box appears. Type the replacement text, and then choose whether you want Excel to replace only the first occurrence of the text or every occurrence in the entire spreadsheet. If, on the other hand, you only want to Find something, click the **Find Next** button now.

The Find or Replace function begins. If you chose Find, the next highlighted cell you see should be the one you were looking for. If you chose Replace, Excel replaces the text automatically.

Clear 'Em Out: Clearing and Deleting

A pop quiz: What's the difference between deleting something and clearing it? Confused? Yeah, you and everybody else. But Excel wants you to learn the distinction. So take a deep breath.

When you *clear* a cell or a range, Excel sweeps out its contents but leaves the actual cell or range in place. When you *delete*, however, it's like taking a pair of scissors to your spreadsheet. Excel actually chops out the cell or range, and the rest of the spreadsheet shifts around to fill in the gaps.

Clearing Cells, Rows, and Columns

Have you ever looked in your closet and wished you could just get rid of everything in it and start over? Although that's not always possible, clearing the contents of a cell, a range, a column, a row you're unhappy with *is* possible. And Excel makes it easy.

First, select the stuff you don't like. Then take your pick of several different ways of making it disappear:

- **The frustration method** Press **Backspace** to mow right over the text. (This works in a single cell only.)
- **The Clear command** You'll find it on the Edit menu. This method gives you the option of clearing all the contents, the formatting commands, the visible contents, or the notes.
- **The right mouse button** When you click the right mouse button, an Excel shortcut menu appears. Choose **Clear Contents** from the menu.
- **Delete** Just press the darned **Delete** key. Hey! Why didn't we think of that earlier?

Slash and Burn Deletion Tips

Deleting is lots more fun than clearing. The adventure! The thrills! The...oops!

Deleting changes relationships between the elements, and physically moves cells, rows, and columns. When you delete cells, you can make fundamental changes to the structure of your worksheet—which makes it all too easy to destroy the whole thing.

If you're bound and determined to delete anyway, highlight the desired cell, range, column, or row. Open the **Edit** menu and select **Delete** or press **Alt+E** and then **D**. If you selected a row or column, Excel deletes it immediately. If you selected a range, the Delete dialog box (shown below) appears, asking whether you want to move the remaining cells up or to the left, or whether you want to eliminate your current row or column altogether.

If you are sure you really want to do this, click on the appropriate button and press **OK**. There. You just destroyed your spreadsheet.

The Delete dialog box.

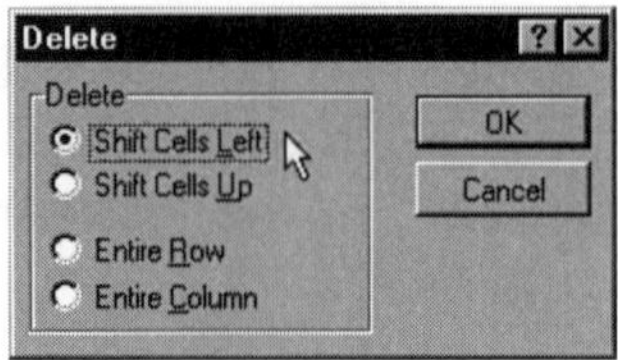

Cool Deletion Tip

Unsure about deleting? Here's a better—safer—way to delete. First, save your worksheet. Then clear a single cell or a group of cells. STOP! Before you do anything else, see if anything went wrong. Did any errors pop up? Move around your spreadsheet and check for other errors. If you find a mistake, press **Ctrl+Z** now to undo the Clear command. Then re-examine your change.

If everything looks good, go ahead and delete the cells and check immediately to see if the spreadsheet died. If it did, press **Ctrl+Z** immediately to recover. You cannot go back later and undo the changes.

The Least You Need to Know

This chapter taught you the basics of Excel editing. With an air of nostalgia and a tender tear in our collective eye, let's look back at what we learned:

- Changing cells is an unnecessarily complicated process. The quick and dirty way to change the contents of a cell is to place the cursor there and start typing. Delete any extra stuff and press **Enter**. There. You're done.
- Spell check is easy. Just press **F7**, and away it goes.
- The AutoCorrect feature corrects your typos and misspellings on the fly, but you need to add your own entries to the list for it to be effective.
- Clearing and deleting are not the same thing. When you clear a cell, only its contents are removed. When you delete a cell, the entire cell disappears, and the rest of the spreadsheet moves in.

Chapter 9

AutoPilot: Excel's Automatic Features

In This Chapter

- Filter tip
- Get in (AutoOut) line
- Sum it up
- Macro economics
- You auto know better

As automatically as tears appear in the eyes of an impoverished televangelist, Excel's best features can have you moving along to the next channel in no time! Watch as columns add themselves and outlines create themselves. In fact, keep watching as everything you ever wanted happens with almost miraculous regularity.

Shifting to Automatic

Hey, Detroit did it! So isn't it about time the computer industry figured out how to do automatic? Excel's auto features are designed to get you out of the kitchen fast. Top 10 lists, outlines, subtotals, macros—Excel's got 'em all. We start this chapter with an examination of the AutoFilter feature.

AutoFilter

Imagine that the list of employees at your widget company has grown from half a dozen salesfolk to several hundred worker bees. That's one long list on your spreadsheet, and when it comes time to check up on individual performance, you certainly don't want to look through all those names. You're only interested in finding the top and bottom 10 percent. Great news! AutoFilter is the answer to your prayers.

AutoFilter enables you to enter criteria for searching and viewing spreadsheet data. Based on your selections, it filters out the details that don't interest you.

Now You See It; Now You Don't

To work through this section, you might want to create a small test spreadsheet of your own. You can work with something similar to the spreadsheet you created in Chapter 6: a couple of columns, one with names and one with numbers. (A dozen or so of each will suffice.) Label the top of each column with a name that describes its contents. Or you can label it "Elephants on the March" if you like, because Excel can't read English and won't know the difference. You must put a label at the top of each column, because AutoFilter considers the first entry in a column a *non-event*. Follow along, and we promise not to ask you to sing with the bouncing icon.

Click on any cell that contains data to make it active. Then open the **Data** menu, choose **Filter**, and click on **AutoFilter**. When you begin the AutoFilter, arrow buttons appear at the tops of the columns in your worksheet (see the following figure). Click on the arrow at the top of the column you want to filter. A pick list appears containing all of the values found in the column, an All selection, and Top 10, Custom, Blanks, and Non-Blanks.

It's a Chameleon
The AutoFilter arrow button changes color when that column is an active filter column.

We'll start with an easy filter. From the pick list, select one of the items that originated from your column, an employee name for instance. AutoFilter hides all rows in that column that do not contain the selected employee name. Click on the arrow button again and select **All**. The filter is turned off, and everything returns to normal.

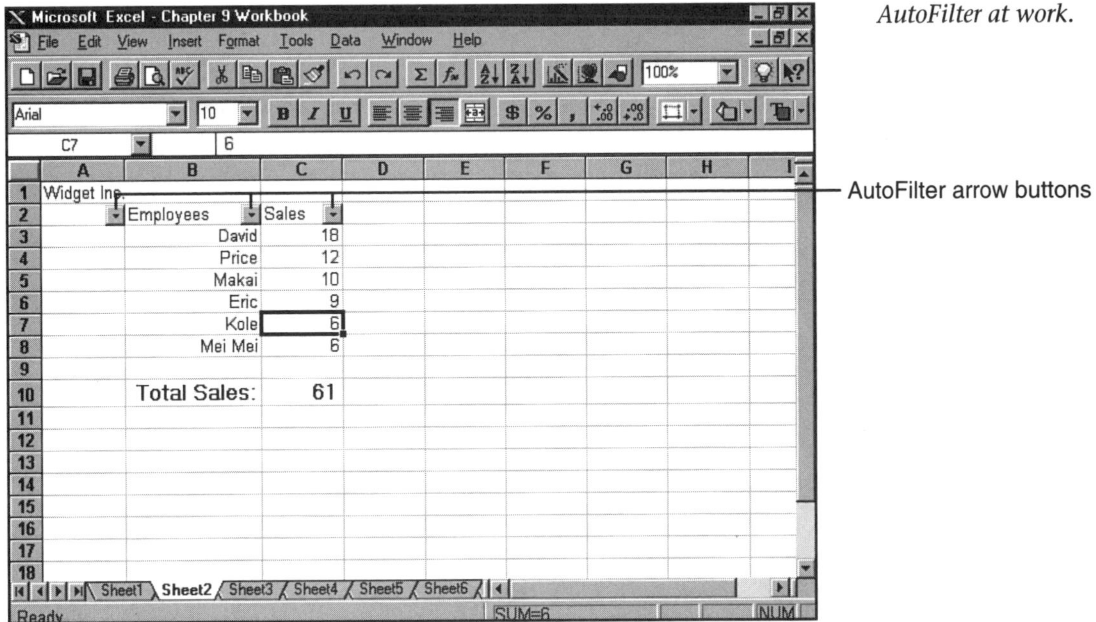

AutoFilter at work.

Only the Good Get Viewed

Let's move on to the features that really make AutoFilter special. Click on an arrow button at the top of a column containing number values—no names, please. Choose **Top 10** from the pick list, and Excel displays the Top 10 AutoFilter dialog box.

The Top 10 dialog box.

This dialog box contains three controls you use to make your AutoFilter selections. In the first box (on the left), indicate whether you want to filter from the top or the bottom (the highest or the lowest values). In the second box, you can make an adjustment to the number 10. Do you really want to see 10? Or do you need to see the top/bottom 5, 100, or 500 values? The third box enables you to control whether the numbers in the second box represent real numbers or percentages. (For example, do you want to find the top 10 or the top 10 percent?)

When you've made your selections, click **OK**. Excel hides all rows that don't match the selected criteria. To re-expand the column, click on the arrow button again and select **All**.

To disable AutoFilter, open the **Data** menu, select **Filter**, and choose **AutoFilter**. The check mark disappears, and the AutoFilter arrow buttons disappear. Don't you wish there were some way to get children to behave so well?

Exactly What You Were Looking For

If you'd like to have an even more precise view of your data (if, for example, you want to see a list of employees who sold more than 217 widgets this month or a list of employee names that start with the letter P), you'll want to investigate the Custom AutoFilter function.

This time around, click the arrow button and choose **Custom** from the pick list. The Custom AutoFilter dialog box appears (see the following figure) with two boxes from which you select the filtering criteria.

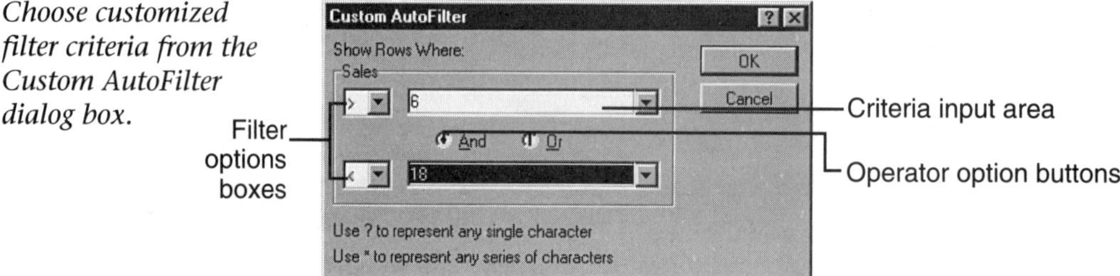

Choose customized filter criteria from the Custom AutoFilter dialog box.

Click on the down arrow of the top left filter options box. Excel displays a list of mathematical symbols you can use to indicate the criteria for your filter. Choose from = (equal), > (greater than), < (less than), >= (greater than or equal to), <= (less than or equal to), and <> (not equal to). For example, if you were really trying to find which employees had sold more than 217 widgets, you would select > (greater than). But it's a free pick, and this is only a demo, so choose one.

Next, click on the down arrow of the top box on the right (criteria input area). Excel displays a list of the values in the selected column. Pick one (such as 217). If you want, you can enter a number that does not appear in the list. For instance, if you're looking for all items with a value of 100, just enter 100. There is no need to go up and down the list searching for the closest value. Why settle for 101 or 99 when you can have exactly what you want? If you've finished selecting your filter criteria, click **OK** to start your custom AutoFilter.

If, on the other hand, you want to add another filter criteria, don't click OK. For example, if you want to see not only the top performers but also those at the bottom of the barrel, you need to use the other options in the Custom AutoFilter dialog box.

In the center of the Custom AutoFilter dialog box are two option buttons, And and Or, which you use to tell Excel what kind of logic you want to use. Use the And operator to make each item on the list fit *all* the criteria. You'll get a small list of possibilities. Use Or to select items that fit *any* of the criteria. Your list of possibilities is larger. If, for example, you want to see who sold more than 217 widgets *and* who sold fewer than 190, you enter filter criteria for greater than 217 and less than 190 and select Or, as shown in this figure. Click **OK**.

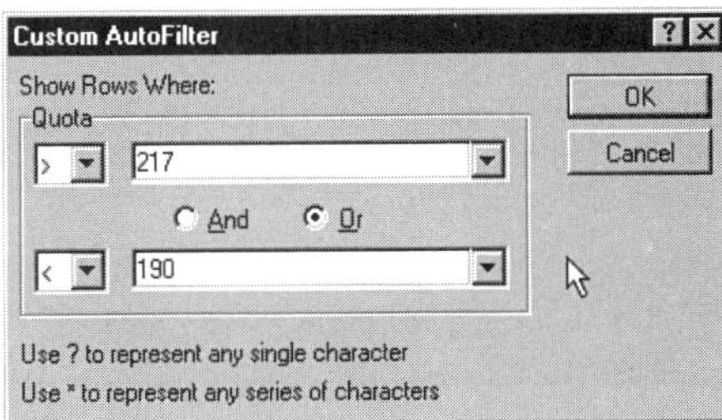

The Custom AutoFilter criteria.

AutoFilter finds all values in that column that are greater than 217 and all that are less than 190, and hides all other rows. The following figure shows the result of such a filter.

Use Wild Cards in Your Criteria

You can use wild-card characters in the Custom AutoFilter dialog box to broaden your filter criteria. Suppose, for example, you want to filter employee names or towns where your employees live. You could enter a partial word, instead of a number, in the Custom AutoFilter criteria box. Here's how the wild cards work.

The question mark represents any single character in a sequence of characters. For example, you can enter **P?st** to find Post and Past. The asterisk represents one or more characters in a sequence of characters. For example, you can enter **Sunny*** to find Sunnyvale and Sunnybono. If you really want to use a question mark or asterisk in your string of characters, preface it with the tilde (~) character. For example, enter **Whatthe~?** to find "Whatthe?"

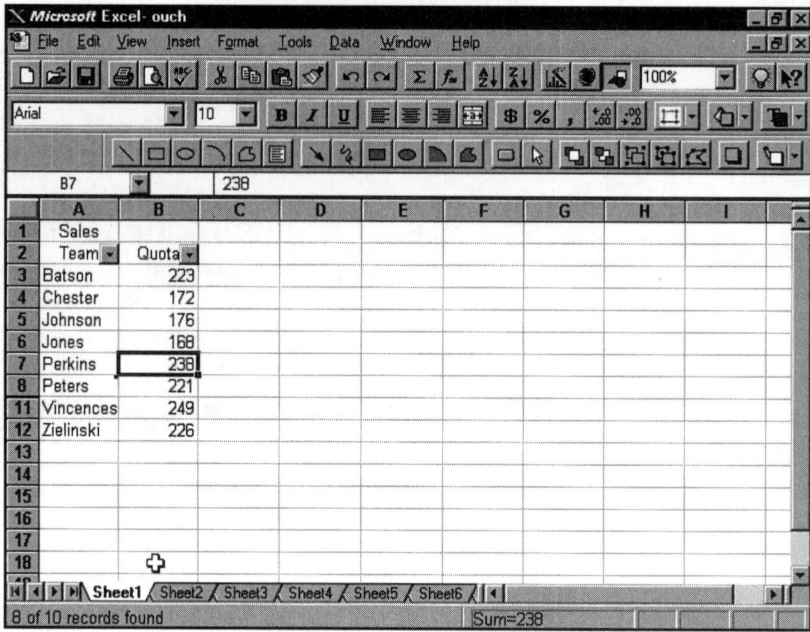

The completed custom AutoFilter.

Putting a Stop to It

At any time, you can restore the complete list by clicking on the AutoFilter arrow button in the selected column and selecting **All** from the pick list. To turn off AutoFilter itself, open the **Data** menu, select **Filter**, and select **AutoFilter** to remove the check mark.

AutoOutline

My, how your widget factory has grown: a list of six employees has grown into a list of 6,000. But you don't need to spend time scrolling through these seemingly endless rows and columns. It's 3 o'clock in the morning, and your eyes are about to pop out of your head now. Put any more caffeine in your system, and you'll be dead three weeks before you can get any sleep. What to do? You use the AutoOutline feature to view employees by department, by job title, or by any other system you've arranged to give you summary statistics.

Getting to the Bottom Line

AutoOutline offers a quick way to jump to the all-important bottom line on your worksheet: the sums, averages, and percentages that "auto" be the final result of all your calculations. Having traveled a mile for that bad pun, you should be ready to begin. How many widgets did everybody sell?

AutoOutline collapses entire sections of data and leaves behind only summary information, taking you right to your bottom line quickly and easily… well, sort of. This feature does have a few requirements of its own.

- Your data must be organized into, say, departments or product lines or age, and each category must be subtotaled.
- The subtotals for the data in the columns and rows must be located in the same columns and rows as the data. In other words, the sum of the entries in column B must be located at the bottom (or top) of column B. The rule concerning rows is similar: the sum of the entries in row 3 must be at the end (or beginning) of row 3.
- Your layout must be consistent from section to section: all subtotals must be located consistently. You can choose top or bottom but not top and bottom. (This is also true of rows. Put all your subtotals at either the beginning or the end.)

To automatically outline a worksheet, be certain that all subtotals are located in the same row or column as the data they total. Then click on any cell, open the **Data** menu, select **Group and Outline**, and choose **Auto Outline**.

That's it! If your totals and subtotals are located at the bottoms or tops of your columns, the Outline symbols appear to the left of your worksheet. If your totals and subtotals are to the right or left side of row entries, the Outline symbols appear above the worksheet. It is possible to have outline symbols on both the top and left of the worksheet.

The scale bars give you an indication of what will be hidden. In the figure, rows 3 through 9 will be hidden. Click on the + sign, the – sign, and the number buttons in the outline symbols area to display different views of the worksheet. When you click on **1** or the + button in the outline symbols area, Excel displays only the number that you are interested in. The following figure shows the spreadsheet after we clicked on the + button to see Total Sales.

AutoOutline view with outline bars in place.

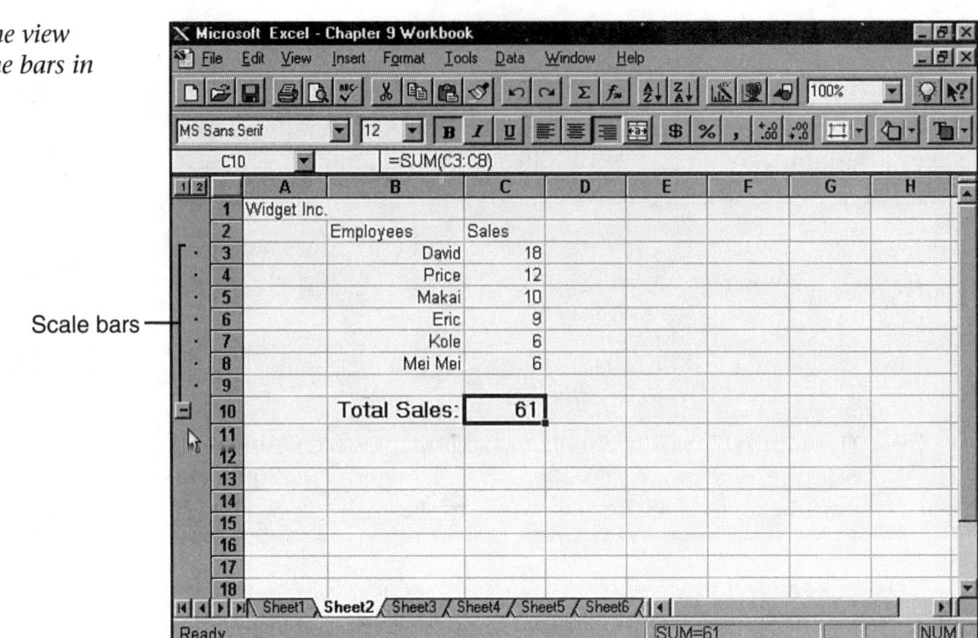

To turn off the AutoOutline feature, open the **Data** menu, select **Group and Outline**, and click on **Clear Outline**. It's over. Bag the coffee and get some sleep.

AutoSum

At last: an automatic feature that's really automatic! AutoSum couldn't be easier. Select a cell or a block of cells, and the sum of the numbers in that block appears in the AutoSum area on the right side of the Status bar (see the following figure). When you select a different block of cells, AutoSum... guess what?... figures the new sum.

AutoSum does several other tricks, as well. Right-click on the AutoSum block, and a shortcut menu appears. You can select Count to have AutoSum automatically count the number of filled cells in any given selection. Average gives the numerical average of the numbers in a block of cells. Count Nums counts the cells in a highlighted block that contain numbers only (no text). Max and Min show the maximum and minimum values in a range.

To insert the results of the AutoSum into your worksheet, simply click on the **AutoSum** button on the Standard toolbar or press **Alt+=**.

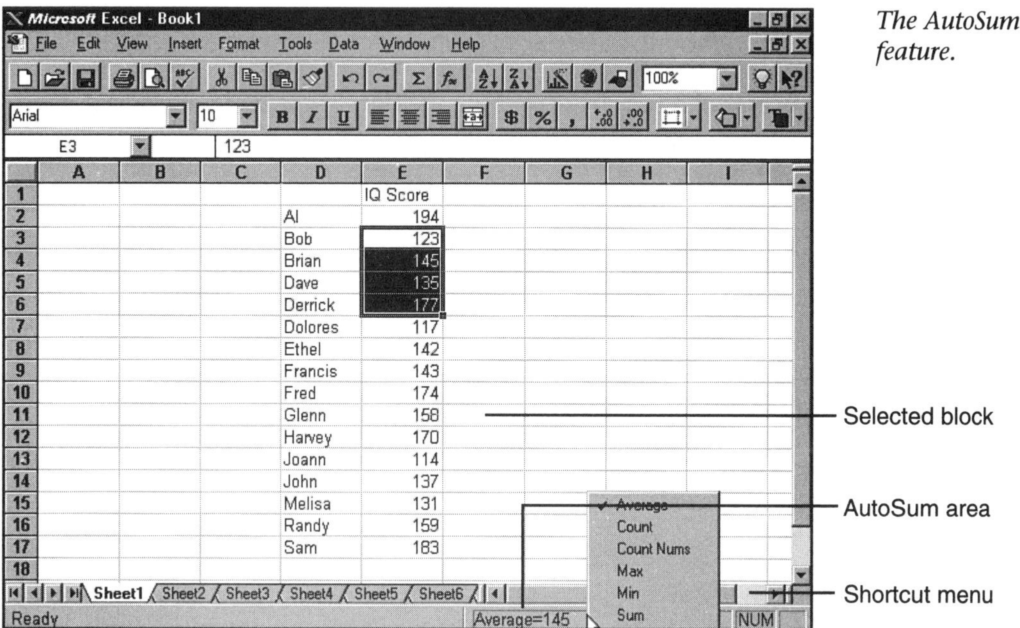

The AutoSum feature.

Automate with Macros

The only thing worse than that feeling of déjà vu that you get when you perform a task is that feeling of déjà vu that you get all over again when you repeat that same time-consuming task time after time. Or did we already say that?

Anyway, macros can fix all that. A *macro* enables you to record a multiple-keystroke process that you use repeatedly and reduce that process to a single keystroke or menu command. Any task that contains a finger-numbing series of keystrokes or that you do more than five or six times a day is a good candidate for turning into a macro. But, because what is mindless repetition to one person is a great Bruce Willis action flick to another, we won't try to anticipate what combinations of operations make worthwhile macros. We'll just point the way and silently step aside.

Macronucleus

Start out by opening the **Tools** menu and selecting **Record Macro**. In the submenu that appears, select **Use Relative References**. (If there is a check mark next to Relative References, the feature is already active; selecting it again deactivates it.) If the Use Relative References option is active, the macro you build can function in any area of the worksheet. If the Use Relative References option is inactive (there's no check mark), the macro functions only in the cells in which you build it.

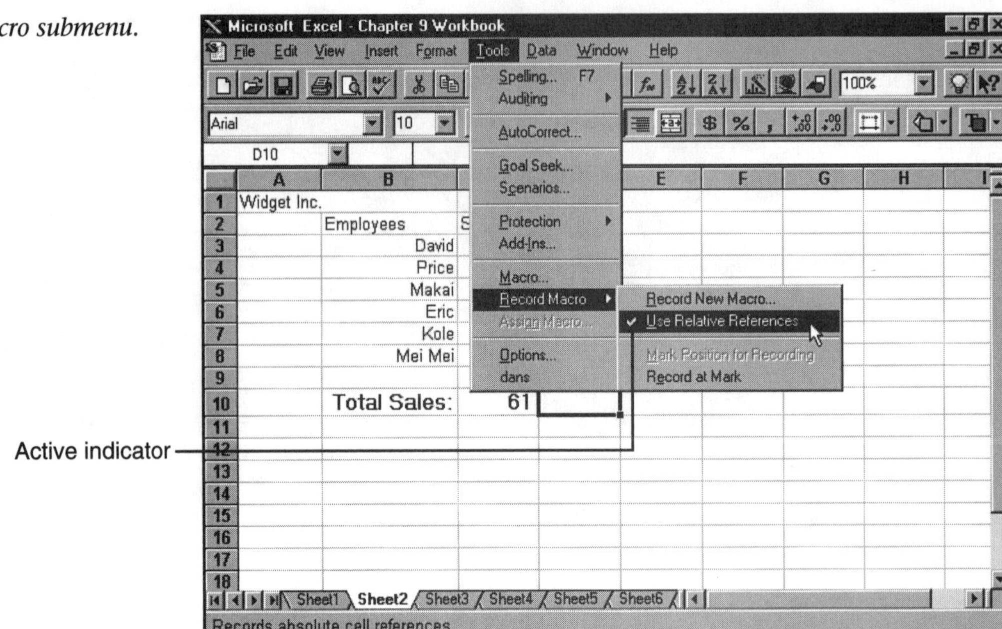

The Macro submenu.

With the Relative Reference selection active, you're ready to start building a macro. Open the **Tools** menu again and select **Record Macro**. This isn't tedious. This is déjà vu, remember? In the macro submenu, click **Record New Macro**, and the Record New Macro dialog box appears. From here you can choose a macro name and include a description if you want. To make your macro truly worthwhile, click on the **Options>>** button. Excel displays the screen shown in the following figure.

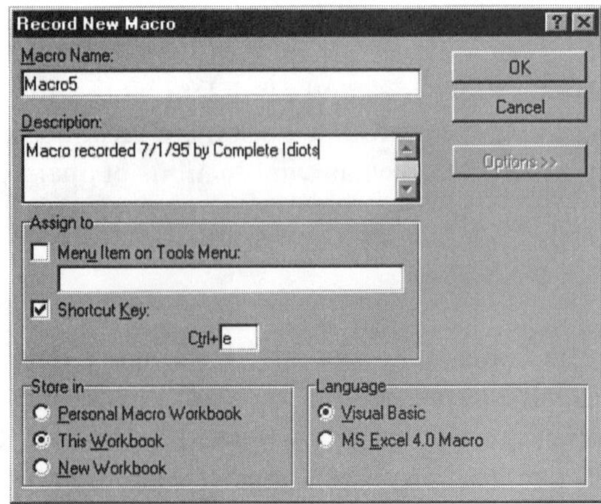

Enter a name, description, and shortcut key in the Record New Macro dialog box.

In the Assign to box, you can choose to assign a shortcut key for the macro or have it listed as a menu entry on the Tools menu. For the example that follows, click on the **Shortcut Key** check box to select it. A letter appears in the box to the right of Ctrl+. That key combination (Ctrl+*letter*) is the shortcut key you press anytime you want to run this particular macro. If this is your first try at creating a macro, it's probably the letter e. If not, type E now. Click **OK**, and the screen view returns to the normal worksheet, except that a small Stop Record button appears in the top right corner.

Work through the following steps to create a sample macro that changes the format of a selected cell:

1. Click on any cell.
2. Click the right mouse button.
3. From the shortcut menu, click on **Format Cells**.
4. In the Format Cells dialog box, click on the **Number** tab if necessary, and then select **Currency**.
5. In the Format Cells dialog box, click the **Font** tab.
6. Change the Font style to **BOLD**.
7. In the Format Cells dialog box, click **OK**.

8. Click the macro **Stop Record** button.

Now go back to the worksheet and try running your macro. Enter a list of random numbers and activate any cell in the list. Then press the shortcut key (**Ctrl+E**) for the new macro to reformat the cell's contents. The value in the cell changes to Currency format and becomes bold.

You have successfully completed your first macro. Give yourself a pat on the back.

Other Automatic Excel Functions

Excel has other automatic functions as well, all of which are covered in more detail in other chapters of this book. For more information on one of these features, skip to the chapter listed below.

AutoComplete — This feature tries to complete words for you as you type. Bothersome, don't you think? The suggestions come from a list of words already entered in the same column. See Chapter 6.

AutoCorrect — This function corrects your errors as you type. Fortunately, you can choose the list of errors you want AutoCorrect to correct. Chapter 8 explains how.

AutoFormat	Got a range? Change it to a table with AutoFormat. Just select the range, open the **Format** menu, and choose **AutoFormat**. Turn to Chapter 10 for more explanation.
AutoTemplate	When you begin building worksheets so that novice users can enter data, you need AutoTemplates. You'll find a complete description in Chapter 20.

The Least You Need to Know

- Use AutoFilter to quickly view the most, the least, or the best matches. AutoFilter works only in columns, and each column must have a label.
- AutoOutline telescopes worksheets into a more manageable view. Each section you want to outline must be formatted identically, with subtotals in the same place in each section.
- AutoSum subtotals a block of numbers and displays the sum automatically in its own on-screen box. You can also use AutoSum to display averages or to count the items in a group.
- Macros simplify repetitive tasks. Start a macro, record your keystrokes, and then play them back when you need to repeat that task.
- Excel contains loads of other automatic features, all of which are detailed in related chapters.

Chapter 10

Home on the Range

In This Chapter

- Reference rap
- Keep your options open
- Rang-er Rick

In 1972, the great American Battleship champion Bobby Fissure defeated his Soviet challenger Boris Spatzy in a converted airplane hangar in an inhospitable area of Iceland. Playing before a packed house (they had managed to requisition the only working space heater within 100 miles), Fissure brilliantly attacked Spatzy's formation, picking him apart one cell at a time. After 12 hours, the multitudes in attendance were awakened by the last anguished cry of "You sank my battleship." A thunderous roar filled the arena as a hundred thousand or so Icelanders simultaneously cheered the new champion and plotted ways to relieve him of his space heater.

Imagine how history would have changed if Boris Spatzy had known about ranges. Instead of a lame attack on a single cell, like A3, he could have designated an entire range:

"Boris Number 1"

"What's that?"

"All the cells from A1 to Z99."

"You sank all my battleships!"

But, alas! Poor Boris didn't know the first thing about the power of designating ranges. By the end of this chapter, you will.

Excellent References

Every one of those *cells* (the blocks on the worksheet grid) on your spreadsheet has a life and an address. No, you can't send them e-mail... not yet, anyway. But you can refer to each cell by its address, and that comes in handy when you need to move around, find your place on the worksheet, or write a formula.

This chapter is a brief introduction to references and ranges, including information you need to know before you start writing formulas in the next chapter. While we're at it, we also examine the all-important Options dialog box.

You learned in earlier chapters that each worksheet cell has a unique address that consists of its column letter and row number. The cell in the third row of the third column is—quite naturally—C3. Excel permits as many as 16,384 rows per worksheet, numbered 1 through 16,384 (what did you expect?). You're allowed a slightly smaller number of columns: 256. But column heads don't get numbers; they get letters, and that's a bit more problematic. Once you've gone past the 26th letter, Excel begins labeling columns AA, AB, and so on, right up to the 256th column.

If Excel's column-lettering system is too cumbersome, you can set up your spreadsheet to number the columns instead. In that case, cell B3 becomes R3C2, and you've got some really ugly references. But for a few people, particularly those who are transferring from other spreadsheet packages, this alternative system is easier to understand.

To initiate the alternative reference format, pull down the **Tools** menu and choose **Options**. In the Options dialog box, click the **General** tab. The first option you see there is for Reference Style, and the default style is A1. If you want to change it, click on the **R1C1** option button.

In this text we stick with the A1 reference style.

Other Options Dialog Box Options

While we have this dialog box open, this is probably a good time to explain the other features in the Options dialog box. (This particular dialog box is sort of the Miscellaneous box, and doesn't fit neatly into any particular Excel category. Sort of like a Woody Allen movie.) So we'll continue where we left off, with the General tab.

General Tab

In the Menus area, check the **Recently Used File List** box to have Excel display the last four files you had open in the File menu. This makes it easy to reopen any of the last few files you were using.

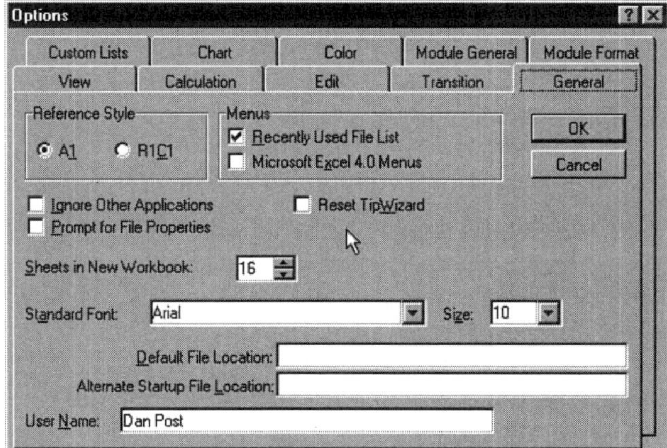

The General tab of the Options dialog box.

If you click in the box for Microsoft Excel 4.0 Menus, Excel makes significant changes to your menu. To return to the Excel 7.0 menus, simply open the **Options** menu and select **New Menus.**

Check the **Ignore Other Applications** box to have Microsoft Excel ignore all requests from other applications. Note, however, that this could cause problems if you have embedded objects in your worksheet.

The Prompt for File Properties option controls whether Excel displays the Properties dialog box when you save your worksheet. In the Properties dialog box, you can enter identifying information about your worksheet.

You can select **Reset TipWizard** to have Excel redisplay tips you've already seen.

At the bottom of the Options dialog box are several data entry areas. There you define the number of worksheets in your workbook, the standard typeface (font) and type size you want to use, the default and alternate locations of your files (which you enter in the format ***drive letter:folder/subfolder***), and your user name.

Transition Tab

The Transition tab of the Options dialog box contains features that simplify the transition from older versions of Microsoft Excel or from Lotus 1-2-3 to Excel for Windows 95.

The infamous slash (/) key should be familiar to all 1-2-3 users. In the Settings area, choose the Help files and menus you want to use and turn on the **Transition Navigation Keys** if you want the home key to move you back to cell A1. If you want to maintain your old formula habits, check the appropriate options in the Sheet Options area.

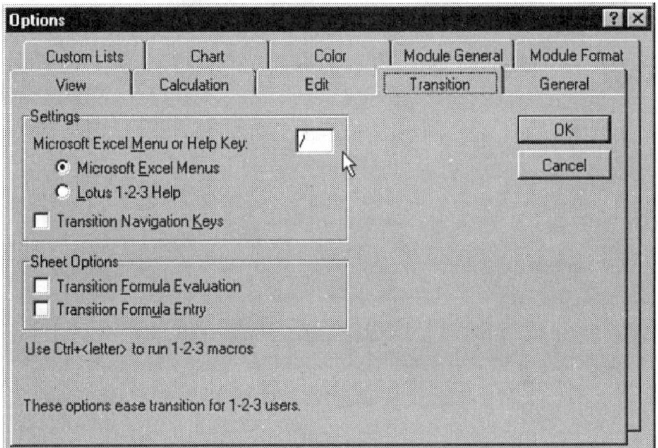

The Transition tab.

Edit Tab

These features enable you to edit your worksheets. For the most part, your best bet is to turn them all on.

You use the Edit tab's settings to control whether you can edit (make changes) directly in a cell or drag-and-drop the contents of your cell with your mouse when you copy or move. You can tell Excel which direction you want to move when you press the Enter key after entering information in a cell.

Use the Fixed Decimal setting to set the number of decimal places in your numbers (usually two). If you select Fixed Decimal and you enter the digits **1 2 3**, for example, Excel records 1.23. When this feature is selected, you can override it by manually entering the decimal.

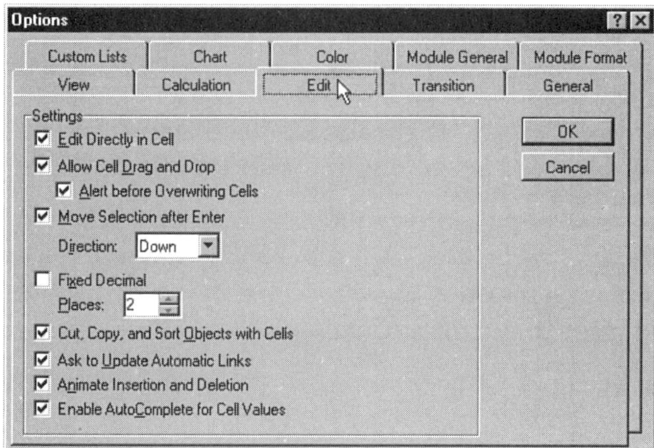

The Edit tab.

This tab also contains an option that allows you to copy the objects (pictures, notes, maps and so on) along with the contents of the cell. Another fun Excel trick you can implement is to animate your insertions and deletions (for example, slow them down so you can watch the progress). This is also the section where you choose to use the AutoComplete feature to automatically fill in cell values. (See Chapter 6 for an explanation of AutoComplete.)

Calculation Tab

Generally, when you enter a formula, Excel calculates the result immediately. If you work in very large spreadsheets, you might find yourself spending a lot of time waiting for Excel to calculate. Use the Manual option (instead of the default Automatic option) to turn off the automatic calculations so you can control when Excel calculates the formulas.

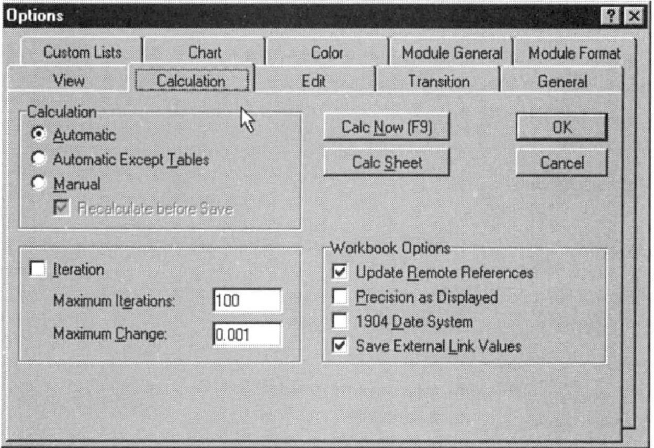

The Calculation tab.

Normally you want Excel to calculate all its formulas just one time. Very rarely, though, you might want it to calculate all its formulas several times. *Iterations* repeat a calculation a designated number of times (in case you want to calculate 1/3 of 1/3 of 1/3, and so on for 10 repetitions, for example). You might also use this feature if you want to see a calculation whose results depend on the results of another calculation.

The Workbook options are obscure, and you probably want to check only the first and last options in this section. Update Remote References enables you to *link* (connect) a cell on your worksheet to a cell on some other worksheet, and Save External Link Values remembers the value of links made to data in programs other than Excel.

The Precision as Displayed option changes Excel so that it calculates based only on the figures you see on the worksheet. If a number has been rounded for display purposes, Excel normally calculates based on the real number instead of the rounded number that appears; this feature changes that. The 1904 Date System is almost never used. It calculates all Excel dates with serial numbers that begin in the year 1904, instead of in 1900 (the default).

Those Other Tabs

The options on the View tab enable you to decide how cluttered your worksheet will be. The default leaves most, but not all, items visible. In the Objects area, you'll probably want to choose **Show All**, which makes all your pictures and maps and graphics visible as you work. Turn the other Show and Window Options features off or on individually.

The features on the Module Format and Module General tabs are useful to software writers, but not to real people. Actively resist the urge to change them. (Join a self-help group if necessary.)

The Color tab contains options you can use to change the colors for your worksheet, charts, and lines. The Chart tab options are available only when you have a chart displayed. (See Chapter 18 for an explanation of these features.) And the options on the Custom Lists tab deal with the AutoFill feature, explained in Chapter 7.

More on References

We return now to our discussion of references. References can be categorized in a couple of different ways: as absolute or relative, and as internal, external, or remote.

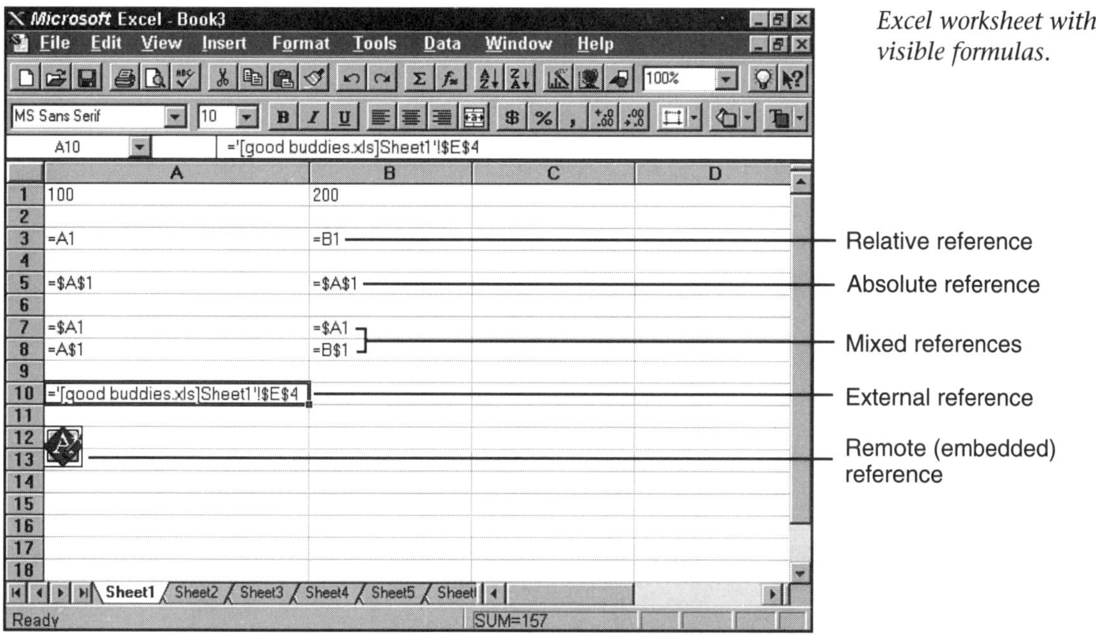

Excel worksheet with visible formulas.

Absolute vs. Relative

In the next chapter, you'll see that instead of calculating formulas like 2 + 2, it's more useful to calculate cell A7 + cell A8. This way of calculating enables you to change the contents of cells A7 and A8, without having to rewrite the formula. When we talk about numbers like 2 and 3, we're using *values*. When we talk about cells A7 and A8, we're using *references*.

When you create an entire column of formulas and use Excel's Copy or AutoFill features to fill them in automatically, you run into some interesting problems. What if, for example, your original formula contains a reference to cell A7, and you copy that formula down a row? Should the copied formula continue to refer to cell A7, or should it now refer to a new cell one row below cell A7?

Most references are *relative*, which means that they refer to a relative location (such as "the three cells immediately above this cell"). For example, when you copy a reference to cell A1 to a location one column to the right, the reference changes to B1, which reflects the amount of the relative change. The default copy status is Relative.

Absolute references, on the other hand, always refer to the same cell (such as cell C3) no matter where they are copied to. You make a reference absolute by including dollar signs ($) in the reference, like this: C3. (When you refer to a cell by clicking on it, instead of actually typing it in, you can make it absolute by pressing **F4** before you enter the next keystroke.)

Mixed references combine absolute and relative (such as $C4 or C$4). You use mixed references when you want a group of calculations to refer to multiple rows in the same column or multiple columns in the same row, but not both.

Internal vs. External vs. Remote

There are some other twists to the story of cell references. It's easy to see where a cell reference like A3 comes from. Sometimes, though, you want to refer to information that's not found on your current worksheet.

Most references are *internal*, that is, they refer to other cells on the same worksheet. To include an internal reference in a formula (a mathematical equation), you can type in the cell reference manually, or you can simply click on the cell you want to reference. A simple formula with an internal reference might look like this:

```
=A1+6
```

The equal sign starts the formula, A1 is a relative reference to cell A1, the + is an *operator*, and the 6 is the next factor (element) in the formula. Chapter 11 explains formula writing in more detail, so all you need to learn now is that A1, in this example, is the moral equivalent of a number, and that worksheet formulas use the Reverse Polish notation of old Hewlett-Packard calculators, where every entry must be preceded by an operator.

An *external* reference refers to cells in another worksheet or even an entirely different workbook. To use an external reference to another workbook in a formula, open both workbooks. (This step is not necessary if your external reference is only to another worksheet in your same workbook.) Start entering the formula, and when you're ready to add the external reference, select the other worksheet from the **Window** menu or use the worksheet tabs at the bottom of your screen to open it. Click on the cell you want to reference. Then continue the formula with the next operator and switch back to the original worksheet when necessary. A formula with an external reference might look like this:

```
='[budget.xls]Sheet1'!$E$5+6
```

The equal sign starts the formula. The portion in square brackets is the name of the second workbook, Sheet1 is the name of the worksheet, and the exclamation point (!)

separates the worksheet name from the cell reference. The E5 is an absolute reference to cell E5, the + is an operator, and the 6 is the next factor in the formula.

Go Outside!

Your formulas can include multiple references. And Excel doesn't even mind if you mix and match internal, external, remote, relative, absolute, and mixed references.

You're limited only by the total number of characters in your formula and the amount of memory in your computer. Remember, though, that exceedingly complex references are difficult to trace and increase the risk of a software crash.

The *remote* reference is highly advanced and has limited use. A remote reference imports data from another application altogether. A formula containing a remote reference might look like this:

=RISKCALC|SMITH.INS!1995+6

The equal sign starts the formula. RISKCALC is the name of an application that supports Object Linking and Embedding (OLE). The pipe character (|) pipes in the document name (SMITH.INS), and the exclamation point separates the document reference from the cell reference (1995). The + is an operator, and the 6 is the next factor in the formula.

Linking and embedding are complicated ways of copying information from other applications. A generally easier (and safer) alternative is to do what you need to do in the other application, and then simply copy and paste the results into your Excel worksheet.

Range Roving

A *range* is a specific group of cells. Ranges most often comprise a group of cells in the same column or row, or in a rectangular block encompassing multiples rows or columns. It is possible, however, to have a range of noncontiguous cells (cells that are not adjacent to one another).

The normal syntax for a range is A1:A10, which means the range includes all the cells in the first 10 rows of column A. Like cell references, range references can be relative, absolute, or mixed. Fortunately, you can assign an English-language name to a range so you don't have to figure out later what you meant when you said BA64:GC72. You might, for example, name a range Oct Expenses, 90 Thru 95 Taxes, Taco Bell, or Yamaha.

You use ranges in a number of ways:

- **In formulas** If you want to add up a column of numbers, use a range so you don't have to enter =A1+A2+A3+A4+A5....
- **To move around** When worksheets and workbooks start getting huge, it helps to give different areas different names. Excel's range-naming command enables you to quickly go to a specific named area of your worksheet.
- **In macros** Simplify macro writing by using range names instead of selecting ranges on the fly. See Chapter 9 to learn how to use Excel macros.

Creating a Range

Here's the process for creating and naming a simple range.

1. Select the range by highlighting a block of cells (as described in Chapter 7). If you intend to use the range in formulas and calculations, make sure the range you select contains only numeric values, and no labels. (Labels don't affect most of your calculations, but they do affect your spreadsheet housekeeping.)
2. Click in the **Name Box** at the left end of the Formula bar, and type in the name of the new range. Excel adds the new name to the Reference List; you can recall it by clicking on the **Name Box** down arrow and choosing the name from the list.

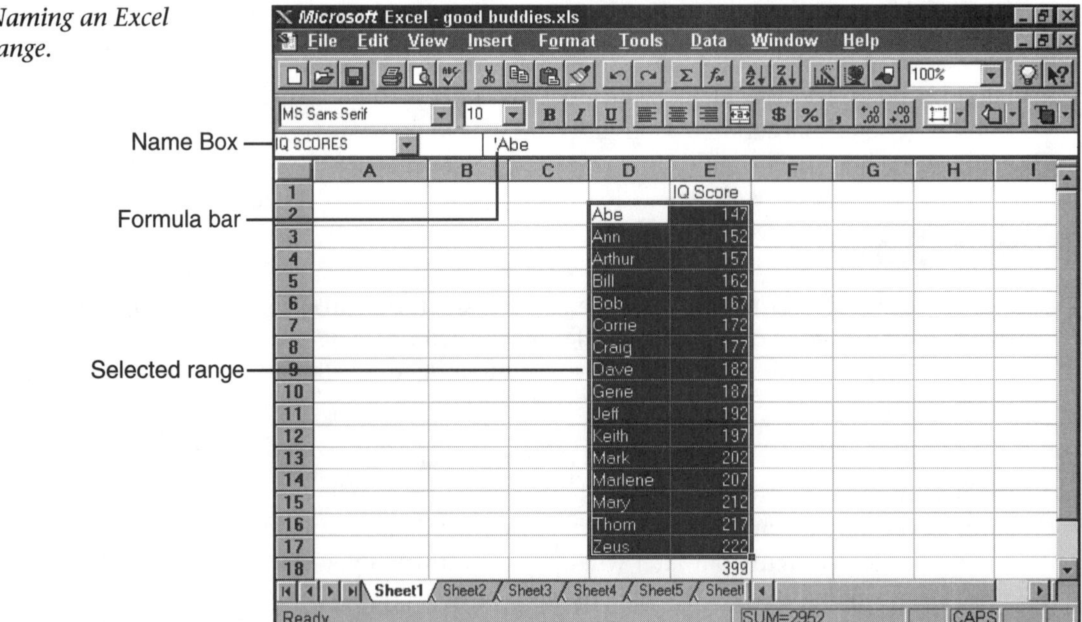

Naming an Excel range.

Alternatively, you can select the range, open the **Insert** menu, and choose **Name and Define**. In the Define Name dialog box, type in the new range name, click **Add**, and click **OK**.

Selecting Non-Adjacent Cells

You can create a range that contains not only multiple cells, but also multiple blocks of cells. To do so, select the first block (click on the corner cell and drag to the cell at the opposite corner), press and hold down the **Ctrl** key, and select the next block. You can add as many blocks as you want using this method. Then name the new range, as described earlier in this chapter.

Keep Your Head Up

If you want to use existing labels that are at the top of a column or the end of a row to name a range, you don't even have to type the name. Just select the cells that contain the headings, open the **Insert** menu, choose **Name**, and select **Create**. The Create Names dialog box appears, asking where you want the names to come from. Each column or row label becomes a separate range.

Look Ma! No Hands! The AutoFormat Function

Never downplay the importance of style when making any kind of presentation. (After all, what would Robin Hood have been but another thief in the forest if he hadn't slipped on those kelly green pantyhose?) When you've got nice, neat ranges, rows, and columns, it's time to add some… Pizzazz!

There's no Pizzazz command exactly, but AutoFormat comes pretty close. AutoFormat can invigorate your ranges by adding color and depth. It can help get rid of that tired, old—uh—worksheet look.

The Look That Says You

Before you start AutoFormat, you must select the range of cells you want to dress up. Then open the **Format** menu and select **AutoFormat**. The AutoFormat dialog box appears.

Use the scroll bar in the Table Format list box to select a format. In the Sample area, Excel displays a sample of what you will see. Click on the **Options** button to open the Formats to Apply section of the dialog box. This section contains options you can use to customize the look of your display. Again, you can view the effects of each option in the Sample area, so experiment a little. Click **OK** when you've settled on a look that you like.

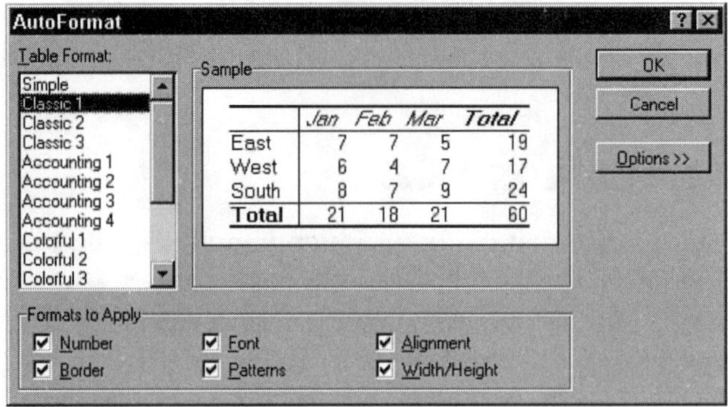

The AutoFormat dialog box with options selected.

Back to the Past

To clear the effects of AutoFormat, go through the same steps again: select a range of cells, open the **Format** menu, and click on **AutoFormat**. In the AutoFormat dialog box, select **None** from the Table Format list and click **OK**. The cells revert to their dull, drab, uninspired, unformatted selves.

The Least You Need to Know

- References describe the location of a cell or a group of cells.
- References take the form A1, where A is the column and 1 is the row number.
- Relative references change when they're copied. Absolute references, which contain a dollar sign in their address, don't change.
- The Options dialog box (select **Tools**, **Options**) is the place for modifying the way Excel operates. If you don't know where else to go to make a change, try the Options dialog box.
- A range can be a block of cells or multiple blocks of cells. If you want to remember later what data the range contains, you can name the range.
- When it's time to pretty up a range of cells, choose **AutoFormat** from the **Format** menu.

Chapter 11

The Winning Formula

In This Chapter

- Form-ula feed
- Work it out
- Stop problems dead
- Juggling in a jumble of formula junk

Oktoberfest arrives in Munich in late September. It's an occasion for drinking, eating, drinking, merrymaking... and drinking. The most significant part of Oktoberfest is, of course, the beer. And if that's the case, the second-most-significant part would have to be what goes in the beer.

Brewers pitch their tents side by side, competing for the accolades of Germans and beer-guzzling tourists. Within the strict rules regulating the ingredients, there is still room for individuality. As a result, a large tent with no waiting will probably remain empty while a small tent will be stuffed well beyond capacity. Brewing beer is an art, they say. There are basic formulas, bizarre formulas, and of course, winning formulas.

Fortunately, you don't have to travel to Munich to brew up a few formulas of your own. Get the spreadsheet formula right, and you'll find yourself with all the right numbers in all the right places—and with a good aftertaste in your mouth. Choose the wrong formulas, and you'll face an illogical maze of values—a conglomeration that will soon have you in a stupor, unable to tell what's happening, and suffering a sure-fire morning-after headache.

Brewing instructions follow.

Formula for Success

Formulas. They're the heart and soul of spreadsheets; without them, you might as well use a pocket calculator, a tablet of paper, and a pencil with a good eraser. Formulas give Excel's worksheets the power to compare, select, calculate, iterate, manipulate, and eliminate the data you put into its grimy little hands.

What Is a Formula?

A *formula* is a mathematical computation involving multiple factors: values, references, names, operators, and functions. To qualify as a formula, the equation has to return new information from the data you enter. In Excel, all formulas begin with an equal sign (=).

Some Definitions

Before we get too far into this discussion, let's establish a few definitions. We'll do these alphabetically, shall we?

Formula Jargon

Term	Definition
Address	The location of a cell or a group of cells. Takes the form B3, where B is the second column, and 3 is the third row. You can also call it a reference.
Argument	The part of the equation that's not an operator. How's that for a bum definition? Okay, it includes constants, functions, names, cell references, and values.
Constant	A number or text that you type directly into the formula (as opposed to something like a cell reference, which tells Excel where to find its own numbers or text).
Equation	You learned this in the third grade, right? Something equals something else. In Excel, however, you don't know what it equals until you hit the Enter key. You might also call this a formula.

Term	Definition
Factor	An element of a formula; can be a value, reference, name, operator, or function. Yeah, you're right: that's the same thing as an argument.
Formula	A mathematical computation involving multiple factors and resulting in a new value. Pretty much the same thing as an equation.
Function	A built-in formula. (You'll learn to use functions in Chapter 12.)
Label	Text—not numbers. Okay, maybe numbers and text together. For our purposes, labels are the words at the top of a column or the left end of a row that describe the contents of the column or row.
Name	The English-language name that identifies a particular range. (French and Spanish names work, too. But no Chinese names unless you know how to Romanize them, like this: Hau Bu Hau?)
Operator	The mathematical symbols that tell Excel how to calculate a formula. The operators include Add (+), Subtract (–), Divide (/), Multiply (*), Percents (%), Exponents (^), and Equivalencies (equal [=], not equal [<>], greater than [>], and less than [<]).
Range	A cell or a block of cells identified by a name or an address. (See Chapter 10 for more information on ranges.)
Reference	The name or address of a cell or a range. (See Chapter 11 for more information on references.)
Result	The answer you get after Excel calculates your formula.
Syntax	The rules about where to put the parentheses, commas, asterisks, and operators within a formula.
Value	Numbers—not text.

Working Through Formulas

Now that you can talk the talk, let's walk through a simple formula. In this example, we'll add up a column of numbers.

On a blank worksheet, enter the numbers 1, 2, and 3 in the first three rows of column A. Draw a line through cell A4 to indicate the end of the data.

The Bottom Line

If you have a column of numbers you need to total, and you want to draw a line in the cell above the total, select the cell and type a backslash and a hyphen (\–). Excel fills the cell with dashes, creating an underline that expands and contracts automatically when you change the width of the column.

In the same way, you can use any character to fill a given cell. If you want a line of asterisks, for example, just type *.

Your formula can contain numbers or references (addresses that tell the formula where to find the numbers). For our sample formula, we want to add the numbers 1, 2, and 3 (the data in column A). Instead of typing the formula =1+2+3, we'll tell Excel to go find those numbers itself.

Go to cell A5 to begin writing your formula. Enter an equal sign (=) or a plus sign (+) to let Excel know you're starting the formula. To tell Excel what three numbers you want to add, move to cell A1. (A moving line around the current cell indicates where you are.) Press + to enter the reference. Your formula now reads =A1+. Move up to cell A2 and press + again, and then move back up to cell A3. This is the last entry in your formula, but don't enter anything else yet. Instead, read on for more useful information.

The Formula Bar

Before we continue, take a look up north at the Formula bar (the line above the column headers). There you see a duplicate of the formula you're entering in your active cell. Later, you can edit your formula in the Formula bar by adding to the formula or deleting parts of it. Characters you type will be inserted at the location of the blinking cursor in either the Formula bar or the active cell. Use the I-beam-shaped mouse pointer to click on the spot in the Formula bar where you want the cursor to appear. Once you have a cursor, you can press **Backspace** to remove the character to the left of the cursor or **Delete** to remove the character to the right.

Let's complete the formula now. Instead of pressing + again (which will confuse Excel to death), press the **Enter** key to tell Excel you've finished. Your formula disappears, and in its place you find your result: 6. You can click in cell A5 at any time, and the formula reappears in the Formula bar, while the result remains unchanged.

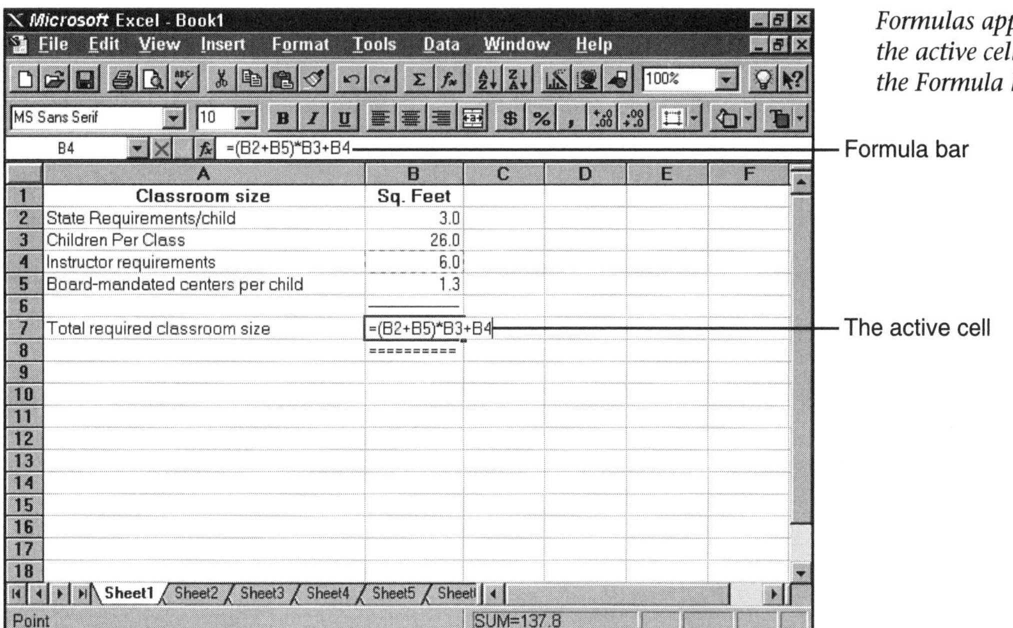

Formulas appear in the active cell and the Formula bar.

Now What?

Now that you've entered your first formula, it's time to see the power of Excel. If no formula did more than this sample did, well… you'd be better off doing your math in your head. But, suppose that instead of the numbers 1, 2, and 3, you wanted to figure the total of all your annual income, the total of all your annual expenses, and the rate of tax on the difference.

In that case, you'd find yourself writing a formula that looked more like =(A1–A2)*A3 or, if you named your cells, your formula would be =(INCOME–EXPENSES)*TAXRATE. Then you could subtract your TAXDUE from your GROSS to find your NET and suddenly, things get much more interesting.

Imposing a Syntax

Poor Mr. Hartman. He was the high school algebra teacher of one of the authors of this book, and for an entire year, he had to do daily battle with the plaintive whining of "Why do I need to learn this stuff? What good is it in real life?" Mr. Hartman, if you're reading this, you can relax now. All the rules of precedence and order and logic finally make sense. Too bad you couldn't demonstrate a spreadsheet in 1977!

Remember these basic principles when you enter formulas:

➤ **Formulas have order.** In Excel, formulas begin with an equal sign (=). If you cannot afford an equal sign, one will be appointed for you when you enter a plus sign (+) at the beginning of your formula.

➤ **Operators have order.** Multiplication (*) and division (/) take precedence over addition (+) and subtraction (–). In addition to those four basic operators, there are other operators that control the order in which a calculation is performed. We've included a handy table in this section to remind you of the order of operations. The table shows you the order of operators, listed in order of precedence. (For example, arguments in parentheses are calculated before negative arguments.)

➤ **Calculations are performed logically.** When operators are equal, Excel calculates left to right.

➤ **Ranges can operate like single cells.** In Excel, the address A1 is as valid as the number 6, which is as valid as the range name "DOGFOOD."

Priority Order of Operators

Operator	Symbol
Parenthetical calculations	( )
Negative numbers	–
Percentages	%
Exponents	^
Multiplication and division	*, /
Addition and subtraction	+, –
Equivalencies	=, <>, >, <, >=, <=

Following the priority order of operators, consider these formulas and their results.

Formula	Returns
=–2+4*3	10
=–(2+4*3)	–14
=–(2+4)*3	–18
=(–2+4)*3	6
=1*(–2+4*3)	10
=(–2+4*3	Error

Note that, unlike what you learned in your high-school algebra class, you cannot use a number followed immediately by parentheses as a substitute for the multiplication symbol. Every argument in an Excel formula requires an operator.

Changing the Contents

Even after you create a formula, you have the freedom to change the referenced cells at will. Excel cheerfully accommodates your fickleness and recalculates the formula with every change. So you can edit to your heart's content (Chapter 8 explains how) and witness the true power of spreadsheets as Excel changes factors and updates results. And you never again have to retype the formula.

A Cell by Any Other Name

Okay, you're probably wondering what the excitement over Excel is all about. So what if Excel gives you the ability to add 1+2 and A1+A2? You could probably do that on your own. Right? But it gets better than that. If you name your cells and ranges, you can also add DOG+CAT and RUSH+HILLARY. (Try that without Excel!)

The simplest way to use the naming power of Excel is to first input your data into the spreadsheet. For example, if you want to list square footage requirements for a building project, you list several categories along with the corresponding numbers. Then you name each of the *ranges* (which can be as small as a single cell). Chapter 10 explains the procedure for naming ranges.

In the formula shown in the following figure, we used the rather long labels in column A to name each corresponding cell in column B using the **Insert**, **Name**, **Create** command. We could have assigned short names (State, Kids, Teacher, Centers) instead, but this way we didn't have to type anything in twice. (Call us lazy.)

Later, as we created the formula, we selected each range name from the Name Box in the same manner we would have selected a cell from the spreadsheet (by clicking on each one when it was time to enter its reference in the formula).

Naming ranges and cells before you enter them into formulas has a couple of advantages:

- **Location** There's no risk of entering the wrong cell address or column number if you're simply picking a range or cell from a list.
- **Documentation** If your worksheet is complicated, it will be much easier to remember six years from now what you intended to do with that formula if you can see a descriptive name instead of a cell or range reference.

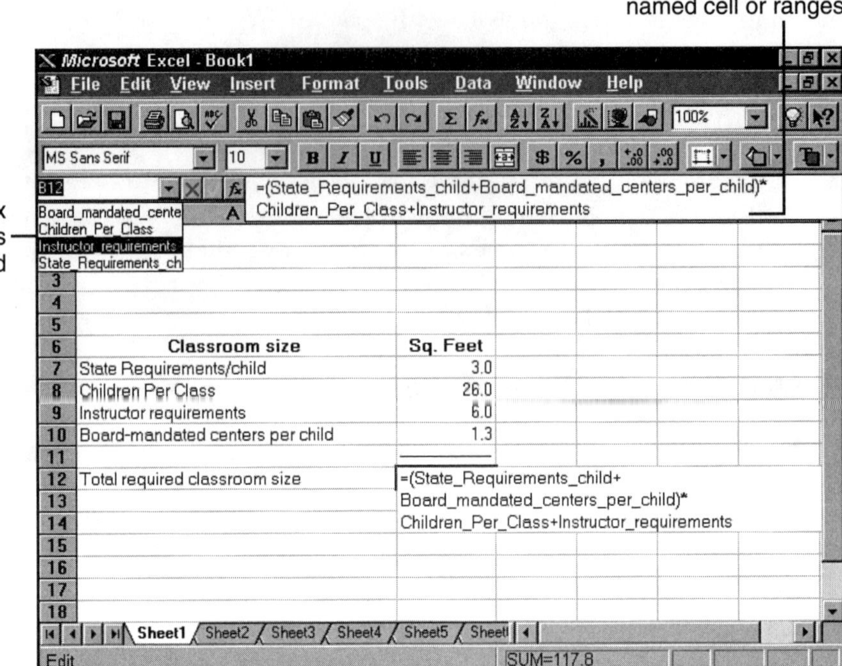

You can easily add named cells or ranges to your formulas.

The Nesting Instinct

Remember the example formulas we used earlier to show the order of operators? Those formulas indicate the importance of parenthetical arguments. A formula is a routine, and parenthetical formulas within the larger formula are called *subroutines*. By "nesting" subroutines (such as 2+4) within a larger formula, you give Excel even more power.

The rule is that you can have subroutine within subroutine within subroutine, but you must be precisely accurate with your parentheses. If you misplace or neglect even one, your entire formula will be either incorrect or incomplete. Hope for the latter, because Microsoft displays a warning message when you don't have an equal number of opening and closing parentheses. If you've just put the parentheses in the wrong place, you get no warning, and you probably won't know.

You can nest subroutines up to seven layers deep. Here's an example of nesting:

=1+(2*(3+(4*(5+(6*(7+8))))))

Notice that each opening parenthesis has a corresponding closing parenthesis. This formula returns the result 767.

Preventing Formula Problems

Preventing formula problems may sound like an impossible task—and maybe it is—but that doesn't mean you have to give up the fight. Here are a few things to look for that might help you along. But don't fret if none of these solutions solve your problem; there are some great problem-solving tools up ahead in Chapter 13. However, the suggestions in the following sections could help keep those formula problems from ever appearing.

Circular References

A circular reference can be thought of as the spreadsheet rendition of the classic chicken-and-egg problem. A *circular reference* occurs when a formula refers to itself, either directly or indirectly.

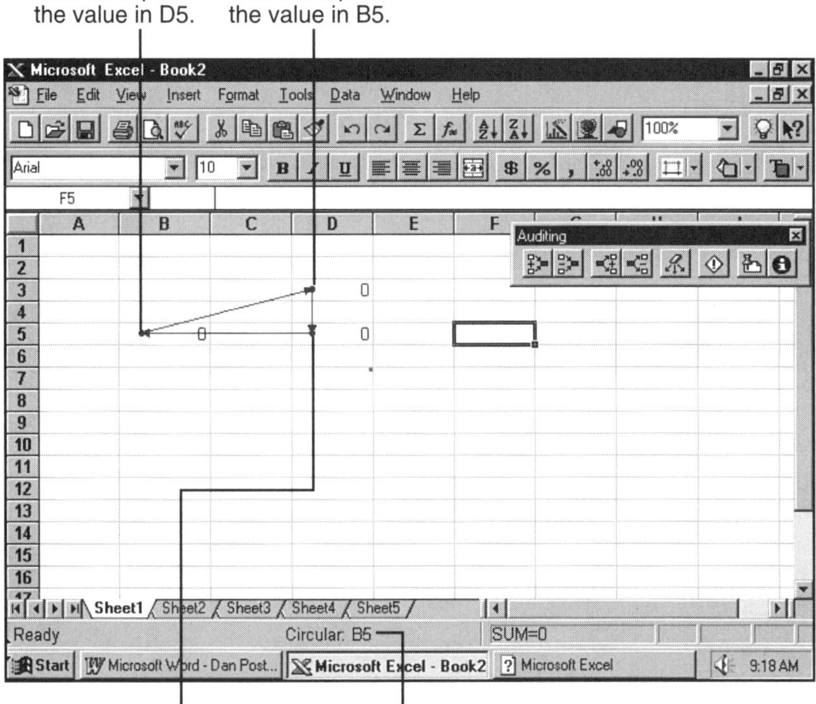

A circular reference.

Anytime you create a circular reference, Excel alerts you by displaying a warning message in the Status bar, and then it lets you continue on your merry way. Unless it was your intention to create a circular reference, you should rewrite your formula to break the circle.

Circle Cycle

Not all circular references are accidental. However, if you want to try using them, there are a few things you should know.

Excel cannot use normal calculation to solve formulas with circular references. Therefore, Excel stops recalculating the value of the cell after 100 iterations or anytime the value in the cell changes by less than .001. To change these defaults, open the **Tools** menu and select **Options**. In the Options dialog box, click the **Calculation** tab. Then select the **Iteration** check box and modify the default values as desired for Maximum Iterations and Maximum Change.

Unexpected Error Messages

Error messages are ever-looming possibilities. You can enter all the right values and punch all the right keys, and still there is a chance you'll end up with some unexpected results. No, we're not just talking about the negative numbers that sometimes appear when balancing a checkbook—although they are often unexpected. We're talking about results like **#####**, and **#NUM!**, and other cryptic error messages. The following table shows a few of those unexpected error messages, most of which are left over from a time when computers had 48KB of memory and when a portable PC was one you could fit in the back of your truck.

Excel Error Messages

Error Message	Description
#####	This indicates that the results of your calculations are too large to fit in the cell. Although it might be annoying, it's not exactly an error. The correct answer is in the cell, Excel is just unable (or unwilling) to display it on your screen in the space allotted. All you have to do to correct this is make your column wide enough to accommodate the answer. (See Chapter 16 for instructions.)
#DIV/0!	You get #DIV/0! when you attempt to divide by 0. It couldn't be done when we were in school (at least one of us has the test scores to prove it), and it can't be done now. The only solution is to track down the formula in which you are attempting to divide by 0, and correct it. One last vital hint: Excel interprets empty cells as 0.
#N/A	This is not an error. In fact, it isn't even a message from Excel. This is just a note that you write to yourself when you don't have a real value to enter. If the value for a cell is not available, enter #N/A. If you leave the cell blank, Excel interprets its value as 0. If you enter text into the cell, you'll get another type of error (#VALUE!).

Error Message	Description
#NAME?	The #NAME? error value indicates that you have used a name Excel doesn't recognize. Maybe you entered a typo, or maybe you meant to enter it that way. Either way, you need to correct your formula to include only those references that Excel recognizes. And don't despair over a simple spelling error; you might still become vice-president one day.
#NUM!	#NUM! indicates that the cell contains a number too large to handle. Unlike ####, which represents a value that's just too large to display, #NUM! tells you that the value is beyond the bounds of what Excel can deal with. Try to re-create the formula to produce an acceptable lower representation of the number.
#REF!	The #REF! error occurs when your formula references cells that are no longer valid (such as cells you have deleted, but which are still referred to in formulas). This error also appears in any cell that refers to a cell with the #REF! value. All references to cells that have been deleted must be changed to valid cells.
#VALUE!	This message appears if you try to use the wrong type of value in your formula (if you attempt to add text to numbers, for instance). Check the referenced cells and confirm that all cells are formatted as required by the function and formula.

The Least You Need to Know

In this chapter, you learned how to write and repair a formula. If you've mastered these points, you've mastered Excel:

- Formulas are the power spot for Excel. Learn how to use them, and you've learned the most important part of spreadsheeting.
- Formulas contain operators and arguments. The operators are the math symbols you learned in elementary school. The arguments are everything else. All Excel formulas begin with an equal sign (=).
- An argument can take the form of a number, a range name, a cell reference, or a function. Functions are explained in the next chapter.
- Careful planning prevents problems with your formulas.

Chapter 12

Fully Functional

In This Chapter

- Function fun
- The function whiz
- Key function keepsakes

We had two pizzas delivered today. After all, we couldn't take the time to grate the cheese and slice the mushrooms ourselves when we had so much work to do. That's why our kids love us: toss 'em a pizza and a video, and let 'em party. We're on auto-function!

Functional Family

At last! The fun part of Excel: *functions*. Functions are built-in formulas that enable you to automatically total, convert, calculate, and manipulate all the values on your spreadsheet.

Excel has more than 300 functions at its beck and call. Among those are functions with particular appeal to engineers, statisticians, accountants, and mathematicians. But a large number of the functions are immediately useful to just about anybody who has to deal with numbers. We detail some of the most useful functions in this chapter. If you need to learn about any of the others, flip to Appendix B of this book.

Before we demonstrate how functions work, let's examine some of the leading lights in the world of Excel functions.

Getting to Know You

Nobody, but nobody, can remember all of Excel's functions. To make it easier, though, Excel has grouped them into these categories:

- **Financial** This group contains more than 50 functions for tracking loans and investments. Use these functions to calculate principal and interest, yield, depreciation, time periods, and present and future values.
- **Date & Time** Excel can show the time and date, of course. That's no big deal. But Excel can also tell you the number of workdays between dates, the number of minutes that have elapsed since your birth, and the day of the week of any particular date (and that's just the beginning). Groovy, don't you think?
- **Math & Trigonometry** A grind?! No, this stuff might actually make math fun. Use these functions to calculate all kinds of logarithms, round off numbers, generate random numbers, and find square roots, tangents, sines, cosines. Heck, you can even generate Roman numerals.
- **Statistical** These functions are really obscure: Weibull and Poisson distributions and even a Pearson product moment correlation. But wait! There's useful stuff here, too. You'll find all kinds of averages, trends, and rankings, as well as probabilities, bell curves, and standard deviations.
- **Lookup & Reference** These functions can look up information in a table for you and give you information about where a certain reference is located on the spreadsheet. Unfortunately, they can't find your car keys. That's a feature in the next upgrade of Excel.
- **Database & List Management** You can use a database from outside of Excel or a database from within Excel (any table you can assign a name to), and then use these functions to count the elements that meet your standards, add them up, or filter them.
- **Text** Most of the Text functions operate like the word-processing features of Excel. Use them to find or search, replace, and adjust the capitalization of your text. The other Text functions are useful mostly to software programmers.
- **Logical** Put on your Vulcan ears. You can use logical functions to create if/then statements with all the best Boolean statements: AND, OR, NOT and TRUE/FALSE.
- **Information** Most of these functions check a cell to see whether or not it IS something (an even number, logical, blank, or whatever). These functions test the cell and tell you "Yep, the thing you're looking for is there," or "Nope, it's not."

- **Engineering** Check your pocket protector. A *few* of the 40-some engineering functions in Excel do simple things (such as finding the square root of a number and multiplying it by Pi), and there are a couple of comparison functions. All the rest of the functions are high-end engineering functions that normal people (those of us who hate polyester) can't even pronounce.

Form Follows Function

Now that you know the categories, it's time to examine a few of the most useful functions. The following table outlines the most common functions, their categories, usage, and syntax. (We explain syntax in the section "The Wages of Syntax," later in this chapter.) If you don't find the function you're looking for here, look in Appendix B, which lists all of the Excel functions. For even more help, press **F1** from almost anywhere on the worksheet, and look for the Help topic "Worksheet Functions Listed by Category." You can also find help under each of the category heads, as listed previously.

Excel's Most Useful Functions

Category	Function	Task	Syntax
Financial	DB	Finds depreciation of an asset for a specified period using fixed-declining balance method	DB(cost, salvage, life, period, month)
Financial	EFFECT	Finds effective annual interest rate	EFFECT (nominal_rate, npery)
Financial	PMT	Finds periodic payment for an annuity	PMT(rate, nper, pv, fv, type)
Financial	YIELD	Finds yield on a security that pays periodic interest	YIELD (settlement, maturity, rate, pr, redemption, frequency, basis)
Date & Time	NETWORKDAYS	Finds number of whole workdays between two dates	NETWORKDAYS (start_date, end_date, holidays)

continues

Excel's Most Useful Functions Continued

Category	Function	Task	Syntax
Date & Time	TODAY	Finds serial number of today's date	TODAY( )
Math & Trig	INT	Rounds a number down to nearest integer	INT(number)
Math & Trig	PI	Finds value of Pi	PI( )
Math & Trig	RAND	Finds a random number between 0 and 1	RAND( )
Math & Trig	ROMAN	Changes an Arabic numeral to Roman, as text	ROMAN (number, form)
Math & Trig	ROUND	Rounds a number to a specified number of digits	ROUND (number, num_digits)
Math & Trig	SQRT	Finds a positive square root	SQRT(number)
Math & Trig	SUM	Adds up arguments	SUM(number1, number2, ...)
Statistics	AVERAGE	Finds average of arguments	AVERAGE (number1, number2, ...)
Statistics	PERCENTILE	Finds k-th percentile of values in a range	PERCENTILE (array, k)
Lookup & Reference	VLOOKUP	Searches first column of an array and moves across to find related data	VLOOKUP (lookup_value, table_array, col_index_num, range_lookup)
Database	DGET	Extracts from a database a single record that matches specified criteria	DGET(database, field, criteria)
Database	DSUM	Adds numbers in field column of records in database that match criteria	DSUM (database,field, criteria)

Category	Function	Task	Syntax
Text	REPLACE	Replaces characters in text	REPLACE (old_text, start_num, num_chars, new_text)
Text	TRIM	Removes all spaces from text except for single spaces between words	TRIM(text)
Logical	IF	Performs logical test	IF(logical_test, value_if_true, value_if_false)
Information	CELL	Finds information about formatting, location, or contents of a cell	CELL(info_type, reference)
Engineering	GESTEP	Tests whether a number is greater than a threshold value	GESTEP (number, step)

Now we'll prepare to make a function work. First, the rules.

The Wages of Syntax

Every Excel function has certain *syntax*, or formatting, requirements. To use functions in formulas, you begin with the usual equal sign, add the name of the function, and add some parenthetical *arguments*.

The arguments are pieces of information that the function uses to perform its duty. For example, if you use the SUM function, your argument will be a list of numbers (or, more likely, a range) that you want the function to add together. Some arguments are required; others are optional. The syntax for the SUM function, for example, is

SUM(number1,number2,...)

This means that to enter a formula using SUM, you enter **SUM** (the name of the function), no space, and immediately follow that with the arguments, which are separated by commas. The argument number1 represents the first number to be added, and number2 is the second. You can continue adding numbers to the series if you want. In this particular function, the second and following numbers are optional. You can SUM a single number (we can't imagine why you'd want to do this, but you could) or multiple numbers, or you can insert a whole range in place of number1. Then you can do the same thing with number2, if you want.

Let's return to the spreadsheet we started in the last chapter and use the SUM function to total that column of three numbers. This time, however, we'll work in a neighboring column, just to compare. Enter the numbers 1, 2, and 3 in the first three rows of column C. Draw an underline in cell C4 with the **\–** key combination. Then watch what happens when you use a function.

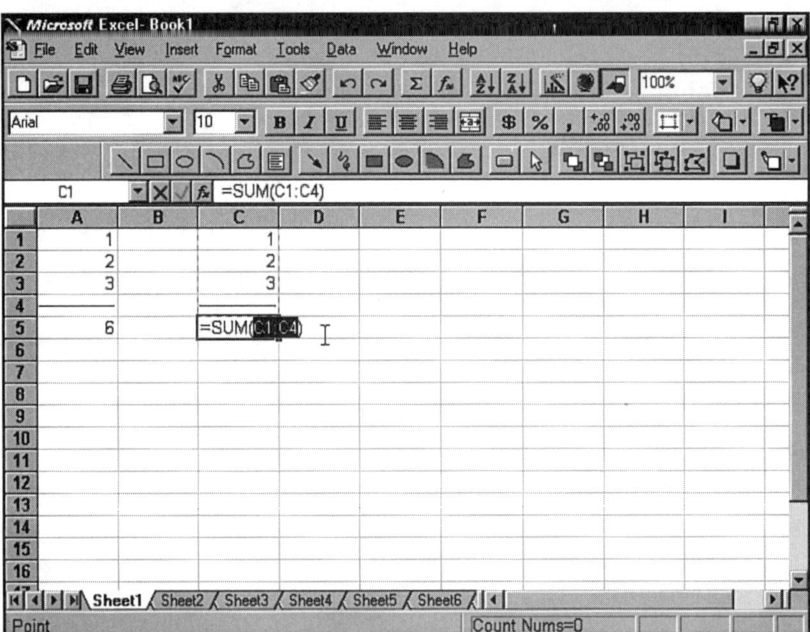

The SUM function at work.

A Manual Tour

We'll continue with functions by walking you through the manual process. This is a little complicated, but once you've done it, you'll understand how functions work, and you'll be able to use the automatic functions more efficiently.

Follow these steps to manually insert a function (in this case, the SUM function):

1. Select cell **C5** to make it the active cell. Enter an equal sign (=) to notify Excel that you intend to begin a formula.

2. Type **SUM**, immediately followed by an opening parenthesis. You've started the function. (The word "sum" can be in any combination of upper- and lowercase letters.)
3. Enter your argument. For our example, you need to enter the range of numbers from C1 to C3. You can do this in either of two ways:
   - Simply enter **C1:C3** and be done with it.
   - Move your active cell indicator to cell C1 (a moving line surrounds cell C1 when you get there) to indicate that it's the beginning of your range. Enter a colon (or a period, if you want) to separate the first cell from the last cell. Then move your cursor to the end of the range, cell C3. This method seems more complicated at first blush, but if your ranges become immense, it comes in handy.
4. Finish the formula by typing a closing parenthesis. Your formula should look like this:

   =SUM(C1:C3)
5. Press **Enter**, and Excel calculates the formula. Once again, the formula disappears, and the cell shows the result: 6. You've now manually entered a function.

The AutoSum Button

As a reward for your hard work, you can now learn the easiest way of all for finding the total of a column or a row: Excel's AutoSum toolbar button.

To automatically total a list of numbers, enter your data in the usual way. (In this case, enter the numbers 1, 2, and 3 in the first three rows of column E and draw an underline if you want.) Then move your active cell to the bottom of the numbers (cell E5, in this case).

Σ It's time now to get automatic: click on the **AutoSum** button, press **Enter**, and watch the result magically appear. The AutoSum button works at the end (not the beginning) of any line of numbers. If your active cell is in the middle of several numbers, the AutoSum button totals the column up to that point: above or to the left of the active cell.

Now that you've seen how easy automatic functions can be, let's move on to the Function Wizard to see how you can perform other functions automatically.

The Function Wizard

Like all great wizards, the Function Wizard *pretends* to have great power. In fact, it can't do anything you couldn't do for yourself. Don't sell the Function Wizard short, though, unless you really feel confident about the requirements for all those gauges and knobs behind the curtain.

Off to See the Wizard

There are several ways to get to the Function Wizard, and in only one of them is a tornado required. We'll stick to the simpler methods.

The Function Wizard performs its magic on the active cell. To see how it works, select a blank cell now. Then follow one of these four paths, and you're off to see the wizard.

- Click the **Function Wizard** button on the Standard toolbar.
- Click the **Function Wizard** button on the Formula bar. (This button, which looks just like the one on the Standard toolbar, is available only after you enter the equal sign to activate the Formula bar.)
- Open the **Insert** menu and select the **Function** command.
- Press **Shift+F3**.

Whichever path you choose to get to the wizard, the results are the same. A dialog box called Function Wizard - Step 1 of 2 appears (see the following figure). Smoke and flames are options reserved for later, more interactive versions of Excel.

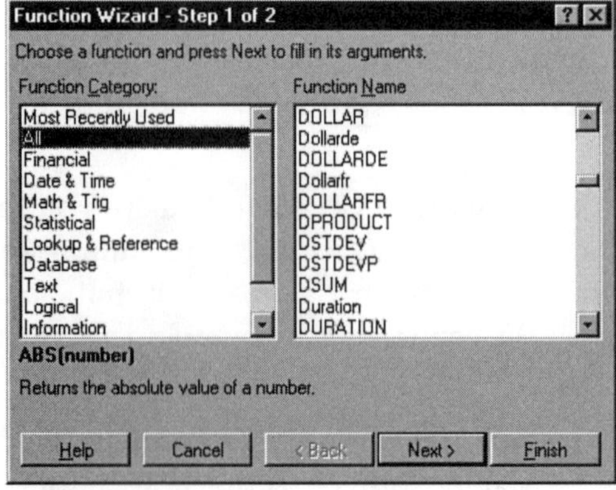

The Function Wizard - Step 1 of 2 dialog box.

In the Function Category list, you select the function that best represents the nature of your task. If you are unsure which to choose, select **All**. Then select a function from the Function Name list.

Once you select a function, Excel displays the correct syntax, or formatting, for the function directly below the Function Category list. Required arguments appear in bold type; optional arguments appear in regular type.

Having chosen the function, you need to start adding arguments. Click the **Next>** button to move on to that step.

> Check This Out...
>
> **Functional Help** As you scroll slowly through the list in the Function Name box, a brief description of each function appears in the area above the command buttons. If you need further information on using one of the functions, click the **Help** button in the Function Wizard dialog box to view a detailed explanation of the function currently highlighted.

There's No Place Like Step Two

The Function Wizard - Step 2 of 2 dialog box contains one or more blank text boxes for your arguments (see the following figure). To the left of each blank box is an additional Function Wizard button. You use these buttons to create nested functions. You'll learn more about nesting in the next section.

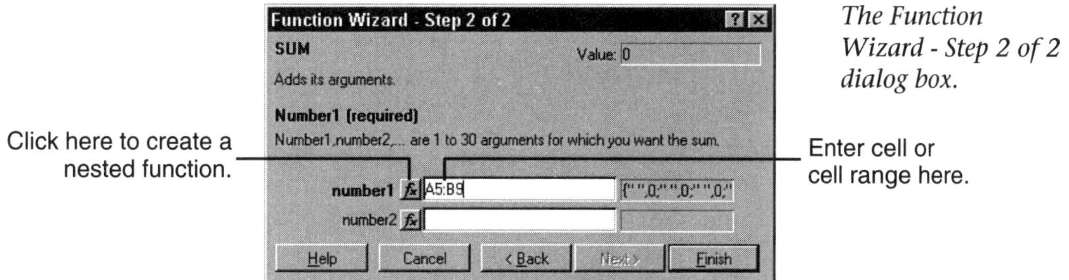

The Function Wizard - Step 2 of 2 dialog box.

For now, enter a cell reference, a range name, or a constant number in the first box. If you need to enter information in another box, click on the appropriate box or press **Tab** to move to it. When you finish entering information, click **Finish**, and your work is done.

> Check This Out...
>
> **Out of Line** Instead of directly entering information about the cell or range of cells in the Function Wizard - Step 2 of 2 dialog box, use your mouse to select the range on your worksheet. The correct values appear automatically in the Function Wizard dialog box.

A Function in a Function

This section is for fun-loving nested-function fanciers and Peter-Piper-picked-a-peck-of-pickled-peppers aficionados only.

In the Step 2 of 2 dialog box, you saw Function Wizard buttons to the left of each text box. You use those buttons when you want to nest a function within the current function.

To create a nested function, first decide which part of your formula will contain the nested argument, and then click the appropriate **Function Wizard** button. A new Function Wizard - Step 1 of 1 dialog box appears. (The only giveaway that it is not the original box is the word "Nested" in the title.)

From this point, carry on exactly as you would if this were the first Function Wizard box: select the function and click **OK**. The original Step 2 of 2 dialog box returns to the screen (note the absence of the word "Nested" in the title, and the fact that the OK button is replaced by the Finish button). Finish your function and click the **Finish** button. Excel displays your nested formula in its cell and returns you to your home screen—and you didn't even have to close your eyes or click your heels.

The Least You Need to Know

This chapter taught you the basics of using Excel functions (the built-in formulas that give Excel its power). Here's what you need to remember:

- Functions are built-in formulas. Excel has more than 300 of them.
- You can enter functions manually if you stick to the correct formula syntax conventions.
- The arguments in a function can refer to specific numbers, other cells, or even whole ranges.
- You can enter many, but not all, functions with the help of Excel's Formula Wizard.

Chapter 13

Keep It Clean, Keep It Accurate, Keep It Safe.

In This Chapter

- Ya oughta audit
- Vacuum that worksheet
- Leave a lasting luster on lovely worksheets

Audit! It's an ugly word, ain't it? Sends your skin crawling and your heart racing. Those awful men from the tax bureau are panting at your door like hell-sired pit bulls... no, stop! That's not the kind of auditing we're doing here. This is light, breezy, fun stuff! (Oh, and we're just joking about the "pit bull" part. You hear that, Mr. Taxman? Just JOKING!)

You're Being Audited

No, not by the IRS—at least not yet. The only auditing going on here is the kind you can accomplish within an Excel workbook. So sit back and relax. That knock on the door is not the IRS. They use certified mail—or so we're told!

When something goes wrong in your worksheet (you get an error message, a circular reference, or an unexpected result, for example), you've got to pull out the auditing tools to get it back to rights. This section explains how to use Excel's auditing tools to repair those mistakes.

Visual Auditing

It feels silly to say this, so please excuse us if we sound maternal, but it's mandatory:

> Make sure you visually scan your worksheet for obvious errors before you start pulling out the big auditing guns.

There, we said it. Now let's move on.

The Auditing Process

Anyone who has ever attempted to put together a family tree knows that the difficulty is not so much finding the names of ancestors as it is determining which branch to go chasing down. Where do Uncle Harry and his seven wives fit in? Are they ancestors or anecdotes? Do you trace back the ancestry of extended siblings, cousins, best friends, or cousins of best friends?

Tracing the pathways of a worksheet can be just as complicated and not half as much fun. All the twists and turns are decided by calculations that use values resulting from the calculations of other values. We suppose that's why the folks who brought you Excel decided to provide a simple method of tracing the paths your formulas follow. That method is called *auditing.*

Auditing is a system that traces the genealogy of your spreadsheet problems. It shows you, visually, where all the cells that feed into your formula come from. Just as you might with a family tree, you can follow the graphical auditing lines to see the source of your mistake. Unlike your pedigree chart, though, with Excel you can correct mistakes and get on with your work.

Auditing has its own unique language. Before we go much further, you'll need to know these words:

Auditing toolbar A group of buttons you can use to simplify the auditing process.

Dependent Any cell that descends from another cell. The dependent is the offspring of the original cell. (Hey, maybe those IRS guys really are watching!)

Direct Dependent Any cell that descends in whole or in part from the active cell. This is the child of the original cell.

Indirect Dependent The grandchild of another cell. It descends from a direct dependent.

Precedent The first ancestral line of a formula. The parenting cells. There are two types: direct and indirect.

Direct Precedent The first ancestral line of the formula in the active cell (the daddy cell).

Indirect Precedent The entire ancestral line of the formula in the active cell (the grandpa and great-grandpa cells).

Now that that's clear as mud, let's start auditing!

The Auditing Toolbar

Using Excel's audit commands, you can trace the stuff that leads into your formula (the *precedents*) and the stuff that comes out of your formula (the *dependents*). You can also trace errors, attach notes, and display all the available status information about a cell.

All of Excel's audit features are accessible from the Auditing toolbar or via the Auditing command on the Tools menu. For this section, we'll work from the toolbar. To view the Auditing toolbar, open the **View** menu and select **Toolbars**, choose **Auditing**, and click **OK**. Excel displays the Auditing toolbar, shown in the following figure.

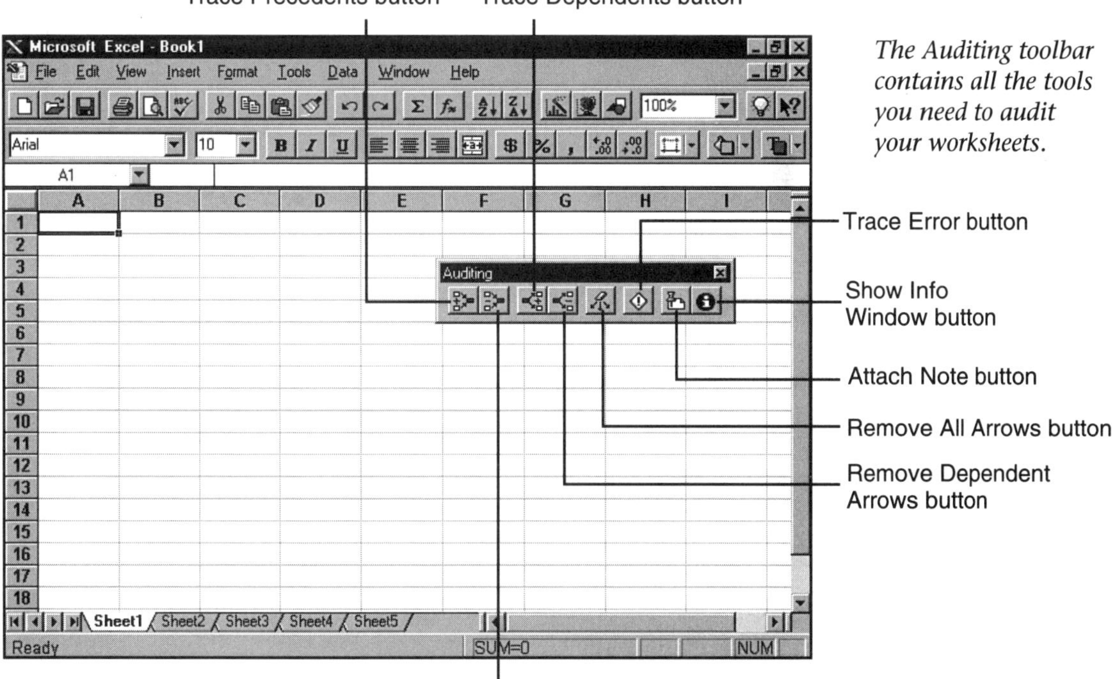

The Auditing toolbar contains all the tools you need to audit your worksheets.

Let's examine each of the auditing elements individually.

Tracing Precedents and Dependents

Tracing relationships has never been easier. First, open the **Tools** menu and select **Options**. The Trace Properties dialog box appears. Click on the View tab and make sure the **Hide All** option button is cleared. You're ready to begin.

Click on the cell that's giving you problems to make it active. To start off, you'll want to view all the formulas and data that feed into the problem cell. To do so, click the **Trace Precedents** button. Excel displays a blue arrow connecting the problem cell to its *direct precedents*. You can follow the blue line to find out how the problem formula or value was created.

No problems? Then click on the **Trace Precedents** button again, and Excel points out any *indirect precedents*. The original direct precedent lines stay visible, and they are joined by additional indirect precedent lines. Follow these lines to see whether you can track down the problem. Click on the **Remove Precedent Arrows** button to clear the worksheet of all arrows.

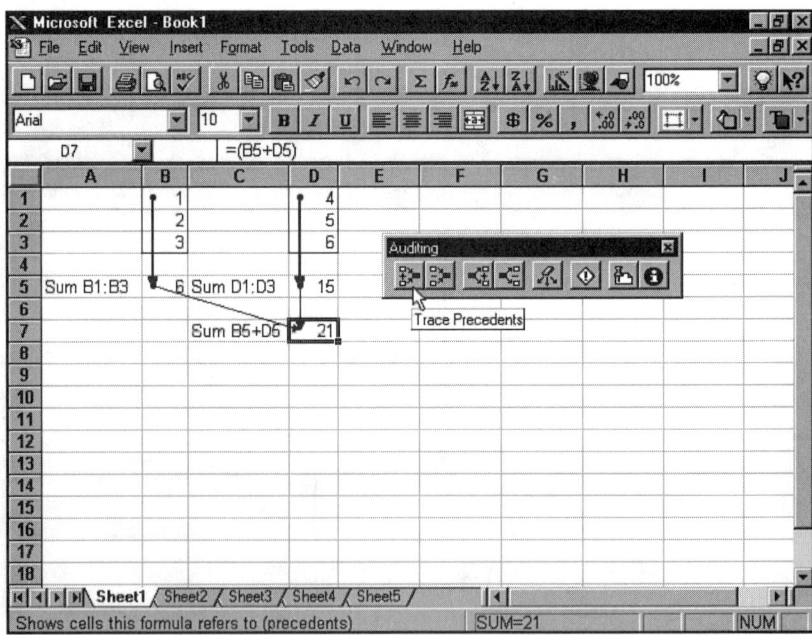

Excel displays arrows to point out direct and indirect precedents.

Sometimes you may want to work in reverse. You've got a piece of information, and you want to know where it's being used. In this case, you'll use the Trace Dependents button. The procedure is identical. Click on the information in question to make it active, and then click the **Trace Dependents** button on the Auditing toolbar. Excel shows the direct dependents with blue arrows leading out of the active cell.

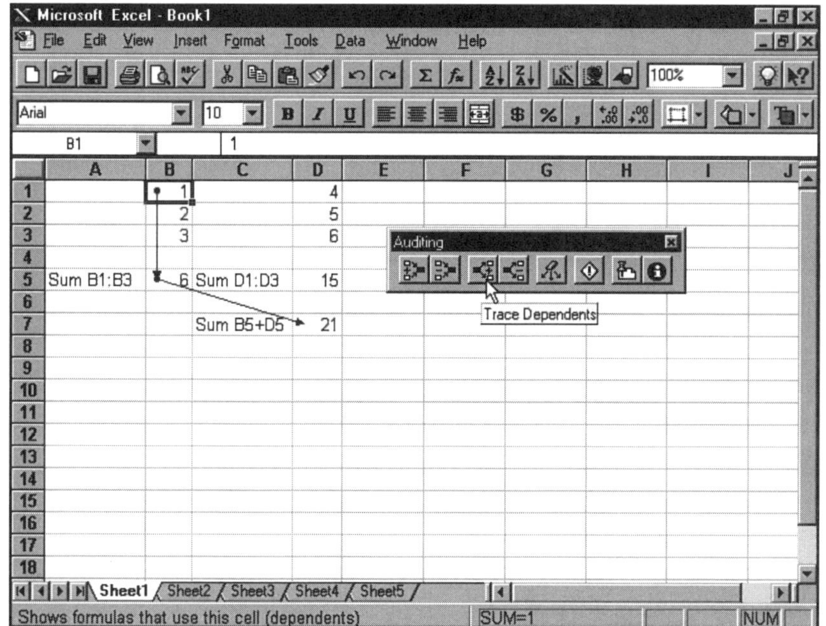

Use the Trace Dependents button to see which cells' contents depend on the value in the selected cell.

Dependents and precedents are very similar functions and can be intermixed on the same screen.

Phase in the Tracers

There's a popular—but errant—belief that Captain Kirk was in the habit of ordering his troops to "Set your tracers on stun." He's being misquoted. Captain Kirk never had the power of the Trace Error button at his command.

On those rare occasions when an error message appears in a cell in place of a legitimate value, activate the cell and click the **Trace Error** button. Excel highlights all of the precedents of the troubled cell with blue and red arrows. A red arrow indicates the source of the error condition; blue arrows highlight the remainder of the precedent.

Other Useful Auditing Buttons

Now seems like as good a time as any to go through the remaining buttons on the Auditing toolbar.

- **Remove All Arrows** What's in a name? In this case, everything. Click on this button, and all the tracer arrows disappear.

- **Show Info Window** When you click on this button, Excel displays a window that contains everything you ever wanted to know about the active cell but didn't know who to ask. You can view notes, formatting, formulas, and so on.
- **Attach Note** Click this button and you can attach a note to a cell. You'll learn more about that process in the section "Attach Notes to Cells," later in this chapter.

Good Housekeeping

Now that you've learned how to clean up your worksheet messes, it's time to learn how to stop them before they start. Using a spreadsheet productively starts with planning—take it from us. We've spent hours and hours looking for lost yellow sticky notes and puzzling out scribbled notes like: "Work in that insurance figure from I.T."

If you're producing a spreadsheet of any size, take a moment before you start and plan (at the very least) how you want to label all your columns and rows, and what information belongs in separate ranges and tables. Resist the urge to jump right in. Good planning prevents circular references, error messages, and incomprehensible formulas, and saves hours of wasted time.

Good Advice for All Computer Users

Some housekeeping practices make good sense for any piece of software you touch. These include:

Save, save, save. Sure, who doesn't know this? And yet, whether it's a natural disaster that knocks the power out all across the city, or a cat that knocks the power cord out of the wall, you're still going to end up wishing you'd saved more often.

Fortunately, you can have Excel save your work automatically with just the flip of a switch, and you even get to tell it how often to save. To do so, open the **Tools** menu and select the **AutoSave** command. The AutoSave dialog box appears.

The AutoSave dialog box.

Can't Find It?

If the AutoSave command is not on the Tools menu, you must install the AutoSave add-in. Add-ins are programs that perform highly specialized tasks. When you first install Excel (see Appendix A), you see several options for choosing which add-ins you want to have available. Other add-ins will be available as shareware or separately purchased software.

Here's how to install AutoSave, or any other Excel add-in. Go to the **Tools** menu and click on **Add-Ins**. The Add-Ins dialog box appears, with a list of available add-ins. Click on any item on the list, and you'll see an explanation of that add-in at the bottom of the dialog box. Click on any item on the list to select it, and then click **OK** to add it. You can back out of the dialog box with the Cancel button.

In the AutoSave dialog box, check the **Automatic Save Every** check box. In the Minutes box, set the time interval at which you want Excel to save your workbooks. Make other selections as desired. Then click the **OK** button, and prepare to be saved.

Techno Talk

Name That File The file names you see in Excel's Open dialog box aren't exactly identical to their actual DOS-level file names. If you're still working in DOS, you'll see the actual file names as *FILENAME*.XLS for the original file and *FILENAME*.XLK for the backup file.

Back Up. You need to do more than save your work. You also need to back it up on floppy disks, another computer, or a tape backup. At the very least, you'll want to keep a backup of your files on the same hard disk as your original files—just in case. You keep backups because things burn, things crash, things get stolen, things get corrupted, and things (like files and minds) get changed.

In the favored backup system, you keep your files on a series of floppy disks that you rotate in and out of your building. This is the "In Case of Fire" or "In Case I Get Fired" scenario. (We understand there are some who advocate keeping one copy of your work on a space shuttle. That's the "In Case of Nuclear War" scenario, and we don't recommend it.)

In any event, most modern software, including Excel, has a backup feature that enables you to save not only what you're presently working on, but the previous edition of that file as well. When you turn on Excel's automatic Backup feature, it saves a copy of your file, "CATFOOD," for example, under the name "Backup of CATFOOD."

To recover your work after a power failure or a close encounter with a clumsy child, you must have already enabled the Backup feature. In addition, you must have saved a document more than once for Backup to have a back up of it. (The first time you save, there's nothing to back up.) What that means is, if you haven't done so already, you should turn on the Backup feature now and leave it on. If you wait until you need it, you will have waited too long.

To enable the Backup feature, open the **File** menu and choose **Save As**. Select **Options** and click on the **Always Create Backup** check box. Then click **OK** and click **Save.** Easy enough!

If you ever experience a power failure, you'll find that recovery is just as simple. Click on the **Open** button to access the Open dialog box, and in the Files of type box, choose **Backup Files (*.XLK, *.BAK)**. Look through the folders to find your missing document, select it, and click **Open**.

Long vs. Short File Names Keep in mind that although Excel for Windows 95 accepts long file names, previous versions don't. If you're exchanging data with people who are stuck back in Windows 3.1-ville, you should stick with good old DOS file names: eight alphanumeric characters, followed by a period, followed by Excel's .XLS extension (which it adds on its own). Let it go at that.

Use Sequential File Names. Choose a system for naming your files, and use file naming conventions that reflect the sequence of versions.

We've found it useful to name each worksheet with a recognizable English name, followed by a number that indicates its stage of revision. Each time you open your worksheet for another shot at building it, give it a new revision number. That way, if something goes terribly wrong, you can fall back to the previous version.

Keep your hard drive cleaned off. We know this is a frustrating piece of advice, but Windows 95 requires acres of disk space to run efficiently. (We've found that anything less than 100MB of free space sets Excel and all other applications to crawling.)

All the other hints in this section are specific to spreadsheets, and some apply only to Excel. Follow the advice to see your productivity soar.

Plan the Worksheet

Yeah, yeah... we already told you this. But we can't say it firmly enough. Drag out a piece of paper, jot down the column and row labels you want to use, write down the source of your range and table data, and block out the size of various areas that will later become ranges. You can even give them names right now, so you're working efficiently before you even start working.

Work in Byte-Sized Pieces

Set one part of your spreadsheet in motion before you add in new parts. If you have planned thoroughly, this step is easy. If you ignored our incessant nagging, you may find yourself trying to juggle all the bits of the spreadsheet at the same time. Remember that it's easier to back up one step than to start all over when nothing comes out right.

Know As You Go No need to pull out a calculator to check your work as you build your worksheet. Use Excel's AutoSum feature instead. The AutoSum area is located on the right side of the Status bar at the bottom of your Excel screen. You'll find an explanation in Chapter 9.

Use the Undo Command

Excel enables you to correct mistakes you enter in your formulas or cancel a formula altogether if necessary. To cancel an error before you actually enter it (for example, while the formula itself—and not its result—still appears in the Formula bar and the cell), press the **Esc** key or click on the **Cancel** button in a dialog box or on the Formula bar.

If you actually enter a formula and then realize you made a mistake, you can undo the change. To do so, simply click on the **Undo** button on the Standard toolbar immediately, and Excel reverses the previous change.

Note, however, that Excel has an upper limit on what it can undo. If you attempt to clear too many cells at once, they may be lost forever. In addition, Undo is limited to one level, which means that if you make an error, and then go on to something else, you can't back up two steps and undo the error.

Understand Toolbars

We've covered each toolbar in detail as we've come to it, but we'll recap that information here because understanding Excel toolbars from top to bottom can really boost your productivity.

A toolbar is simply a collection of task-related buttons that represent common commands. By nature, toolbars simplify your work.

Hide-Away

If the Windows 95 taskbar gets in your way, you can temporarily hide it. To do so, click on Windows 95's **Start** button and select **Settings and Taskbar** to access the Taskbar Properties dialog box. Click on the **Taskbar Options** tab, and select **Always on top** and **Auto hide**. Then close the box. Until you give Windows further notice, the taskbar remains hidden unless you drag your mouse pointer to the bottom of the screen and call it up.

Excel has a built-in collection of more than a dozen toolbars. To see the list, open the **View** menu and choose **Toolbars**. Then, to display any given toolbar, click on the check box next to the toolbar's name.

You can move a toolbar out of harm's way by "docking" it at the edge of Excel. To dock a toolbar, click on its Title bar and drag it off the worksheet. When toolbars are floating, you can resize them by dragging any side; you cannot resize a docked toolbar.

In addition, you can change any toolbar or create new toolbars by adding, deleting, and rearranging buttons. You'll learn how to customize your toolbars in Chapter 16.

Protect Cells

Okay, maybe you're no longer a complete idiot about spreadsheets, but one day you're going to do something completely idiotic to a spreadsheet. At that point, you will wish you'd remembered cell protection.

Cell protection is a process by which you can keep other people's grimy hands off your work. More significantly, it keeps your own grimy hands (and your own errant formulas and macros) from destroying existing parts of your worksheet.

When your spreadsheet starts getting cumbersome (as in, larger than the screen), it's probably time to consider locking it up. With Excel, you can lock up the entire spreadsheet, and then selectively unlock the cells or areas where you want to enter data, edit existing cells, or continue building the spreadsheet.

The Theory

If you grew up with older non-Excel spreadsheets, you might find Excel's protection features disappointing. On those old kludge-y programs, you had no trouble locking and unlocking cells all over the spreadsheet. However, Excel works a bit differently. You can protect cells in two ways: by hiding them or by locking them. And instead of choosing a handful of cells and locking them up (as you did in other spreadsheets), Excel requires that you first *unlock* some cells, and *then* protect the rest of the worksheet.

Unfortunately, Excel provides no visual indicator to tell you whether or not a particular cell is locked. The only way to find out is by trial and error: you try entering information in a cell, and if it's locked, Excel displays an error message.

The Practice

To protect an entire worksheet, open the **Tools** menu, select **Protection**, and choose **Protect Sheet** from the submenu that appears. To unprotect a worksheet, repeat those steps but choose **Unprotect Sheet** from the submenu that appears.

Check This Out...

Do Not Pass(word) Go

That Password option in the Protect Sheet dialog box looks mighty tempting, doesn't it? We advise that you pass it by. Do not enter anything in that Password box. Why? Once you've assigned a password, you're under a lifelong obligation to remember it. You cannot, under any circumstances, talk Microsoft into removing it for you. And if you forget the password, the worksheet is as good as gone forever. You cannot access it through any other source.

The Locking Thing

To keep a few cells unlocked so you can continue to enter information in them, you must first remove protection from the worksheet. To do so, follow these steps:

1. Open the **Tools** menu and select **Unprotect**.
2. Select the cells you want to keep unlocked. You can select multiple ranges by dragging over the first one, pressing and holding the **Ctrl** key, and dragging over any others. Repeat this process as often as necessary, until all your ranges are selected.
3. To actually mark the cells as unlocked, open the **Format** menu and select **Cells** (or press **Ctrl+1**). The Format Cells dialog box appears.
4. Choose the **Protection** tab.
5. Click on the **Locked** box to remove the check mark, and then click **OK**. Your cells are unlocked.

Of course, everything else is also unlocked right now, so you have to lock the worksheet again. Open the **Tools** menu, select **Protection**, and choose **Protect Sheet** again. Excel locks all but your chosen cells. That's it.

The Hiding Place

Sometimes you have confidential information on an otherwise great spreadsheet. You'd love to show off your spreadsheet to, say, your boss, but you don't paticularly want her to see the part where you calculate your spouse's annual income.

You can hide and unhide cells in much the same way you locked and unlocked cells. First, make sure the worksheet is not protected by selecting **Tools, Protection, Unprotect Sheet**. Select the cells that contain the information you want to hide. Then open the **Format** menu and select **Cells** (or press **Ctrl+1**), and click on the **Protection** tab of the Format Cells dialog box. On the Protection tab, check the **Hidden** option, and click **OK** to save your setup. Protect the worksheet again, and you're all set. These features *toggle* on and off like light switches, so you can retrace your steps to undo them.

Attach Notes to Cells

In older spreadsheets, attaching a note to a cell was a complicated process that was rarely carried out and was almost always regretted. Not so, anymore. Attaching notes is easy in Excel for Windows 95, and it enables you to leave a "paper trail" for others who may use your worksheet and—believe it or not—for yourself. (Just try to remember six weeks later why you used a particular cell reference in your formula or where you got the data for a certain range of numbers.)

Too much trouble to type out a note? That's okay. Excel permits you to be excessively lazy: it includes an option for recording spoken notes! "I assumed an inflation rate of 280 percent because I think the chairman of the Federal Reserve is an idiot," you say, and forevermore you'll remember why you made the assumptions you made. Be a prolific note attacher, and one day you may find yourself rolling around in the happy mud of pig heaven when the boss asks "Hey! Why'd you do THAT?"

To attach a note to a cell in an Excel worksheet, open the **Insert** menu and select **Note.** (Alternatively, you can click on the **Attach Note** button on the Auditing toolbar.) The Cell Note dialog box appears. By default, Excel automatically attaches your note to the active cell. To attach a note to a different cell, click in the **Cell** box of the dialog box and enter that cell's address.

If you have a sound card and a microphone, you can attach audio notes to a cell. To attach an audio note, click the **Record** button in the Sound Note box. Then record your message, or click on **Import** to include a sound file from another source.

When you finish entering your selections, click **OK**. Excel displays a small red dot in the upper right corner of the cell to indicate that a note is attached to the cell. Anytime you select a cell with a note attached, a pop-up box displays your note on-screen. If you've attached an audio message, Excel sings out the message for all the world (or all your colleagues) to hear.

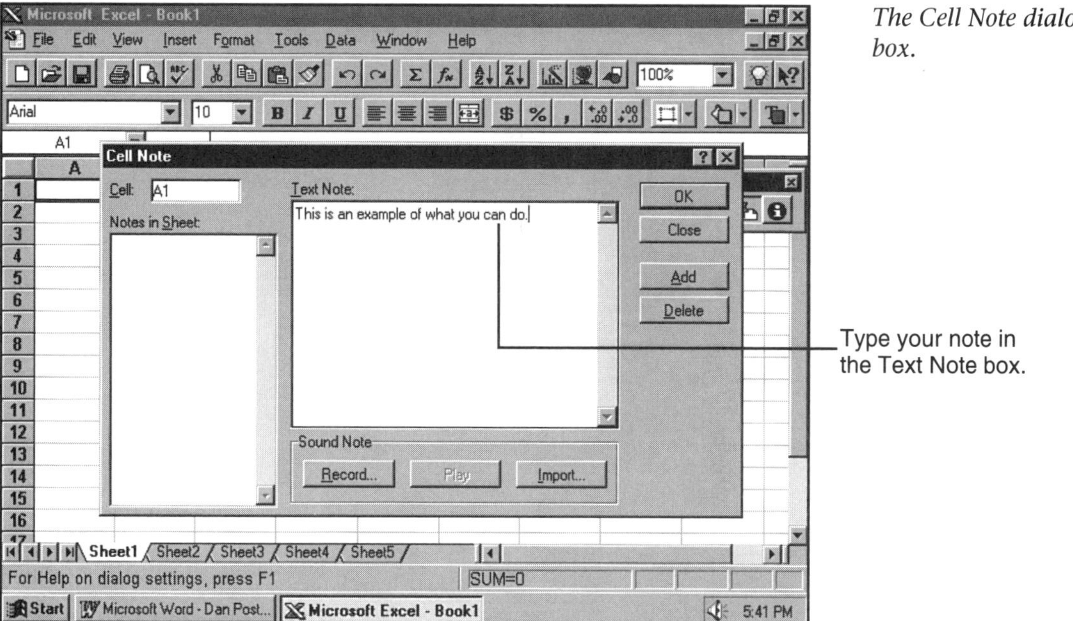

The Cell Note dialog box.

To edit or remove notes from a cell, access the Cell Note dialog box. In the Notes in Sheet box, select the cell you want to change. The text note for the selected cell appears in the Text Note box. You can edit the note by clicking in the Text Note box, making the necessary changes, and clicking **OK**. To delete the note, click the **Delete** button in the dialog box. Excel deletes all notes, including sound notes, from the selected cell.

Fill in Workbook Properties

Workbook Properties give you tracking information about any worksheet. Excel fills in some of the properties automatically. If you manually fill in the rest, you have a good record of who has worked on a file, what the file contains, and how it's connected to other information on your computer.

To access Workbook Properties, open the **File** menu and choose **Properties**. The Properties dialog box appears (see the following figure).

You enter most of your tracking information on the Summary tab of the Properties dialog box. The General tab describes file creation information; the Statistics tab tracks editing time; the Contents tab tells you how the entire workbook is structured, in outline form; and the Custom tab enables you to pick from a long list of other categories you might want to track. To see those categories, click the Name down arrow.

When you finish viewing the Workbook Properties dialog box, click **Cancel**.

Track the use of each worksheet using the Properties dialog box.

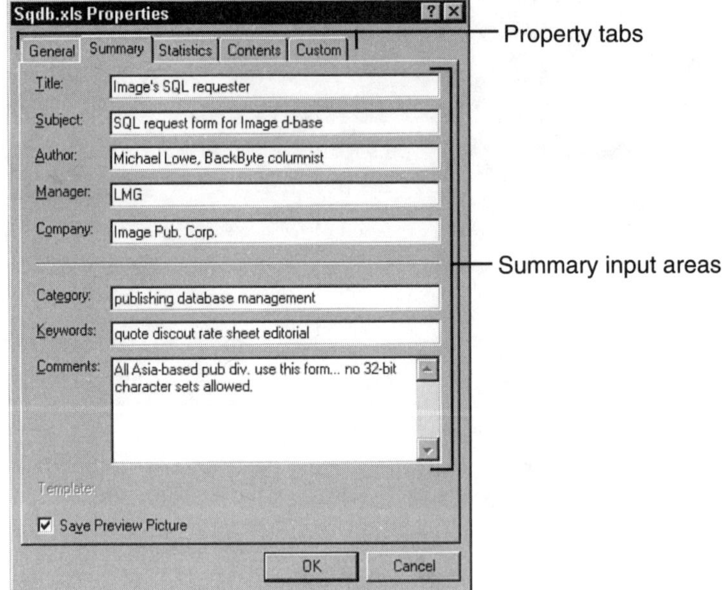

The Least You Need to Know

In this chapter, you learned how to keep your spreadsheets neat and tidy. Keep these points in mind, and you'll never have a problem:

- Excel's audit functions can help you find errors quickly.
- You can access all auditing functions from the Auditing toolbar.
- Plan, plan, plan. It prevents auditing, auditing, auditing.
- Save and back up your files regularly, and follow other basic housekeeping hints to keep your Excel files safe and clean.
- With Excel, you can attach either written or audio notes.
- Careful handling and labeling of your worksheets can save you hours of trouble later on.

Chapter 14

Managing in Multiples

In This Chapter

- Workbook fun for the whole family
- Swapping sheets
- Booking books
- Multiple management miracles

Ever listen to a child whine? He acts almost as if his problems were somehow... significant.

"Hey kid!" you want to holler. "Do I care about your broken gummy worm when I've got a mortgage payment to make and two guys trying to break into my Ford Escort Pony?! No, I think I do NOT!"

Welcome to Workbooks

In this chapter, Excel makes you grow up. We advance from working in a single worksheet to working with entire workbooks and even multiple workbooks. This chapter focuses on two subjects: moving around in multiple work areas and linking those multiple work areas.

The Workbook Metaphor

Until a few years ago, every worksheet was an independent unit, with no obvious connection to any other worksheet. That made it tough for people who wanted to, for example, produce a separate report for each department in a division, have the results of each department feed into the divisional report, and have the divisional reports feed into a company-wide report.

Excel provides workbooks to simplify all that. Because you can have many worksheets in a single workbook, you can have backups for backups for backups. And you can keep all the information related to a single topic in the same workbook. No chasing around the hard disk to find a lost payroll calculation. Of course if you really liked the old system....

Workbooks also enable you to put your graphic reports—charts, graphs, and tables—on worksheets separate from those containing the underlying calculations. And that simplifies all your reporting and printing work.

How They're Built

By default, a workbook contains 16 worksheets. Excel displays the worksheet numbers on tabs near the bottom of your screen. These tabs make it easy for you to link one worksheet to any other worksheet using references in your formulas.

In the following section, we explain how to work with multiple worksheets. Later in this chapter, we'll show you how to work with multiple workbooks.

Managing Worksheets

By working with multiple worksheets, you can break your work down into logical segments. That's a good thing, because it keeps you from creating overwhelming worksheets that are larger than Oprah on a bad day. The following sections outline a few methods you can use to successfully juggle multiple worksheets.

What was that old joke about the word assume? (It wasn't a great joke, but it helped us remember how to spell the word.) Anyway, instead of assuming that worksheet tabs are visible at the bottom (black patent-leather shoes won't help here), you may have to make those worksheet tabs come and go.

To have Excel display the worksheet tabs, open the **Tools** menu and select **Options**. In the Options dialog box, click on the **View** tab. Then click on the **Sheet Tabs** check box at the bottom of the Window Options section, and click **OK**.

Well, aren't we moving right along with this chapter?

Assign Worksheet Names

Direct from the manufacturer to you, Excel worksheets arrive with clever names like Sheet1 and Sheet2. You can let Excel go on like this for 255 worksheets, or you can give your worksheets names filled with meaning and personality. For us, names like AMEX, Visa, Mastercard, and Repossessed immediately spring to mind. The names you choose should be appropriate for your worksheet.

To name or rename a worksheet, double-click on the tab for the desired worksheet. The Rename dialog box, shown in the following figure, appears in the center of the screen. (No need to measure; these positions are approximate.) Type in the new name for your worksheet and click **OK**.

Enter a new name for your worksheet in the Rename dialog box.

Switch to Another Sheet

There isn't much point in coming up with brilliant names for worksheets if you can't choose from among them. You learned in an earlier chapter that you can select a worksheet by clicking on the numbered worksheet tab. But naming the worksheets may have added a few wrinkles you didn't have to contend with before.

When you first opened your workbook, the worksheet names were short, and all the tabs were clearly visible near the bottom of your screen. That has all changed now. With longer worksheet names like "Bill's Bank Accounts" and "Nixon's Enemies List," you'll be lucky to see more than two of the tabs at a time.

> Check This Out...
>
> **Double Trouble?**
> If double-clicking has got you down, you can just as easily change the name of your tab by clicking on it just once with the right mouse button. Select **Rename** from the shortcut menu that appears, and Excel displays the Rename dialog box. Ain't it nice to have choices?

If the tab you are looking for is not readily visible, do one of two things:

- Use the tab scrolling buttons (shown in the following figure) to display the tabs. When you see the tab you want, stop and click on it.
- Right-click on the tab scrolling button, and a list of all the worksheet names appears. Select the one you want from that list.

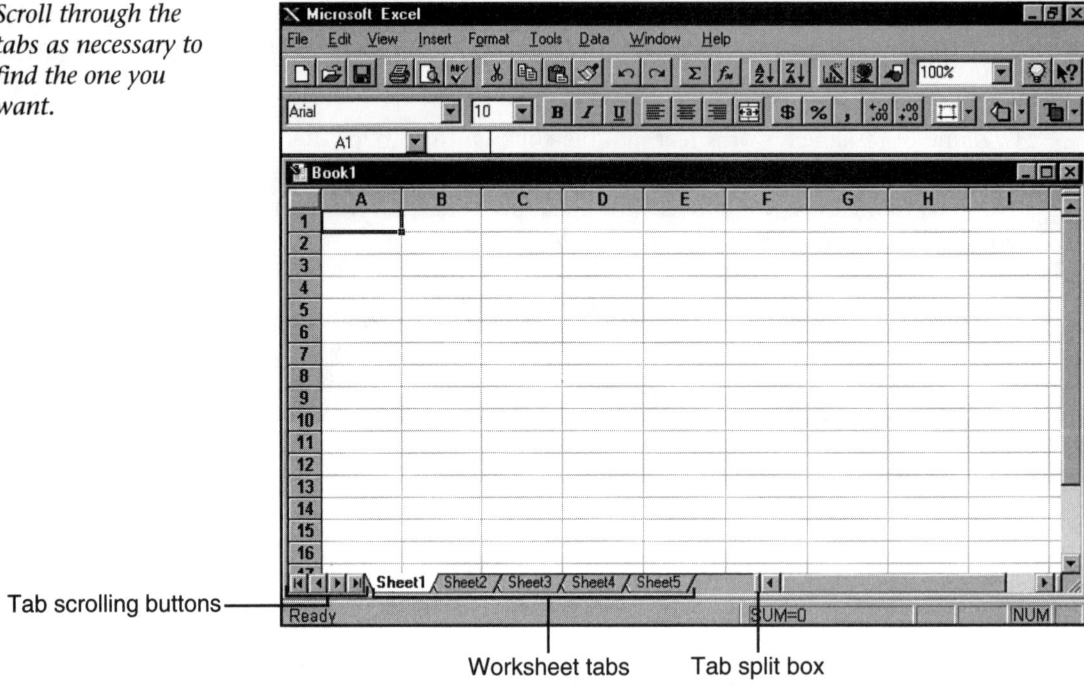

Scroll through the tabs as necessary to find the one you want.

Change the Number of Visible Tabs

One thing that might prove helpful is to open up the area where the tabs are displayed. Don't worry; that's easy to do. Simply click on the tab split box (see previous figure) and drag it back and forth as necessary. To return the box to its original position, double-click on it.

Create Multiple Views

If you're going to take the time to create all of those wonderful worksheets, it's probably safe to say you'll want to have a few of them on the screen simultaneously from time to time. To view two or more worksheets at a time, open the **Window** menu and choose **New Window**. In the new window, select the tab of the worksheet you want to view. (Don't panic if you can't see the window you had open before. We'll get to that in due time.) Repeat this process until every worksheet you want to view is open on-screen.

To arrange the worksheets so you can view them all simultaneously, open the **Window** menu and select **Arrange**. The Arrange Windows dialog box appears, with a few choices as to how the multiple screens are laid out. This is a personal matter; we'll close our eyes while you choose.

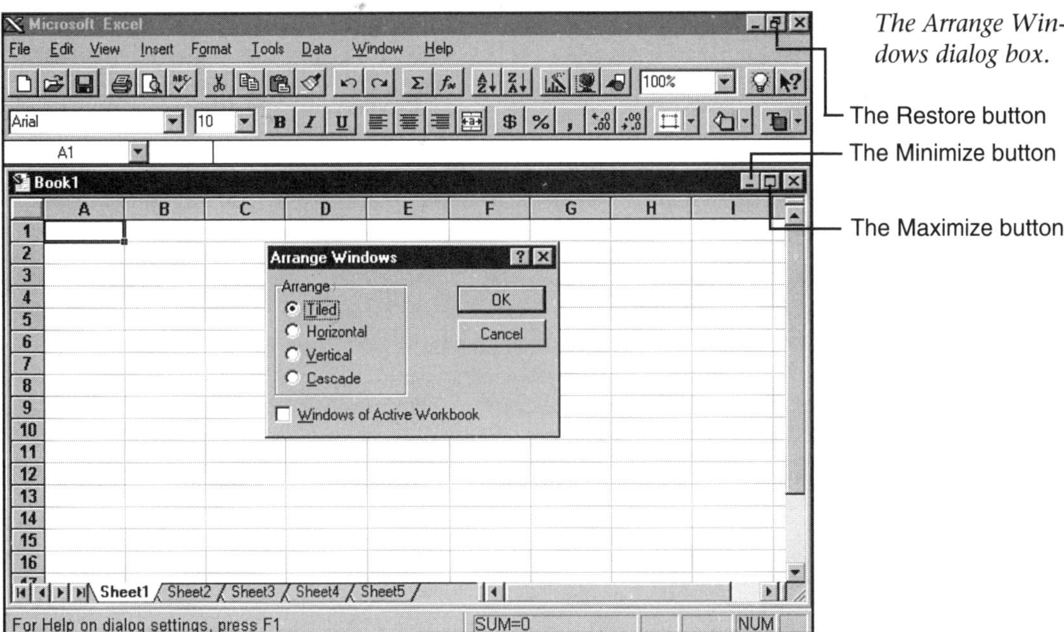

The Arrange Windows dialog box.

Near the bottom of the Arrange Windows dialog box is the Windows of Active Workbook check box. Click on the box to remove the check. (We'll use it later; for now it just muddies the water.)

You can restore worksheets to full size by clicking on the **Maximize** button (the second button in the upper-right corner of the active Title bar). Click the **Restore** button to revert to the multi-worksheet view.

Adding, Moving, and Copying Sheets

Now that you're into this multiple worksheet stuff, the default number of worksheets just won't do. You want one more—at least. Okay. It's your workbook. You can add, move, or copy worksheets at your discretion.

- **Adding worksheets** The first step in adding a worksheet is to mark where you want it to appear. Click on the worksheet to the left of which you want to add a worksheet; that worksheet becomes active. Excel automatically inserts new worksheets to the left of the active worksheet. Try to insert it in the right place, even though you can move it later if necessary.
- **Moving worksheets** If you don't like the order of your worksheets, you can move any worksheet by clicking on its tab and dragging it across the row of tabs to where you want it. A small arrow above the tab indicates where it's going to drop.

- **Copying worksheets** To copy a single worksheet, click on the tab of the desired worksheet. Then press and hold the **Ctrl** key while you drag the worksheet across the row of tabs to where you want to insert it. (If you release the mouse button before you release the Ctrl key, Excel inserts a copy of the original.)
- **Moving or copying multiple worksheets** This is a two-step process: first, you select the worksheets and gather them into a group, and then you move or copy the group as a single entity.

  To select two or more adjacent worksheets, click the tab of the first worksheet in the group and hold down the **Shift** key. Then click on the tab of the last worksheet in the series and move or copy the group as you would an individual worksheet. As you drag across the row of tabs, the mouse pointer changes form to look like a series of pages, which indicates that you are using multiple worksheets.

  To select two or more nonadjacent worksheets, click on the tab of the first worksheet, press and hold the **Ctrl** key, and click on the tabs of the other worksheets you want to include in the group. Then move or copy the group as you would an individual worksheet. The multi-page mouse pointer appears as you drag across the row of tabs. Excel places all of the selected worksheets to the left of the indicator arrow.

Referencing in Formulas

Now that you're using multiple worksheets, you probably want to start writing formulas that cross worksheet boundaries. We're here to help.

To enter a reference to another worksheet in a formula, enter the worksheet name followed by an exclamation point (!) to separate it from any entries that follow. For example, to calculate the sum of cells A1 through A3 on Sheet8 and have the answer appear in cell A1 of Sheet1, enter **=SUM(Sheet8!A1:A3)** in cell A1 of Sheet1.

Managing Workbooks

You may be wondering why you should bother with multiple workbooks if you're allowed to have more than 250 worksheets in a workbook. That's a fair question, and if this were the TV Kung Fu version of this book, we might say something like, "For as the tree grows tall, Grasshopper, the roots wander wide." Then we would leave you to wonder what on earth we were talking about. But we're not like that (at least, not intentionally), so we'll offer an explanation.

The mind generally thinks more clearly when the clutter is compartmentalized. By separating the individual components of, say, a spreadsheet-based accounting system, you can formalize your plan of attack. (There's also the benefit of being able to choose which things you share and which things you keep to yourself.)

Switching Between Workbooks

When working with related workbooks, you'll probably want to view two or more simultaneously. No problem whatsoever.

Open your workbooks by selecting the **File**, **Open** command. Then, to view more than one workbook at a time, open the **Window** menu and select **Arrange**. The Arrange Windows dialog box appears. You can have Excel tile the workbooks (where the resulting patterns are vaguely reminiscent of a bathroom floor), arrange them in vertical or horizontal rows, or cascade them in a virtual waterfall of stacked windows. Choose the window arrangement you want, activate the **Windows of Active Workbook** check box, and click **OK** to have Excel display all open workbooks.

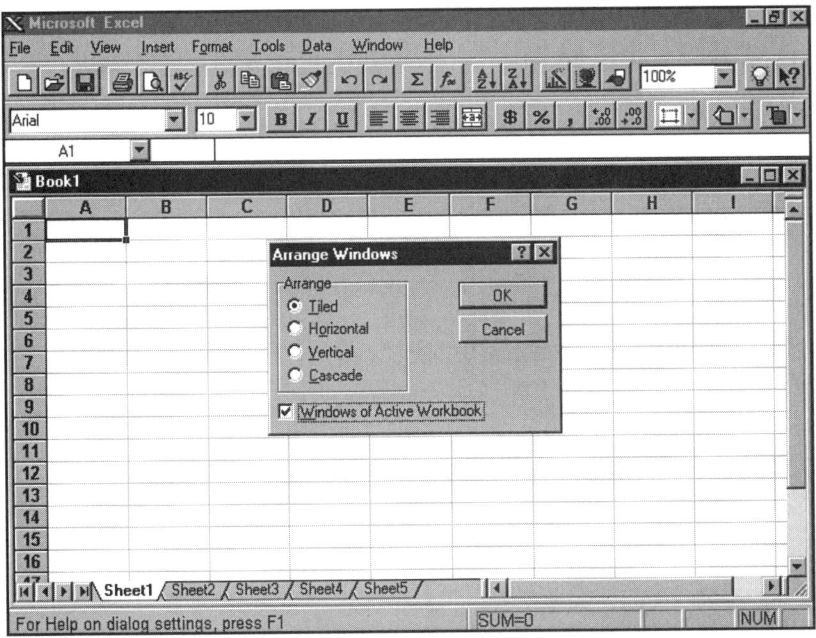

Choose an arrangement for multiple windows in the Arrange Windows dialog box.

You can restore a workbook to full size by clicking the **Maximize** button (the second button in the upper right corner of the active Title bar). Click on the **Restore** button to revert to the multi-worksheet view.

Referencing in Formulas

As it does with worksheets, Excel provides an orderly method for sharing formulas between workbooks.

To enter a reference to another workbook in a formula, enter the workbook name in brackets like this: <[> and]. Then enter the worksheet name and enter an exclamation point to separate that from other entries. Yes, you've seen it all before—almost. To calculate the sum of cells A1 through A3 on Sheet8 of workbook Book1 and have the answer appear in cell A1 of Sheet1 in workbook Book2, enter **=SUM(<[>Book1.XLS]Sheet8!A1:A3)** in cell A1 of Sheet1 of workbook Book2.

Linking

You link workbooks for the same reason you might link your fence to your neighbor's fence: it'd be a waste of resources to run two fences side by side along a common property line. The same is true with workbooks: it would be wasteful and would invite errors to have the same information entered in several areas.

For those times when you want to share data between one or more workbooks, you link. Linking is better than copying because, when you change the source cells in one document, Excel automatically updates the same cells in the second document. Think you could get your neighbor to be that cooperative?

You need two components to link workbooks: a *source workbook* and a *destination workbook*. To create a link between workbooks, select the active cell group from the source workbook and click the **Copy** button. Select the area on the destination workbook where you want to place the selected cells. Open the **Edit** menu and select **Paste Special**, and the Paste Special dialog box appears (see the following figure). Click the **Paste Link** button.

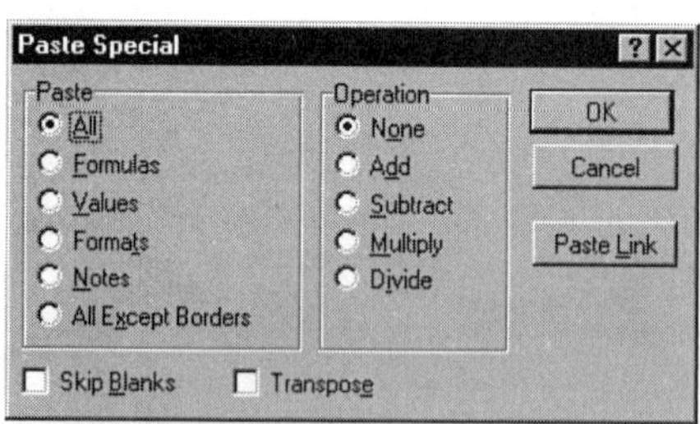

The Paste Special dialog box.

Unfortunately, we're not always happy with our first choices, and neither (we suspect) are you. To change the source workbook, select the linked cells from the *destination* workbook, open the **Edit** menu, and choose **Links**. The Links dialog box (shown in the following figure) appears. Select the **Change Source** button, and a dialog box similar to the Open dialog box appears. Select the new source workbook and click **OK**.

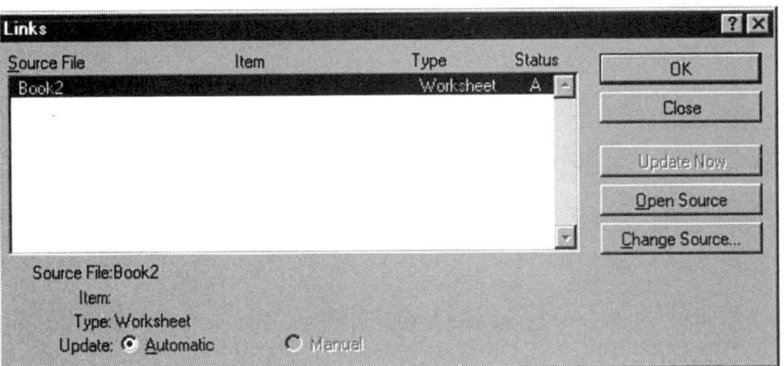

The Links dialog box.

One final note before closing. If you are going to save your source workbooks in directories other than those that contain your destination workbooks, you must save your source workbooks first. If you don't, you could destroy your links.

The Least You Need to Know

- Multiple worksheets simplify complicated spreadsheeting tasks.
- In much the same way as you name cells and ranges, you can name your worksheets.
- You can reference formulas from one worksheet in another worksheet so that one feeds into the next.
- You can simultaneously view multiple worksheets and multiple workbooks.
- Linking workbooks makes it possible to change a formula in one and have it automatically updated in the other.

Chapter 15

An Open and Shut Case

In This Chapter

- Search and rescue
- Open wide
- Protect and serve
- Notable nuggets for notorious novices

It's always a debate: do we drive through and let the kids drip ice cream on our fine Corinthian leather-like seats, or do we let 'em loose on the good people of Taco Bell, who, really, have done nothing to us? Usually the seat considerations win out. So we open the doors, kids spill out all over the parking lot, a few disappear immediately to the bathroom, and the youngest wisely picks a table of her own. In the end, we add an extra 18 minutes to our visit searching for kids, loading them back into the car, and protecting the youngest from a carload of older brothers and their pilfered packets of taco sauce.

In this chapter, we describe ways to keep track of files on your disk, open them up again, and protect your new creations from the cold, cruel world.

In Search Of: Searching for Documents

It's not true, what they say. You actually can teach an old dog new tricks. Excel for Windows 95 has taken that old trick of loading up existing files and thrown in a few extra complications to help you out when you can't remember where on the company network you left your salary calculation.

Tools for Prying Open Files

Opening a file is relatively simple—providing you have a good idea where it is. If you've made it to this point in the book, you've managed to do that quite nicely. To provide a neat opening for this segment (and also so you can't say we never told you anything), here's a quick overview.

To open a file in Excel, select the **File** menu and choose **Open**. The Open dialog box appears. Because we haven't been bouncing around in different folders, anything that you've saved should appear in the display area of the Open dialog box. Select the file you want to open and click the **Open** button, or just double-click on the file name.

The Name Game If you've used previous versions of Excel, don't get confused by the new names you find in Windows 95. Those familiar DOS directories haven't changed one iota. They simply have a new name: folders.

You use this process to open any file you've saved to your current folder. Unfortunately, that hardly ever seems to be the case. On our PCs, for example, we have an average of more than 3,000 files in more than 100 directories—sorry. A slip of the tongue. In Windows 95, directories are called *folders*.

In any event, what this means is that several times a year we are left scratching our heads, trying to remember exactly where we stuffed the workbook we created last April for Auntie Jo's taxes. What seemed to be a totally logical filing system just a year ago has now disappeared forever in some deep recess of the gray matter lolling about within our skulls.

Search Tools: A-Digging We Will Go

When you can't find a file, it's time to call out the search team. Excel provides a number of mechanisms for locating lost files.

To search for a file without the help of Leonard Nimoy, select **Open** from the **File** menu. Once again, the Open dialog box appears on your screen (see the following figure).

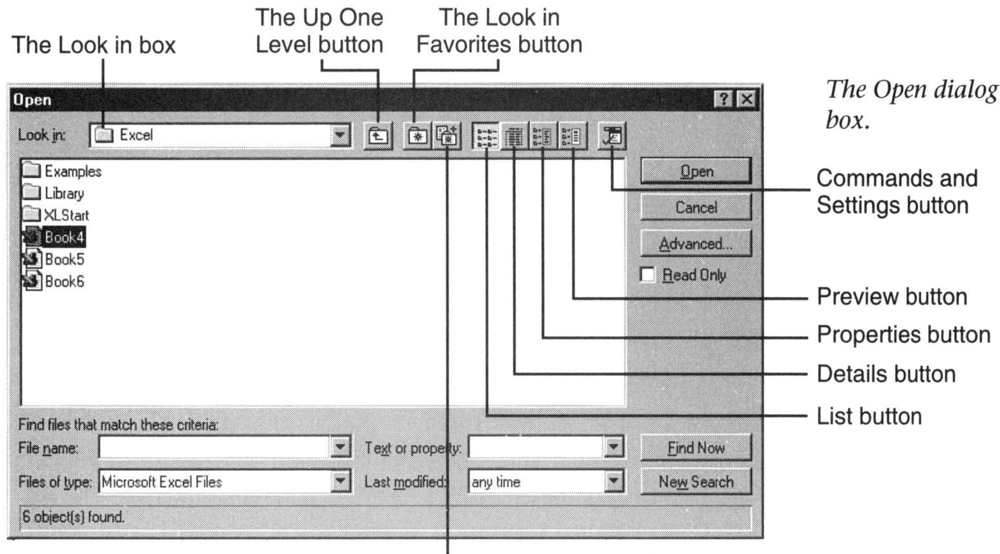

The Open dialog box.

The Look in box at the top of the dialog box contains the name of the current folder, and the display area contains the names of the files and folders in the current folder. If what you're looking for isn't there, it's time to go hunting. Use any of the following methods to change to a different folder:

- Click on the down arrow of the Look in box, and Excel displays all available drives. Select the drive you want to search, and its folders appear in the display area. Double-click the icon for the folder in which you want to conduct your search.
- Click on the **Up One Level** button. The Look in box changes to a folder one level higher than the current folder.
- Click on the **Look in Favorites** button, and shortcuts to folders you have designated as favorites appear in the display area of the Open dialog box. Select from this elite list of folders to conduct your file search.

Add It Up To add a folder to the Favorites list, select a folder from the display area and click the **Add to Favorites** button. Excel creates a shortcut to the selected folder, which will appear whenever you select the Look in Favorites button.

Once you've selected the folder you want to search, think about the file(s) you want to search for. Use the four boxes at the bottom of the dialog box—File name, Files of type, Text or property, and Last modified—to enter criteria to narrow your file search.

Another World

Still no file? There's always the slow and agonizing method. Click the **Commands and Settings** button in the Open dialog box and select **Search Subfolders** from the pop-up menu. This tells Excel to search through every subfolder in the system from the point listed in the Look in box. The actual speed of this search depends on the size and speed of your system. We found the required search time acceptable and, as an added bonus, just about right for a peanut butter and jelly sandwich.

To show all the files in their proper folders, select the **Details** button. Click the **Commands and Setting** button and select **Group files by folder** from the pop-up menu.

Advanced Search

Should you decide that you need to further fine-tune your search criteria, select the **Advanced** button from the Open dialog box. The Advanced Find dialog box (shown in the following figure) appears. You use this box to choose more parameters for your file search. However, this box will probably be of limited use as it takes more time to use it than to simply look through the list of files you found in the previous window.

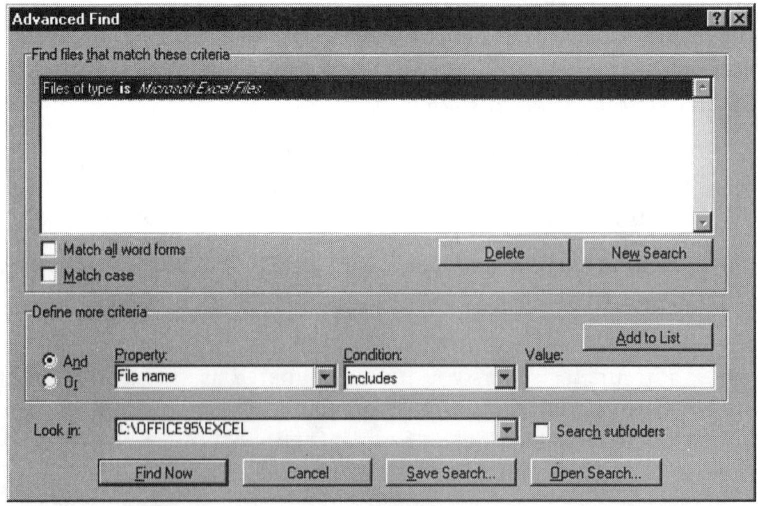

The Advanced Find dialog box.

There is one useful feature in this box, however. In addition to further refining your search criteria, you can also save your search settings for future use. To do so, select the **Save Search** button to access the Save Search dialog box. Enter a descriptive name for your search and click **OK**.

To call up the saved search criteria in the future, select the **Commands and Settings** button from the Open dialog box, select **Saved Searches** from the pop-up menu, and choose the desired search criteria from the displayed menu.

Sneak Views and Previews

Before we continue, let's look at a few other features the Open dialog box has to offer: previews of your files and file sorting.

Excel enables you to take a peek at a file, which can be helpful if you think you've found the file you're looking for, but you want to preview it to make sure. To catch a glimpse of what the file will look like before you actually load it up, select the file and click the **Preview** button.

Excel also enables you to control how the file names are displayed in the display area of the Open dialog box. Use the following methods to control the file display:

- To sort files, click the **Commands and Settings** button and select **Sorting**. Then choose whether you want Excel to sort files by Name, Size, Type, or Date.
- To view file size, type, and date modified, select the **Details** button.
- To view file properties and statistics, click the **Properties** button. Chapter 13 explains the workbook properties feature.

The Shortcut Menu

From the Open dialog box, you can now click the right mouse button to access various "shortcut" menus that contain file management options. There are three shortcut menus, and which one you get depends on where in the Open dialog box you click your right mouse button. Here are your choices:

- Right-click in the middle of the file display area to access the shortcut menu in the following figure. This menu contains four options: Explore (which opens the Windows 95 Explorer utility), Send To (which copies the highlighted file or folder to a different disk drive), Create Shortcut (which creates a shortcut icon you can use to quickly reopen the highlighted file from the Programs option of your Windows 95 taskbar), and Properties (which accesses a dialog box showing the attributes of your current folder).

Setting Properties You can lock, archive, or hide all the files in the current folder. To do so, right-click in the middle of the file display and select **Properties** from the shortcut menu. In the dialog box that appears, click on the appropriate check boxes to lock, archive, or hide the files in the current folder.

Shortcut menu 1.

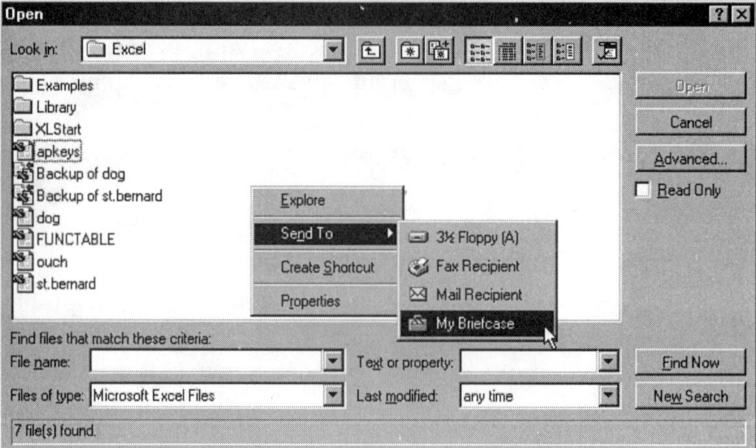

➤ Right-click on a file name. The resulting shortcut menu (shown in the following figure) has the same Send To, Create Shortcut, and Properties options, as well as options for opening the file, opening the file as a read-only file (meaning that it can't be changed), and printing the file. Other options let you cut, copy, delete, or rename the file.

Shortcut menu 2.

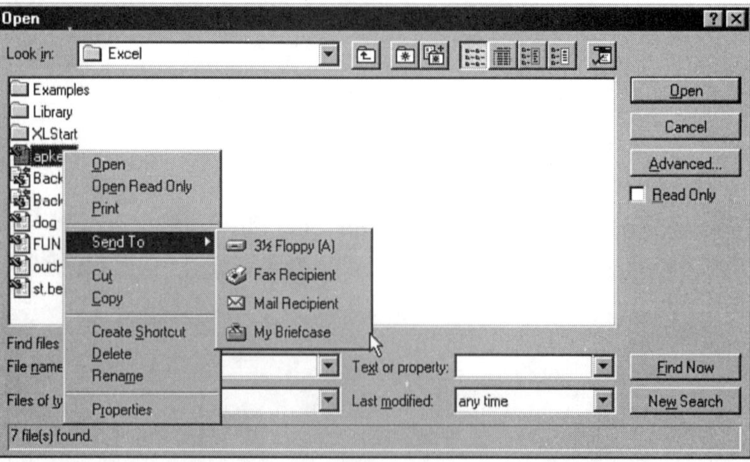

➤ Right-click on a folder. The following figure shows the third shortcut menu, which contains all the options from the first menu, an option for opening the folder, and options for cutting, copying, deleting, and renaming the folder.

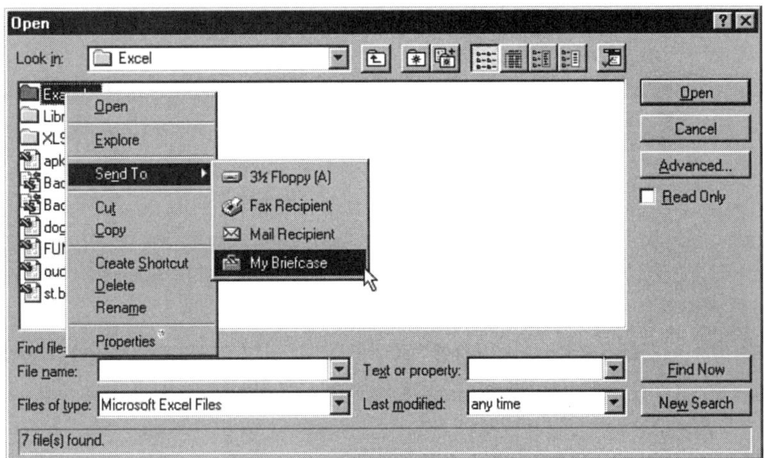

Shortcut menu 3.

Recently Used; Good As New

You'll find people in this world who would tell you that the procedure for opening documents in Excel is really much more complicated than it seems. The folks who would like you to believe this, though, are the kinds who try to impress their dates with snazzy pocket protectors. Do not believe them. Your social status depends on it.

You visited the Open dialog box in the beginning of this chapter. But don't think that's the only way to get to your file. You also have the ultra-easy Recently Used list.

Each time you create or open a file in Excel, the program keeps a little record of your visit. No, it's not a form of corporate espionage. Excel is just trying to make your life a little easier by giving you quick access to the documents you've been using lately.

In the last segment of Excel's File menu is a list of the files you've used most recently. (Go ahead. Pull down the File menu, and you'll see we're not lying.) To re-open one of these files, double-click on its file name.

Opening File Imports and Conversions in Excel

Excel works best on its own files, but if you work with other people or other applications, you'll find that you need to share information from time to time. That's where file imports and conversions come into play. Excel uses something called *import filters* (which you set up when you first install the program) to call up files from other applications. You can call up spreadsheets from other manufacturers, as well as text files, some word processing files, and lots of database files.

Here's the procedure for importing information from other non-database applications (such as word processors, other spreadsheets, and financial packages), text files, and other Microsoft Office applications. What we don't tell you here is how to import from database applications. We explain that complex process in Part 4 of this book. For now, here's the simple stuff:

- To import files from other applications, pull down the **Files** menu and select **Open**. In the Open dialog box, click on the **Files of type** box at the bottom of the screen and choose the file type for the file you are importing from the menu. Select your file and click the **Open** button.
- To import a text file, open the file through the Open dialog box as though it were a regular Excel file, and a Text Import Wizard appears to guide you through the import process.
- To import files from a Microsoft Office application, just open the file. When Excel recognizes the format, it performs the conversion.

Workbook Protection

Because spreadsheet work often deals with finances and proprietary information, it tends to be confidential. For that reason, Excel gives you a number of ways to protect your confidential information from prying eyes.

In the last chapter, you learned how to protect individual cells from change. In this chapter, you learn how to protect the structure of the entire workbook, protect the windows from change, and require a password for access.

Structural Safety

Excel enables you to protect the structure of the workbook so that nobody can hide or unhide certain worksheets, move them, rename them, delete them, or insert others.

But there's more worth protecting. Excel has a good head for figures: each time you open a workbook, it remembers where you left off previously. Your windows retain their position and size, the most recently used page, and even the position of the active cell. You can protect these aspects of a window to prevent other users (or passers-by) from hiding, unhiding, resizing, opening, or closing the window.

Keep It Safe

To protect the structure or the windows of a workbook from unwanted changes, open the **Tools** menu, choose **Protection**, and choose **Protect Workbook**. The Protect Workbook dialog box appears (see the following figure). Select **Structure**, **Windows**, or both. Click **OK**, and your workbook's structure and windows are safe.

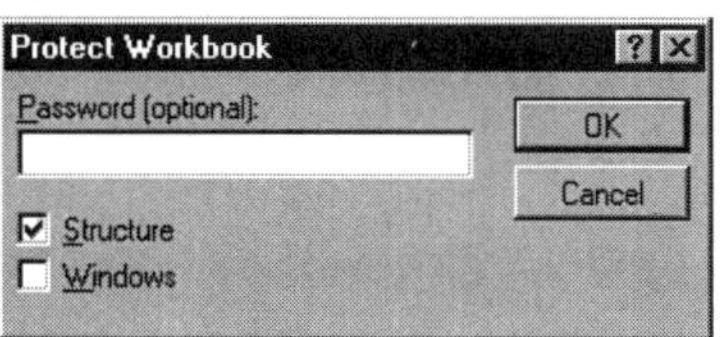

The Protect Workbook dialog box.

Although password protection for the entire workbook is done elsewhere (which we cover later in this chapter), you can enter a password here to protect the structure and windows from being changed. Type a password and click **OK**. Then retype the password to confirm it.

To remove protection, open the **Tools** menu, select **Protection**, and select **Unprotect Workbook.** If you assigned a password when you protected the workbook's structure or windows, you have to re-enter the password to unprotect.

Keep It Hidden

Whether your worksheets contain confidential information or just too much information, there will be times when you'll want to hide part of your work.

Excel makes it easy for you to temporarily hide your workbooks and worksheets to prevent unwanted changes or to cut down on the number of items in your view. The hidden sheets remain open, and all workbooks and worksheets remain available so that they can be referenced from other documents.

Here's how to hide and unhide workbooks and worksheets:

- To hide a workbook, open it and select **Hide** from the **Window** menu. Easy enough.
- To unhide the workbook, you cannot just repeat those steps to reverse the procedure. Most of the menus (including the Window menu) disappear when you hide the workbook, so now you have to open the **File** menu and select **Unhide**.
- To hide a worksheet, first open the worksheet. Then open the **Format** menu, choose **Sheet**, and choose **Hide**. Just like that, it's gone. You can run, but you cannot hide a worksheet if it's the only one in your workbook.
- Unhide the worksheet by choosing **Format**, **Sheet**, **Unhide**. The Unhide dialog box appears, listing your hidden sheets. Choose the one you want to retrieve, click **OK**, and you've got it back.

Learn to Share

Networked users now have the option of sharing files as they work, without wreaking havoc on the files.

The procedure is simple. With a file open, pull down the **File** menu and click on **Shared Lists**. The Shared Lists dialog box appears (see the following figure). This dialog box has two tabs: Editing and Status.

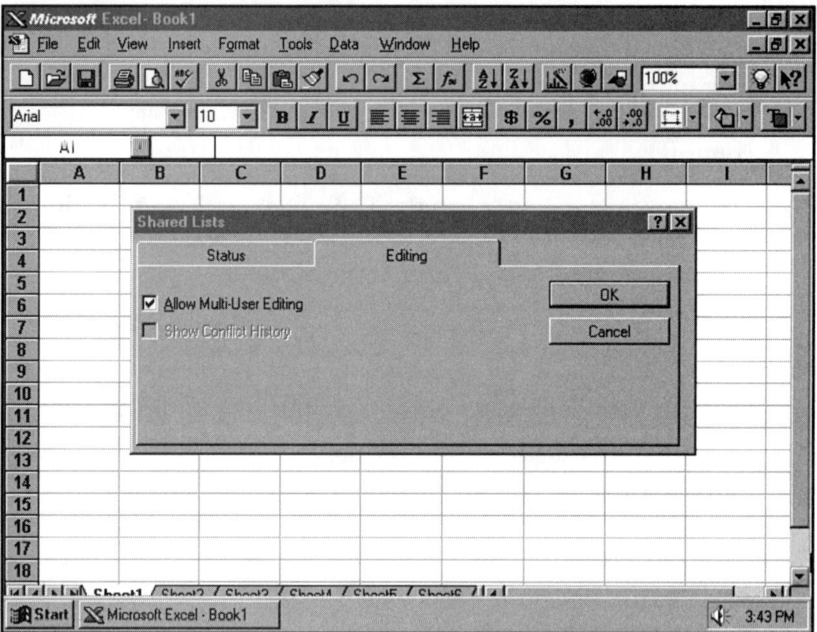

The Shared Lists dialog box.

On the Editing tab, click on the **Allow Multi-User Editing** check box and click **OK**. This turns on the feature that enables you to share your files with other users on your network. Excel saves your new multi-user workbook to the disk and displays a brief welcome message.

Share and Share Alike File sharing is a new feature of Excel for Windows 95!

When multiple users are working on the same workbook, there's bound to be a time when they make dissimilar changes at the same time. Maybe you're planning a trip to Six Flags over Someplace Close, for example, while your spouse is adjusting the workbook to budget a trip to

Brazil. That behavior, of course, causes conflicts. If you re-enter the Shared Lists dialog box, the Show Conflict History option is available. Choose this option, and Excel adds a new worksheet called Conflict History to the end of your multi-user workbook. The Conflict History worksheet lists the following information for each conflict that occurs:

Action Type

Date

Time

Who

Change

Sheet Location

Cell Location

Value

As you work with a multi-user workbook, you'll want to check the Conflict History regularly to ensure that problems are being handled properly.

The Status tab in the Shared lists dialog box shows the identities of users who have access to the multi-user workbook.

To turn off the multi-user option, return to the Shared Lists dialog box, uncheck the **Allow Multi-User Editing** option, and click **OK**.

What's the Password?

The final form of workbook protection is passwords. Excel's password protection enables you to save your workbook with complete password protection (so that only you can get back in) or with write protection (so that other people can read your worksheet, but can't make any changes). Excel also enables you to assign "read-only recommended" protection, which other users can roundly ignore.

When a document is merely write-protected (as opposed to password-protected), anyone who wants to make changes can simply save the workbook under another name. We imagine there's a reason you'd want to do this. Isn't there?

Forgotten Passwords

Hey you! Yeah, you, the guy standing in Wal-Mart reading this book because he forgot his password: Sorry, no. You can't retrieve it. No how, no way, no calls to Microsoft, no crocodile tears on the Internet, no pleas for help from American Express. It's gone forever. We're sorry.

But this is a great book anyway. Feel free to buy it, and read great tips like this:

If you're using a password, print out hard copies of your document formulas as backup in case you lose your password. To view the formulas for printing, open the **Tools** menu, select **Options**, and click on the **View** tab of the Options dialog box. Select **Formulas** in the Windows Options Section, anad then click **OK**. All your formulas are visible, and you can print them as a permanent record.

In Excel, you assign a password during the file-saving routine. Whether or not you've already saved your file, open the **File** menu and choose **Save As**. Click on **Options** and, in the File Sharing area of the Save Options dialog box, choose your level of password protection:

- Protection Password keeps Communist spies out of your entire workbook.
- Write Reservation Password keeps those spies from writing Communist propaganda in your workbook.
- Read-Only Recommended asks them nicely not to write Communist propaganda in your workbook.

Click **OK** and click **Save** to return to your document.

Before you can change or delete a password, you must first prove that you're not a Communist spy by opening the workbook with the password. Once you open the workbook, though, anyone—ANYONE—can change or delete the password. That means you won't want to leave it open while you're visiting the facilities, especially if there are Communist spies wandering around your office.

To change the password, open the **File** menu, choose **Save As**, and click on **Options** again. Click on the hidden password and either delete it or write over it. Then save as before.

The Least You Need to Know

- Excel has a number of complex options for searching for files. You're far better off to keep your files in folders with obvious names and skip the lengthy search process.
- Opening Excel files is easy. Just pull down the **File** menu, select **Open**, and click on the file name in the Open dialog box.
- Importing foreign files to Excel is possible. Choose the file type from your list of import filters in the Open dialog box.
- Protect your files. Hide them or use passwords to maintain confidentiality.

Chapter 16

Customizing the Spreadsheet

In This Chapter

- Back in your cell
- Paging Mr. Formats
- Excel-erate your screen
- Outstanding options offerings

There was a time when the human race was quite content to work with hand-written ledgers and carbon-copied interoffice memos.

Computers have changed all that. Now a memo can't be official unless it's printed in three colors and has a cover sheet, a logo, double bars between the header and body, and at least four different typefaces.

And your spreadsheet? It's gotta have tables, colors, italics!

And you wondered why computers hadn't helped your productivity.

Customs Clearance

There's a bit of artist in all of us. Excel caters to your need to make things look good by giving you all sorts of options for changing the appearance of individual cells and ranges, entire worksheets, and even Excel itself. This chapter tells you how.

Changing Small Things

We start off by describing ways to change the appearance of individual cells or ranges: the fonts, colors, borders, and other formatting features.

Freedom of Choice

You can change the format—the appearance—of cells in several different ways. Throughout this discussion, we instruct you to use the Formatting toolbar. Feel free, though, to use any of these alternatives:

- Open the **Format** menu and select the **Cells** command to access the Format Cells dialog box, which contains a few options (borders and patterns, alignment, and protection) that you cannot change from the Formatting Toolbar. We discuss cell protection in Chapter 13, and we cover borders, patterns, and cell alignment later in this section.
- Right-click on a cell and choose the **Format Cells** option from the shortcut menu that appears.
- Press **Ctrl+1**; that's a shortcut that takes you directly to the Format Cells dialog box.

The Font

The words and letters you type into an Excel spreadsheet have different typefaces, or *fonts*, that change their basic appearance. You can choose your fonts to fit your own style. The following figure shows you some of the fonts and special effects available in Excel.

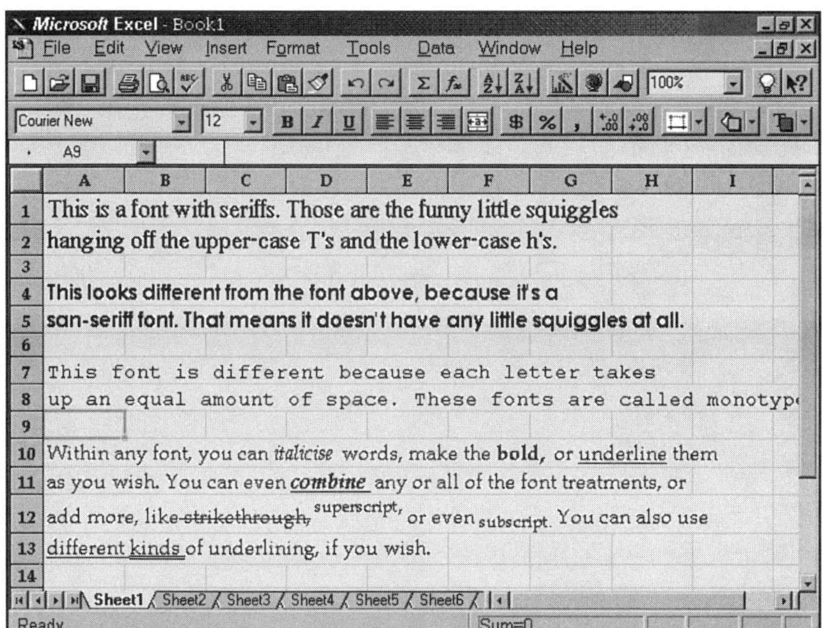

Fonts and special effects change the appearance of text.

Excel uses a default font as the standard typeface for your worksheets. You can change that default font for all of your worksheets, or you can change the font for an individual worksheet, cell, or range. You'll learn later in this chapter how to change the default font. In the meantime, if you'd like to change the font for just some of the cells on your worksheet, follow along here.

Begin by selecting the cells or blocks of text within cells that you want to change. Then pull down the **Font** box on the Formatting toolbar and select a new font. While the cells are still selected, choose your new font size using the Font Size box. You can pick from the drop-down list or enter your own number. Alternatively, you can choose different fonts, sizes, and effects from the Format Cells dialog box, explained at the end of the next section.

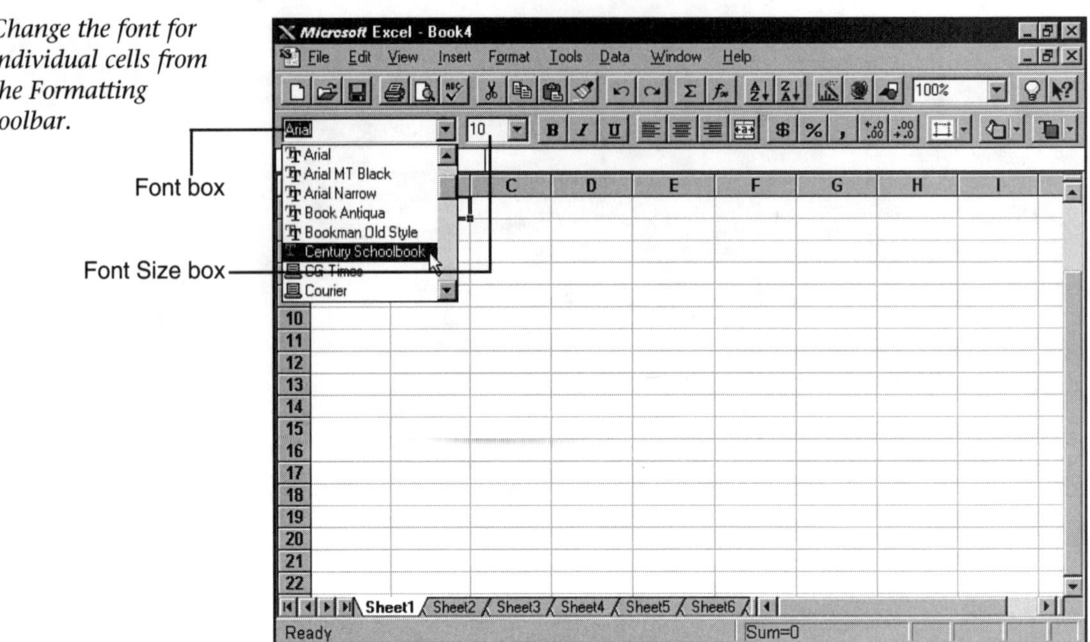

Change the font for individual cells from the Formatting toolbar.

Special Effects

You can add special effects to your text with bold, italic, and underline. Select your text, and then click on any of these buttons on the Formatting toolbar. You can combine them for different effects.

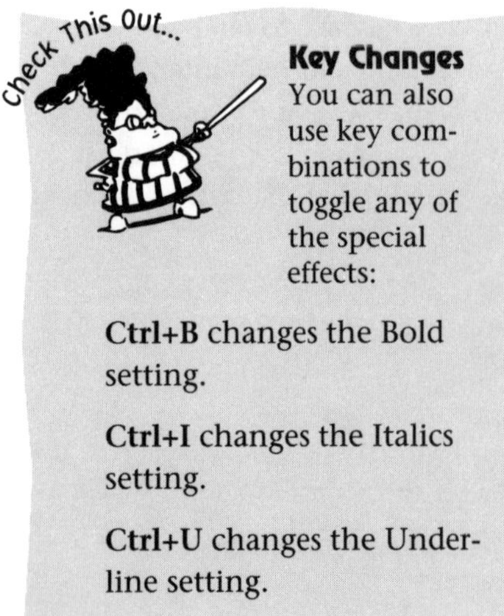

Key Changes You can also use key combinations to toggle any of the special effects:

Ctrl+B changes the Bold setting.

Ctrl+I changes the Italics setting.

Ctrl+U changes the Underline setting.

B Bold

I Italic

U Underline

When you select any of these buttons, the button appears to be pushed in (to indicate that the effect is turned on). To remove special effects, just reselect the text, and click again on the special effects buttons. Excel removes the formatting from your text, and the button no longer appears to be pushed in.

There are other special effects available in Excel, but you have to dig a little deeper to get to them.

Select the text you want to change, and then go to the **Format** menu and select **Cells.** The Format Cells dialog box appears. Click on the **Font** tab to see the options shown in the following figure.

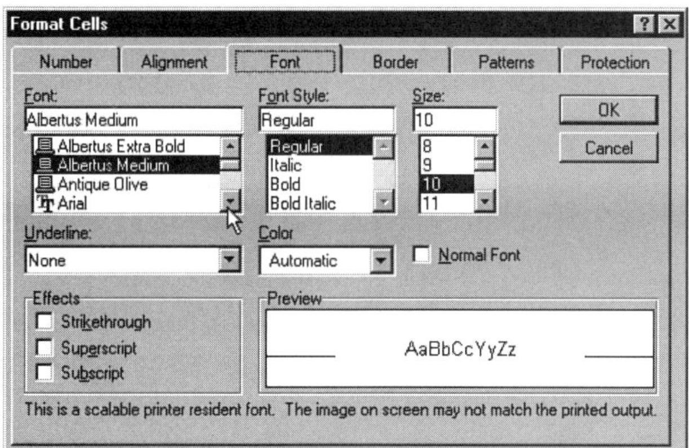

The Font tab of the Format Cells dialog box.

From this box you can change the font, font style (bold, italics, or combination), the font size, the underline settings, cell colors (see below), and other special effects (strike-through, superscript, and subscript). Selecting the Normal Font check box returns all selections to the default, and the Preview window shows you how your changes will appear on-screen. Click **OK** to return to the main Excel screen.

Change Cell Colors

You can easily change colors... twice! Excel allows you to change the color of both the text and the actual cell. Just follow these steps:

1. As usual, select the cell or cells you want to change. You can select non-contiguous areas by holding down the **Ctrl** key as you select additional areas.

2. To change the color of the text, click the down arrow of the **Font Color** button on the Formatting toolbar. From the palette of colors that appears, select the color you want.

3. To change the background color of the cells, click the down arrow of the **Color** button on the Formatting toolbar. Again, select a color from the color palette. The cell changes accordingly.

Color Bind If you're dissatisfied with the color options in your color palette, you can change 'em! Open the **Tools** menu, select **Options**, and click the **Color** tab in the Options dialog box. Then double-click on any color to change it. Click **OK**, and your new color palette is available.

Borders and Patterns

Borders and patterns add more special effects to your cells by allowing you to highlight or outline them. To add a border or pattern, select the cells you want to highlight. As always, you can choose non-contiguous areas by holding down the **Ctrl** key and selecting additional areas with your mouse. When you've selected all the areas you want to highlight, click the down arrow on the **Borders** button on the Formatting toolbar. A small box appears with twelve borders you can choose from (see the following figure).

Select a border for your cells.

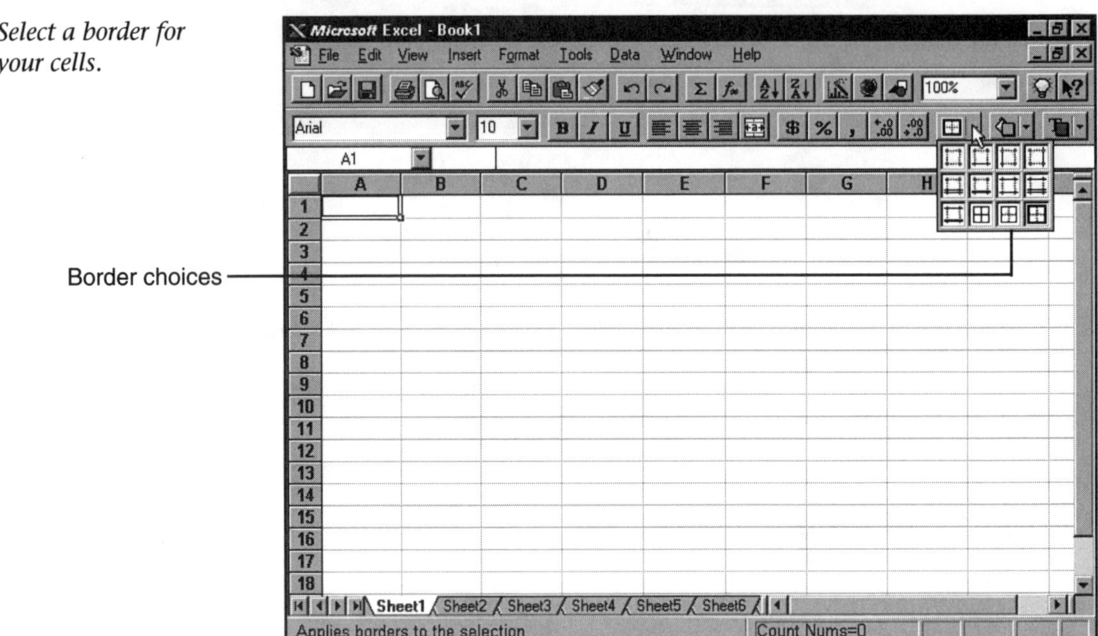

Alternatively, you can open the **Format** menu and choose **Cells**. Choose your border (including color, line style, and placement) from the **Border** tab, and choose your cell pattern (including its color) from the **Patterns** tab. When you finish setting options, click **OK**.

Cell Alignment

You can apply simple cell alignment using the four alignment buttons on the Formatting toolbar. Just select your cells and click on the appropriate button to align the text within the cells. The following figure shows the alignment buttons on the Formatting toolbar.

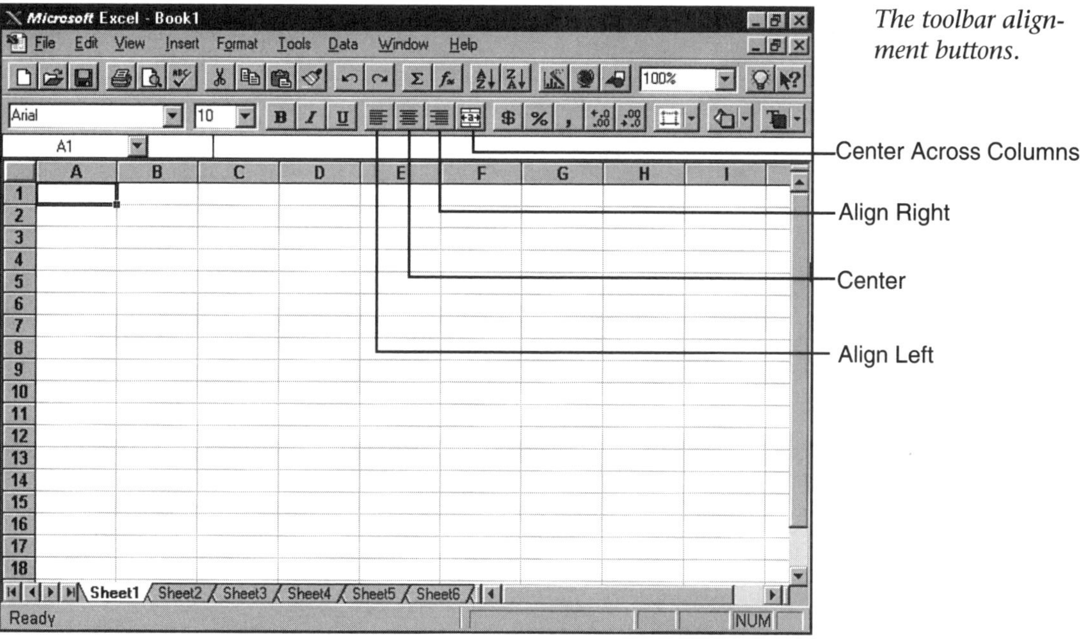

The toolbar alignment buttons.

You can choose from other alignment options as well. Open the **Format** menu, choose **Cells**, and click on the **Alignment** tab of the **Format Cells** dialog box.

From there, you can choose how you want your text to align horizontally. The General setting aligns text to the left, numbers to the right, and errors and logical values in the center. The Left, Center, and Right settings are self-explanatory; the Fill setting repeats the text until the cell is filled; the Justify setting inserts spaces between words to fill the cell; and the Center Across Selection setting aligns the text within a selected block of cells.

The Vertical settings describe vertical placement of text (whether it's at the top, bottom, or center of the page or it's justified), and the Orientation settings control the vertical direction of the text. The Wrap Text check box forces text to wrap within the cell instead of bleeding across blank cells as it usually does.

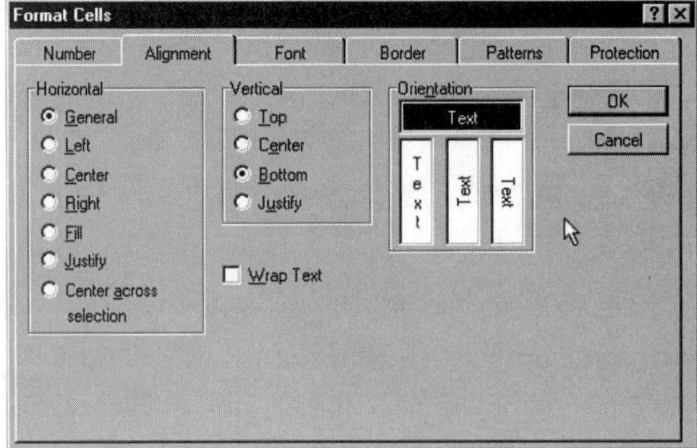

Text alignment options.

Number Formatting

In Chapter 6, you learned how to format numbers using the options on the Number tab of the Format Cells dialog box. You can also format numbers using the five number-formatting buttons on the Formatting toolbar (shown in the following figure).

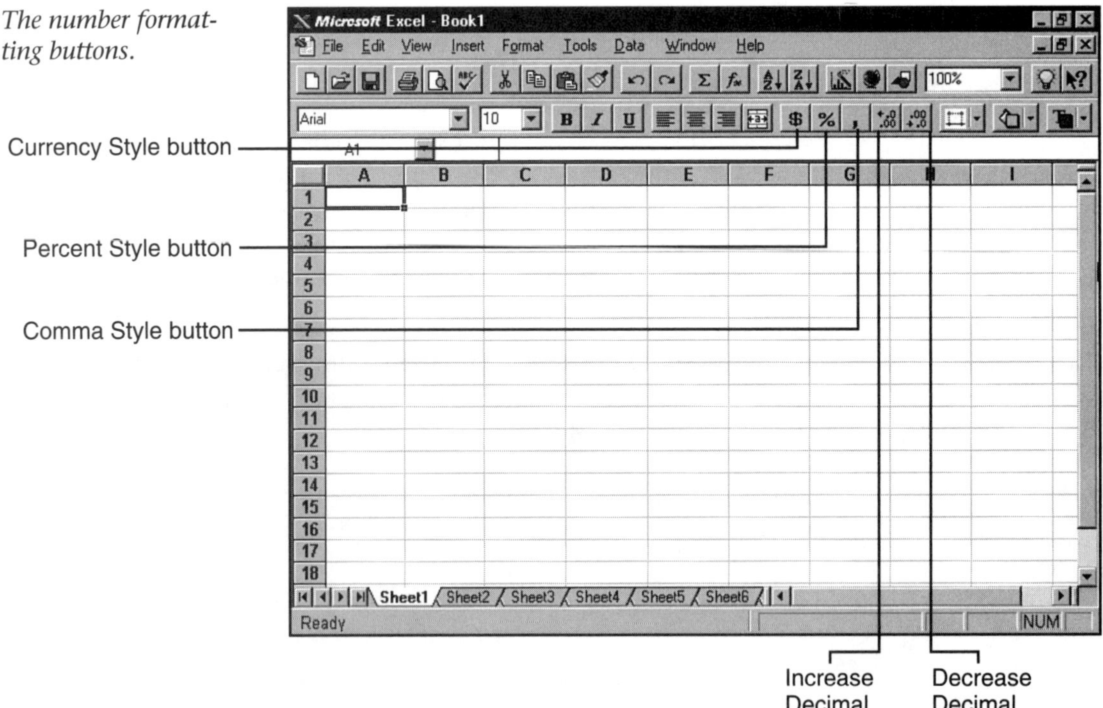

The number formatting buttons.

To use the toolbar buttons, select the cells containing the numbers you want to format, and then click on the button that contains the desired style.

- Currency Style places a dollar sign (or any other currency symbol you used in your original Windows setup) in front of each number in the selected area, and changes the number to two decimal places.
- Percent Style changes to an even percentage without decimal places.
- Comma Style places a comma to the left of every third number (counting from the right, of course), and changes to two decimal places.
- The Increase and Decrease Decimal buttons change the number of decimal places in the selected range. Each time you click the button, the decimal place increases or decreases by one place.

The Format Painter

You can copy all styles, including cell and text colors, from one range to another with the Format Painter button on the Standard toolbar.

First select the text that contains the formatting you want to copy. Then click the **Format Painter** button and select the text to which you want to copy the format. The format changes automatically.

When One Size Doesn't Fit All

Sometimes you'll find that a single column or row is too large or too small. For example, if a column is too narrow for Excel to display a cell's value, Excel simply displays the error message #### in that cell. You can easily resize the column to fit the text.

To adjust column width, move your mouse pointer to the row of grayed-in column headers. Move the mouse slowly to the right, and the pointer changes to the two-arrow beam (see the following figure). Click and drag the two-arrow beam to adjust the column width wider or narrower as necessary.

You can change the size of rows and columns by dragging the two-arrow beam.

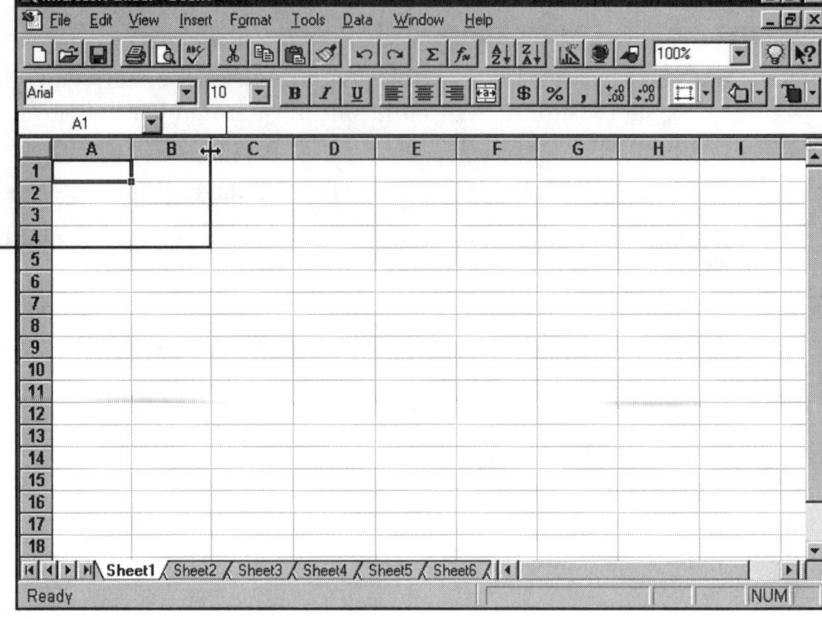

The two-arrow beam pointer

Do It Yourself You can tell Excel to figure out its own column width and row height settings with the AutoFit feature. Just select your columns or rows by clicking on the appropriate headers. Then go to the **Format** menu and choose **Column** or **Row**. Select the **AutoFit** option, and your columns or rows adjust themselves perfectly to accommodate the widest or tallest text in each column or row.

To adjust the row height, position the pointer to the far left in the grayed-in row header area. Move the pointer to the bottom border of the row you want to change. When the pointer changes to a two-arrow beam, click and drag to adjust the row height.

You can also change the size of a group of rows or columns. First, select the group by clicking and dragging across any number of headers. Then move to the edge of the group until the pointer changes to a two-arrow beam. Drag the group as before until it reaches the desired size. All cells in the group become the same height or width.

Changing Larger Things

Most of the changes you make in Excel will affect only individual cells. But there are a few changes you can make universally.

Default Font

Earlier, we showed you how to change the font for a text selection. You can also permanently change the font for both the row/column headers and the worksheet text. To do so, open the **Tools** menu and select **Options**. In the Options dialog box, click the **General** tab to access the options shown in the following figure.

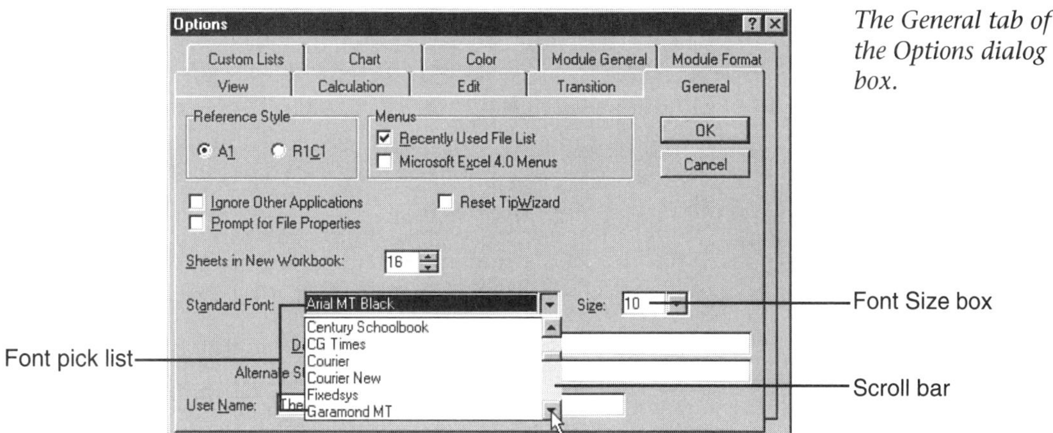

The General tab of the Options dialog box.

For now, click the **Standard Font** down arrow to display the list of available fonts. Move up and down the list as necessary to find other fonts, and when you find the one you want, select it. Choose the font size from the font **Size** box. You can enter a specific size, or you can select the down arrow and choose a size from the list that appears. Click **OK**, and Excel tells you that you must restart your computer for the new default (standard) font to take effect.

Other Options dialog box options are described in Chapter 10.

Column/Row Size Throughout

You learned earlier in this chapter how to change the width of an individual column or a group of columns, and how to change the height of a row or group of rows. You can also change the standard size of all columns and rows in the entire worksheet.

This is the process:

1. Select all the worksheets for which you want to change the row or column size. (Select the first worksheet, hold down the **Ctrl** key, and click on the tabs of additional worksheets.)
2. Click the **Select All** button (the unlabeled block at the intersection of the column and row headers). Excel highlights the entire worksheet.
3. Open the **Format** menu, select **Column** or **Row**, and choose **Height** or **Width**. A dialog box appears. Enter the size of the new height or width. (The height number is measured in points; the width is the average number of characters of the standard font.)

Page Formatting

When it comes time to print your shiny new document, you'll want to set up proper page adjustments: margins, page orientation, page order, and headers and footers. You make all of these adjustments from the same place: the Page Setup dialog box. To access this dialog box, open the **File** menu and select **Page Setup**.

The Page Setup dialog box has four tabs. Although we discussed most of the Page Setup options in Chapter 4, here's a recap to save you the effort of turning a few pages.

- Page Choose your page orientation (vertical or horizontal), page scaling (how much worksheet do you want to cram onto a page?), paper size, print quality (a higher number of dots per inch is a higher quality printout), and the first page number.

  From any page you can also call up the Print, Print Preview, and printer Options screens, all of which are thoroughly explained in Chapter 4.
- Margins Specify how far from the edges you want worksheet and header/footer information to be printed. Choose also whether you want your worksheet to be centered vertically or horizontally on the page.
- Header/Footer Choose from the built-in list of headers and footers, or create your own.
- Sheet This tab lists elements and asks whether or not you want them printed. You can also control your page printing order from this tab.

Changing Excel's Appearance

You change documents for other people. You change Excel for yourself. In this section, you'll learn to customize your own copy of Excel, so that your work environment is friendly, fun, and—depending on the color scheme you pick—safe.

Making It Pretty

Most of your basic screen appearance is determined by your Windows Control Panel settings. The following table shows which Control Panel setting changes each of the aspects of your Excel screen settings.

Changing Excel's Appearance

This Control Panel Setting...	Affects This Excel Screen Element
3D Objects	Color of column/row headers, toolbars, scroll bars
Active Title Bar Color	Title bar color
Active Title Bar Fonts	Title bar fonts
Menu Color	Menu color
Menu Fonts	Menu fonts
Window Color	Workspace, Formula bar, View sizer colors

To access the Windows 95 Control Panel, click the **Start** button on your taskbar, select **Settings**, and select **Control Panel**. Select the **Display** option from Control Panel, and click the **Appearance** tab to change your font and color settings.

Hide and Go Seek: Displaying Screen Elements

In Chapter 2, you learned that the basic Excel screen contains such elements as bars, objects, grids, tabs. You can choose to display or hide most of these elements using the Options dialog box.

Open the **Tools** menu and select **Options** to access the Options dialog box. Click on the **View** tab to see a list of the elements you can change (shown in the following figure). Excel provides a check box for each element you can turn on and off.

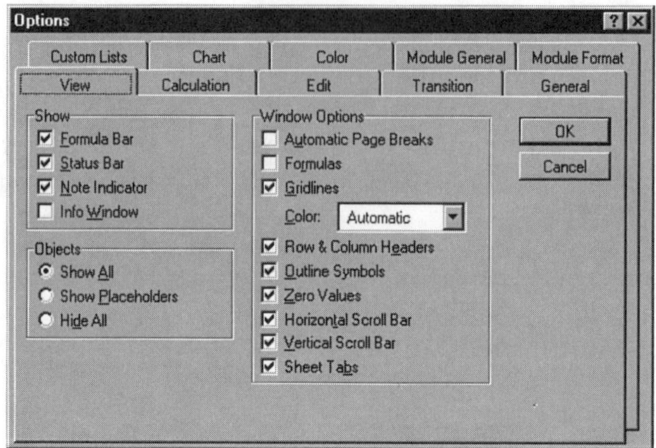

The View tab of the Options dialog box.

- In the Show area, use the Formulas and Status Bar check boxes to turn the Formula bar and the Status bar on and off. The Notes Indicator check box determines whether or not a small red box appears when you attach a note to a cell (see Chapter 13). The Info Window check box controls whether Excel displays information about a single cell (its address, the formula it contains, and the contents of any attached notes).
- The Objects options determine how objects such as imported pictures and Excel charts are displayed. You can show them in full, simply mark their location, or hide them altogether.
- In the Window Options area, you can turn on **Automatic Page Breaks** to prevent printing problems down the road. The Formulas check box changes the display of data in cells that contain formulas; when the Formulas check box is checked, Excel displays the actual formulas instead of their results. This is useful if you need to print out your formulas.
- The Gridlines check box sets grids for each cell in your work area. You can pick a color or let Excel assign a color automatically.
- The other check boxes in this area (Row and Column Headers, Outline Symbols, Zero Values, Horizontal Scroll Bar, Vertical Scroll Bar, and Sheet Tabs) turn the display of each of these items on or off.

Zoom In

There's still one more factor for changing your Excel display: the Zoom feature. Zoom determines how much of the worksheet you see on-screen at any given time. To use Zoom, open the **View** menu and select **Zoom**. Excel displays the Zoom dialog box (shown in the following figure).

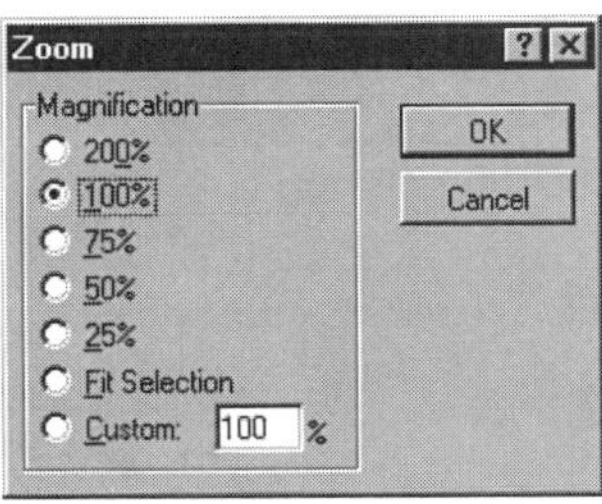

Use the Zoom dialog box to adjust the scope of your view.

Choose a percentage from the list or pick **Fit Selection** to have Excel fit the selected range on the screen. If your selected range is as small as a single cell, the entire cell fills the screen. You can also select your own view percentage from the **Custom** box.

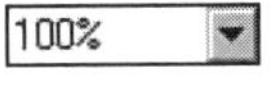

Alternatively, you can adjust the Zoom percentage from the Zoom Control box on the Standard toolbar.

When viewing multiple documents (see Chapter 14), you can size each window individually and zoom each window independently. Simply open the **Window** menu and choose **Arrange**. In the Arrange Windows dialog box, choose how you want the multiple windows arranged: Tiled, Horizontal, Vertical, or Cascade. Check the **Windows of Active Workbook** box to view more than one worksheet at a time. Then, to zoom each window individually, use the Zoom feature for each active window in turn.

New Ways of Viewing Documents

Excel permits you to view your documents in a variety of ways. Each of the screen elements described above is part of the view, as are the Zoom factor and the window size. Once you've determined which elements are best for your active worksheet, you can save them as a "view." Then you can change any or all of those elements and save them again as a new view.

To save a custom view, set up your worksheet display the way you like it. Resize the window, open several windows and tile them, hide the objects, change the font, or do anything else you want. When you're satisfied with the view, open the **View** menu and select **View Manager**. The View Manager dialog box appears (see the following figure).

No View Manager? If the View Manager option doesn't appear on your View menu, you'll need to add it. Go to the **Tools** menu and select **Add-Ins**. Click on **View Manager** and click **OK**. That's all there is to it!

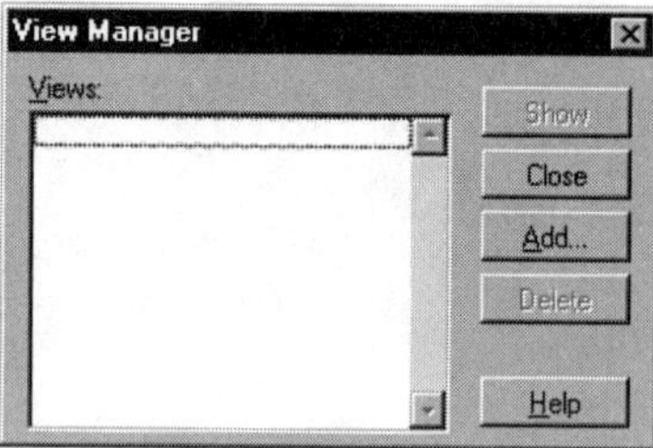

The View Manager dialog box.

The **Views** list contains the names of any existing views. Click the **Add** button to add your new view under a new name. The Add View dialog box (shown in the following figure) appears. Add the view name, choose whether to include print settings and hidden rows and columns, and click **OK** to return to the main screen. Excel saves your view selections, and you can return to them at any time.

The Add View dialog box.

You can change your view—every element if you want—and repeat the process if you want to save that view also.

When you want to recall an old view, go back to the View Manager dialog box, choose the desired view from the **Views** list, and click the **Show** button.

The Least You Need to Know

- You can change the appearance of cells, ranges, worksheets, and all of Excel.
- You can make most cell formatting changes from the Formatting toolbar.
- To make more obscure formatting changes, access the Format Cells dialog box.
- Open the **File** menu and select **Page Setup** to access the Page Setup dialog box, which contains options for most page formatting changes.
- The Windows 95 Control Panel contains controls for most of Excel's appearance settings.

Part 3

Charts, Graphs, Maps, and Other Picture Things

At last! A break from all those numbers!

In this section, you'll learn to build and change charts, graphs, and maps. Flower children from the '60s will appreciate all the available shapes and colors. We wrote this whole section wearing bell-bottom trousers and love beads.

BARRY LOSES THE "TONGUE IN THE DISK DRIVE BET"... AGAIN.

Chapter 17

Graphics Workshop

In This Chapter

- Graphic reminder
- Pulling 'em in
- Draw the line
- Twist and shout
- Perfectly polished prettying-up

Orange crates. Bad posters taped to the wall. Brick-and-board bookshelves. Air mattress.

Yeah, we've done the "I'm single, I'm in college, and I don't care!" school of decorating. Nowadays, though, we prefer glass in our picture frames, counter-sunk screws in our bookshelves, and actual drawers for our undies.

Is it too much to expect the same level of panache from a spreadsheet? We think not.

Welcome to Graphics

As anyone who has ever viewed "Baywatch" knows, there's a lot to be said for visual aids. The right visuals can direct interest where you want it directed.

This section of the book focuses on various sorts of visuals for Excel. These are the features that spice up your worksheets and divert the attention of your audience from the hard cold numbers of your worksheet. Chapter 18 looks at charts, and Chapter 19 explains maps. In this chapter, though, we introduce graphics as a whole, and tell you how to create, import, and manipulate your own.

If you're lucky, you might end up with graphics that are better looking than the lifeguards on... naaaahhhh.

Types and Shadows

Excel enables you to attach graphic objects to your worksheets and workbooks. You can attach existing graphics you've imported from other places or pictures you've drawn yourself, and you can manipulate either kind of graphic. And, of course, you can create charts, tables, and maps, all of which are described in other chapters.

Your imported graphics can take the form of photographs, drawings, clip art, symbols, charts, and software screen shots. Once you've imported or drawn your graphic, you can use Excel's limited drawing features to manipulate them. Let's start by learning to import.

Importing Existing Graphics

You don't have to be a Leonardo, Michelangelo, or any of the other Ninja turtles to place great-looking graphics in your document. There are literally thousands of stock photos and graphic images available from other software packages (including Microsoft's ClipArt collection), online services, electronic bulletin boards, and CD-ROMs located in the "we didn't know where else to put them" rack at local discount stores. Use a classic shot of the Eiffel Tower or a group photo of your kids on vacation. Whatever works best.

You can import any of the bit-mapped Microsoft ClipArt Gallery images that are included with Excel. In addition, Excel allows you to import other bit-mapped (.BMP) files, tagged image format (.TIF) files, PC Paintbrush (.PCX) files, WordPerfect Graphics (.WPG) files, and several other types of graphic files into your documents.

Important Import Info

AlthoughExcel can import several types of graphics files, you must already have installed the proper graphic import filter or translator, usually as part of your original software installation. If you are unable to import a file that's in an acceptable format, run Setup again to install the necessary filters. You can import the following graphics file types into Excel:

.BMP	Bit-mapped image
.CDR	CorelDRAW! 3.0
.CGM	Computer Graphics Metafile
.DRW	Micrographix Designer/Draw
.EPS	Encapsulated PostScript
.GIF	Graphic Image Format
.HPGL	HP Graphics Language
.JPEG	Online compressed graphics format
.PIC	Lotus 1-2-3 graphic
.PCT	Macintosh PICT filter
.PCX	PC Paintbrush
.TIF	Tagged Image Format
.WPG	WordPerfect Graphics

To import a favorite graphic from an outside source, open the **Insert** menu and select **Picture**. The Picture dialog box—startlingly similar to the Open dialog box described in earlier chapters—appears on your screen (see the following figure).

Search for an image in this dialog box just as you would search for any file (refer to Chapter 15 for search techniques). You can preview some images in the Picture dialog box before you load them. Click on the **Preview** button, and then scroll through your graphics images. The viewable images will appear in the Preview window.

Click the **Open** button to copy the image into your worksheet. If Excel does not readily identify the file type, it displays the Convert File dialog box. Select the type of image you are importing and click **OK**.

Select the image you want to import in the Picture dialog box.

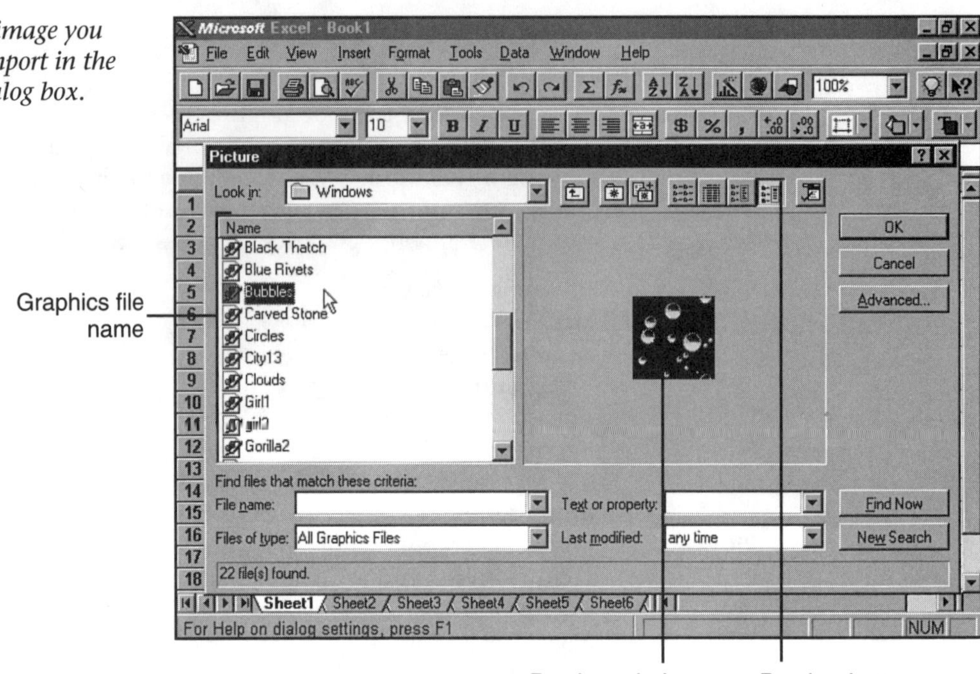

Drawing Your Own

"Everyone's a critic," says the actor. "Everyone's an editor," says the writer. "Everyone's an artist," says... the software developer? Yep. Even if you're awful, Excel gives you the tools to create art that can impress even the most jaded critic: your mom.

The Drawing toolbar contains a great selection of drawing tools. There are tools for drawing lines, boxes, circles, arrows, and just about any variation of those that you can imagine. You can fill in shapes with patterns and colors, change border styles, and have a whale of a good time getting your images just right.

To access the Drawing toolbar, open the **View** menu and select **Toolbars**. In the Toolbars dialog box, check **Drawing**, and click **OK**. Excel displays the Drawing toolbar in the middle of your screen, as shown in the following figure.

On the Drawing toolbar, you find 21 buttons, each with a different drawing function.

The Drawing toolbar.

Basic Shapes, Slings, and Arrows

Trying to master drawing in Excel by reading about it is like trying to learn to play the piano without touching a keyboard. We can tell you all you need to know, but you still need to get in there and fiddle about. So here are a few dry directions to help out when you feel the urge to fiddle (not, we ask, while major Italian cities are on fire).

To draw in Excel, click on one of the shape toolbar buttons. Your pointer changes to a small cross. Move your pointer to the work area of your spreadsheet and position it where you want the shape to begin. Then hold down the left mouse button and drag the shape to the size and position you want.

Some of the shapes have additional tricks. The following table shows each of the icons on the Drawing toolbar and explains its use.

Excel's Drawing Toolbar Buttons

Button	Name	Description
	Line	Draws straight lines horizontally, vertically, or at an angle. Force the line to a 90- or 45-degree angle by holding down the Shift key while creating the line.
	Rectangle	Draws rectangles or perfect squares. Resize by selecting the shape and dragging one of the vertexes at the corner of the shape. Make a perfect square by holding down the Shift key while creating the shape.
	Ellipse	Draws ellipses and circles. To draw a perfect circle, hold down the Shift key while creating or resizing the shape.
	Arc	Draws an arc; for those times when you need less than a full circle, and a straight line won't do. Create a perfect 90-degree arc by holding down the Shift key while drawing.

continues

Excel's Drawing Toolbar Buttons Continued

Button	Name	Description
	Freeform	Creates those shapes that defy easy description (such as that shape you're looking for that's somewhere between a profile of a porcupine and the classic silhouette of George Washington). Pear shapes and un-square boxes are its specialty. As you draw, you'll click on each corner or angle of the shape until you've finished. Get perfect 90-degree angles by holding down the Shift key as you draw. You can mix and match 90-degree and other angles by pressing and releasing the Shift key as you draw.
	Text Box	Opens an adjustable box on your screen, where you can type new text or paste text from another source. You can paste boxes of text anywhere in your document. Hold down the Shift key to make the box perfectly square. The Format Object dialog box associated with Text Boxes has more tabs than the other dialog boxes have. (The Text Box is described in more detail later in this chapter.)
	Arrow	Adds an arrow to point out the obvious, or not so obvious. To force the arrow to a 90- or 45-degree angle, hold down the Shift key while creating the arrow.
	Freehand	Enables you to draw such things as an outline of the east coast, or just make those lines that nature never anticipated; the kissing cousin to the Freeform button, above.
	Filled Rectangle	Creates a rectangle, like the one above, but fills it with patterns and colors that you select using the Pattern button (discussed below).
	Filled Ellipse	Creates an ellipse like the one above, but filled.
	Filled Arc	Creates an arc like the one above, but filled.
	Filled Freeform	Fills your favorite shapes with patterns and colors.
	Create Button	Lets you place and size a button of your own. For fans of self propagation, nothing beats the Create button.

Button	Name	Description
	Drawing Selection	Changes the pointer to an arrow that enables you to select graphic objects and drag them around at will. (You don't really need this button, you know. Just point and click anywhere on the object, and the object is selected anyway.) If you want to select more than one object, hold down the Shift key as you point and click.
	Bring to Front	Moves the active drawing to the front screen position. You can actually layer many drawings in the same area on a worksheet. Most people use this feature so that once they've finished one part of their drawing, they can start working on a new layer without messing up the finished part. Use this button to select the portion of the drawing you want on top.
	Send to Back	Moves the active portion of the drawing to the back position. This is the complement of the Bring to Front button.
	Group Objects	Gathers a collection of drawings made at different times into one group. To create a group, click this button, hold down the Shift key, and click on each object you want in the group. When you finish, click the Group Objects button again. Once you group objects, you can't make changes to individual components of the group without first ungrouping them.
	Ungroup Objects	Disbands a group previously created.
	Reshape	Enables you to twist and bend the active freeform drawing into other shapes. To reshape an object, select the object and click the Reshape button. Drag the black boxes (vertexes) that appear along the borders of the object to achieve the desired shape. When you finish, click the Reshape button again. If you want to resize the entire freeform drawing instead of individual components of it, turn off the Reshape button and click anywhere on the drawing. A rectangle appears around the entire shape with resizing vertexes.

continues

Excel's Drawing Toolbar Buttons Continued

Button	Name	Description
	Drop Shadow	Toggles on or off a 3-D shadow effect for the active drawing.
	Pattern	Contains the patterns and colors you can use to fill in selected drawing shapes.

When you're drawing one of these shapes, don't sweat the details. Just place it in your document. You can always reposition, lengthen, or shorten it later. To do that, just click on the shape, and then drag the black squares, called *vertexes*, that appear at the ends of the line or shape.

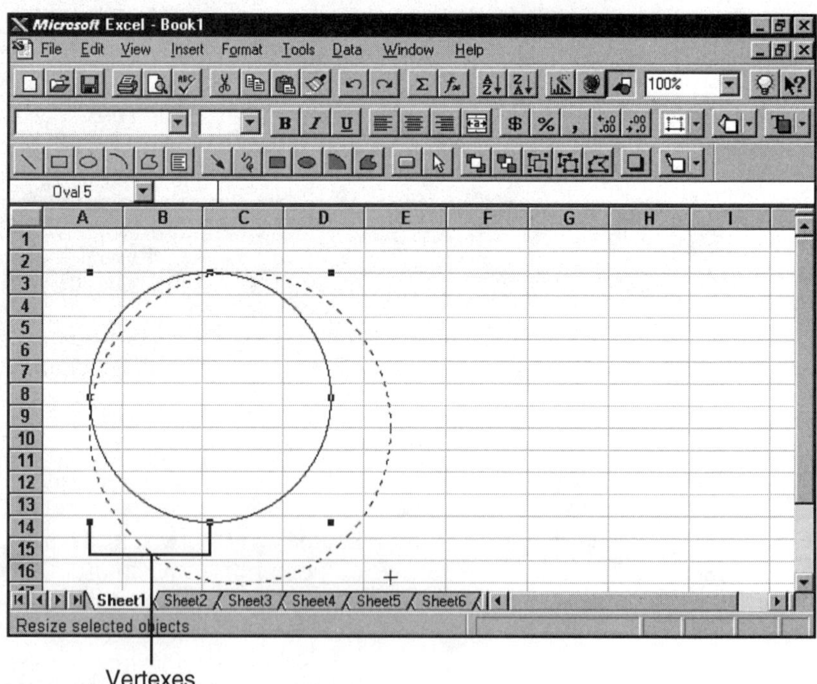

You can resize a shape by dragging one of the vertexes.

You can change the characteristics of a created shape by selecting it (a single click) and then double-clicking on it. When you do, the Format Object dialog box appears.

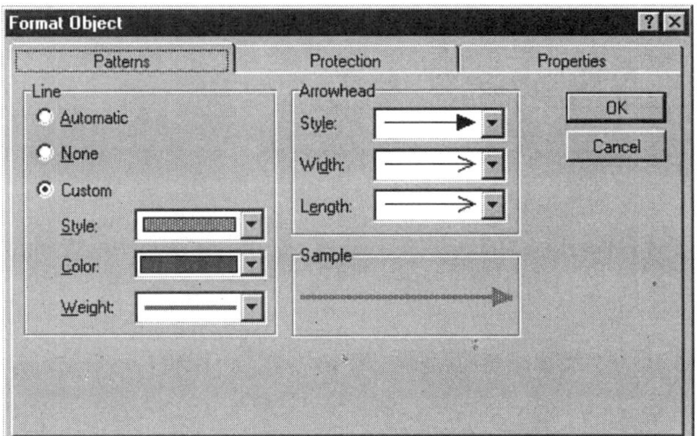

Use the Patterns tab to change the attributes of a shape.

Each shape has its own Patterns tab with options related to changing the appearance of that particular shape. On the Patterns tab for the arrow shape, for example, you can reformat Excel's arrows to make them longer, fatter, greener, double-headed, and so on.

The Format Object dialog box has two other tabs labeled Protection and Properties. Use the Protection tab to protect or unprotect an object from unwanted changes. (See Chapter 13 for more information on cell protection.) The Properties tab enables you to choose what happens to the object if you move or change the underlying cells. You can choose to move the object and resize it with the cells, move it without resizing it, or neither move nor resize it. Use the Print Object check box on this tab to indicate whether or not you want the object printed when you print your worksheet.

> Check This Out...
>
> **World's 'a Changin'**
> Another way to get to the Format Object dialog box is to select the text box or graphic you want to adjust, open the **Format** menu, and select **Object**. The Format Object dialog box appears on your screen. Easier yet, just double-click on the object itself.

Labeling Graphics

You can label your graphics image by placing a text box in the desired area around your image and typing your label or comments into it. Simply click the **Text Box** button on the Drawing toolbar to open up a text box, and then start typing. If you want to adjust the font type and size, select the text box and right-click on it. Select **Format Object** from the shortcut menu, and the Format Object dialog box appears (see the following figure).

You can also call up the entire Format Options dialog box for Text Boxes by clicking once on the edge of the text box to select it and then double-clicking on the box to call up the dialog box.

Make your font type, size, and other format selections here.

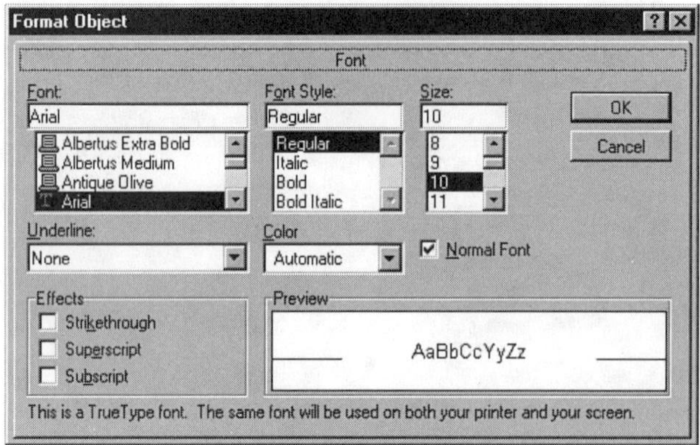

The Format Options dialog box contains the text **Font** and **Alignment** tabs described earlier in this chapter, the **Protection** and **Properties** tabs described earlier in this section, and a **Patterns** tab with options for changing the attributes of the box itself. The **Patterns** tab lists options for changing the appearance of the border (Automatic, for default settings; None, for no border at all; Custom, for changing the line Style, Color and Weight; Shadow to create a three-dimensional shadow effect around the box; and Round Corners instead of the default square corners) and the appearance of the text box itself (Automatic applies the default settings; None gives no color or pattern; the colors change the color of the entire box; and Pattern overlays a pattern or second color that you choose from the drop-down box of colors and patterns). The **Sample** box shows how your choices will appear on the worksheet. Click **OK** to finalize your choices.

Use the Format Options dialog box to change the appearance of text boxes.

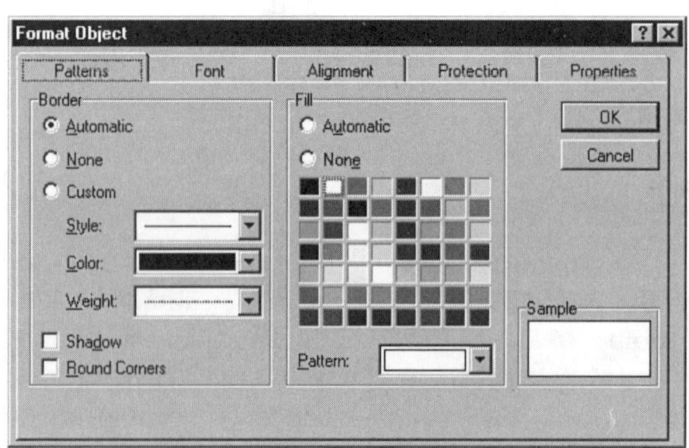

Manipulating from Within

You'll make most of the changes to your graphic objects using the controls in the Format Object dialog box described above. However, you have a few other options for manipulating graphics.

Proportions

You can't do much to manipulate an imported graphics file from within Excel. However, graphic images created in another application are automatically linked to that application so that when you double-click on them, the originating application opens and allows you to make modifications. You'll find it faster and safer to make changes to your object directly from your dedicated graphics package before you import it.

But you can easily make one change to any graphic from within Excel: sizing adjustments. Click on the graphic you want to resize, and a box appears around the graphic with *sizing handles*, small squares located at the corners and midpoints of the box. Click on a sizing handle with your mouse pointer, and drag the side or corner of the graphic to its new size. As you drag, the proportions of the image change in the direction you drag the border. To maintain constant proportions as you resize imported graphics, hold down the **Shift** key as you drag one of the sizing handles.

Drawn Objects

To change the size of an object, click on the object. Sizing handles appear at the edges and mid-way points of the sides of the graphic. Drag the sizing handles to enlarge or reduce the object, fine-tuning its size and position on your worksheet page. To maintain constant proportions as you resize drawn objects, hold down the **Shift** key while dragging one of the corners.

Moving Objects

To move an object within a worksheet, click on it with the mouse and drag it to where you want it to be. To move two or more objects as a set, hold down the **Shift** key, click on each object you want to move, and then drag the objects.

The easiest way to move a graphic to another worksheet or workbook is to select the object and use the Cut and Paste buttons on the Standard toolbar.

Copying Objects

To copy an object within a worksheet, select it, press and hold down the **Ctrl** key, press the right mouse button, and drag the copied graphic to the new location. The original stays put.

The easiest way to copy to another worksheet or workbook is to select the object and use the Copy and Paste buttons on the Standard toolbar.

Exporting

Just as you can import a graphic from another program into an Excel worksheet, you can copy any graphics image in your Excel document (including Excel charts) into another program. To do so, select the image you want to export, hold down the **Shift** key, open the **Edit** menu, and select **Copy Picture**. Then, using the other program's menu commands, paste your image into the other application.

The Least You Need to Know

- Most of your graphics will be imported. They look better than the ones you'd draw in Excel, and you have a wide variety to choose from.
- Some days you won't be able to resist drawing your own object. Excel's drawing tools are very basic, but they're adequate.
- To make changes to a graphic, select it. Then double-click on it and make your changes in the Format Objects dialog box.
- You can resize, move, and copy objects to any place on your worksheet.

Chapter 18

Top of the Charts

In This Chapter

- The chosen chart
- The creation
- Mod-ify squad
- 3-D and 2-D charting

"If it wasn't so rare, we'd all be well done." Or so we were assured by a certain science teacher. A very funny joke we thought, until the day one of our classmates brought in a picture of a person who had actually spontaneously combusted.

The teacher tried to calm the class down. He reasoned with us, explaining that, statistically, the chances of it happening to any one of us were virtually nonexistent. But we weren't listening.

Seeing that his pleas were falling on deaf ears, he began drawing on the walls with bright, bold-colored markers. He drew a great bold line representing most of humanity and a small dot representing the members of humanity that spontaneously combust. We got the picture. The chaos abated, and we returned to our seats for the rest of class. But it was a full week before any of us would sit close to another human being.

Choosing Charts

Why use charts? Because the impact is immediate. Rows and columns are accurate, sure, but they're emotionless. Even when dressed up for readability, they don't jump out and tell you anything. You know: there's a sum... and look over there: an average! Given enough time, your audience could figure out what it is about the numbers that excites you. But do you, or do they, really want to wait?

Charts reach out and grab your viewers by the throat. That thick sky-blue ribbon heading for the heavens—that's sales. The yellow ribbon snaking along at a low level along the bottom—that's cost. This is exciting. This is immediate. This is what charts are all about.

Charts made in Excel have the additional advantage of being able to change as you change the underlying data. Because the charts and the actual data are linked, the chart changes are automatic. So once you create a chart, you never have to go back and change it—unless you want to.

There are 117 basic charts to choose from in Excel, and that's before you do any customization. Which chart will work for you depends on what you're trying to emphasize (or de-emphasize).

Looking for Mr. Good Bar... and Other Types of Charts

In this section, we describe the kinds of charts available in Excel. Later, we'll tell you how to create and modify simple charts of your own and how to create really, really complicated charts—the kind that impress novices and confuse experts.

Here's what you need to know about Excel's selection of charts:

- *Area* charts are great for piling on the data. Area charts are good for illustrating the breadth of change as opposed to a rising or falling rate of change.
- *Bar* and *column* charts emphasize variations among the charted values. The far-reaching bar is generally the most impressive performer. If reaching for the stars is what counts, these charts can emphasize how well you're doing (or not doing).
- *Pie* charts and *doughnut* charts are for more than just law enforcement figures. They provide an excellent way to present such data as resource allocations vs. income and how they relate to the whole.
- *Line* charts are great for showing where you've been, where you are, and where you're going.

- *XY (Scatter)* charts don't look good on-screen. But if you want to know at a glance how your numbers compare to what you expected, these charts are hard to beat.
- *Radar* charts gather the values in a series of numbers and visualize a coverage area.
- You'll find *3-D surface* charts useful in "what if" applications. Resembling topographic maps, they make useful visual aids in determining ideal data combinations.
- *3-D* Bar, Area, Column, Line, and Pie charts are all functionally similar to their 2-D counterparts. However, they offer greater visual impact and clarity.

Creating a Chart

It's not necessary to decide which type of chart you want before you create it; however, it does help to have an idea of what it is you want to do. There are plenty of ways to change your selection later if the chart type you choose doesn't work out.

One choice you should make ahead of time is whether you want the chart to appear on your worksheet or on a page all its own. A chart that exists on your worksheet is known as an *embedded chart*. A chart that exists on a page all its own seems to have gotten this far without a fancy name, but the special page it's on is known in Excel-ese as a *chart sheet*.

Creating an Embedded Chart

Creating a chart in Excel is very much an automated process. Still, it's nice to know where you're headed and what's happening on your trip. We'll start by going through the creation of an embedded chart, which is on the same worksheet with its underlying data.

Embedded charts do not lack any Excel features; they merely share space on a worksheet with some related functions and numbers. You can move and resize embedded charts at will. If you change the worksheet data on which the chart is based, Excel updates the chart immediately to reflect the change. (Okay, almost immediately. Let's not quibble over a few milliseconds.)

To create an embedded chart, you start with chartable data arranged in a tabular format. Any column(s) or row(s) of numbers will do. Charts work best if you've labeled the rows and columns. The following figure shows a range of cells that contain chartable data. Each of these items of data will become a *data point* on the chart.

Chartable data arranged in a table.

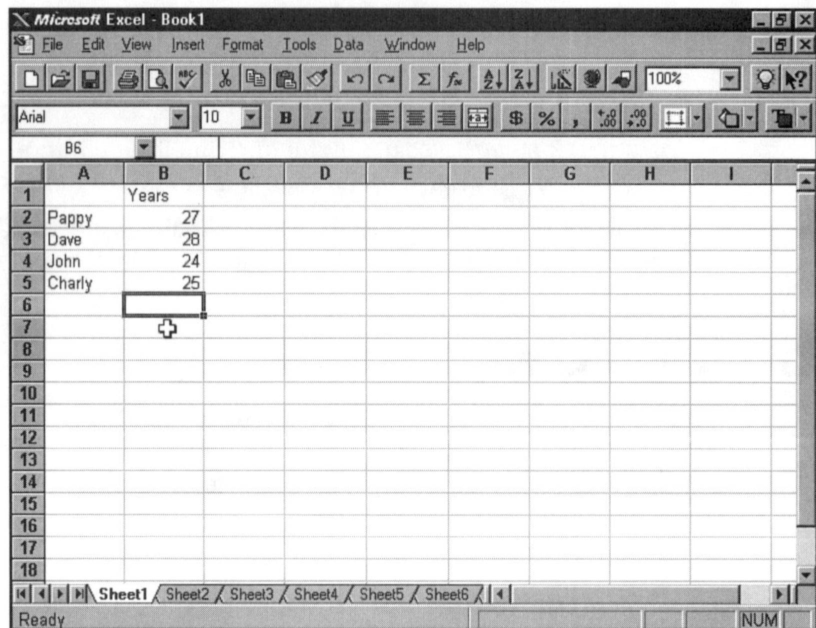

Select the rows and columns you want to include in your chart, including any labels. With the cells still active, start the Excel ChartWizard by clicking on the **ChartWizard** button on the Standard toolbar. The pointer changes to the ChartWizard cross-hair pointer shown in the following figure.

Drag the cross-hair to the position on your worksheet where you want to place the chart. Click the left mouse button to position one corner of the chart. Hold down the left mouse button, drag the pointer to the opposite corner to size the chart, and then release the left mouse button. The ChartWizard - Step 1 of 5 dialog box appears on your screen.

In this dialog box, you see instructions for changing the cell range you've defined. The Range box displays the cell addresses for the range of cells (including labels) that you've selected for your chart. Click on **Next** if the range is correct. The second ChartWizard dialog box appears.

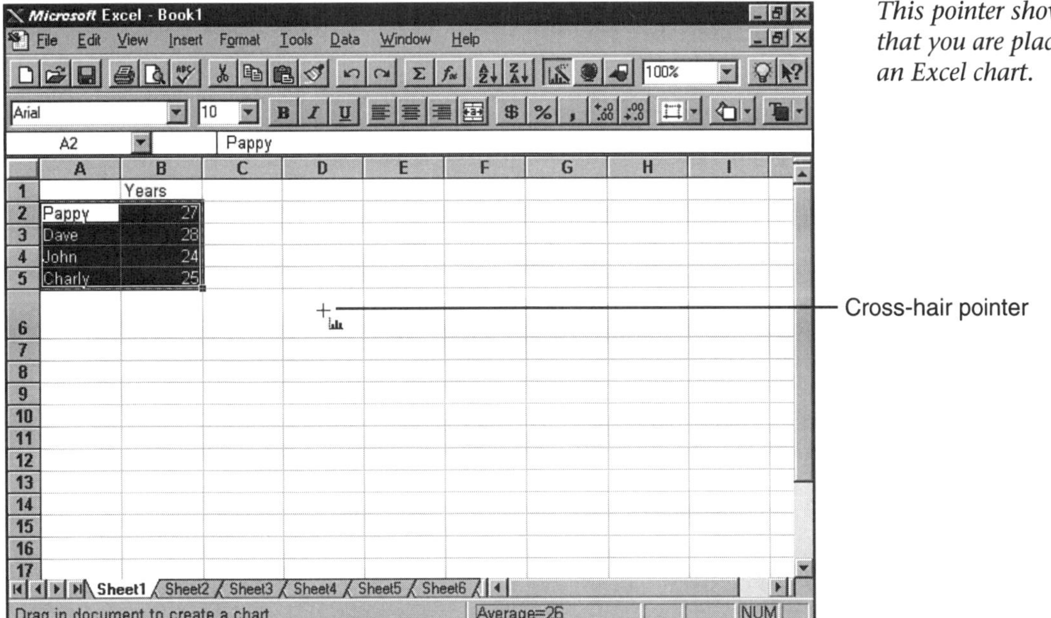

This pointer shows that you are placing an Excel chart.

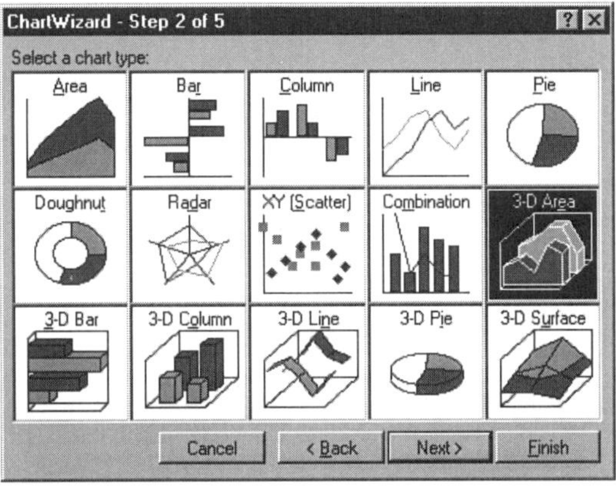

ChartWizard - Step 2 of 5

From the ChartWizard - Step 2 of 5 dialog box, choose a chart type. Don't agonize over which chart type to use at this point; you'll be able to change it later. For now, pick one of the first six charts to keep things simple. When you've selected one, click on **Next**.

Navigating in ChartWizard
You can select the **Back** button at any time to back up a step and change a selection.

The third ChartWizard dialog box illustrates subsets of the selected chart type. Choose from the available formats and select the **Next** button to continue.

The chart modifications featured in the fourth ChartWizard dialog box depend on the chart type you initially selected. The following figure shows the options we got when we chose to create a 3-D bar chart from our sample data.

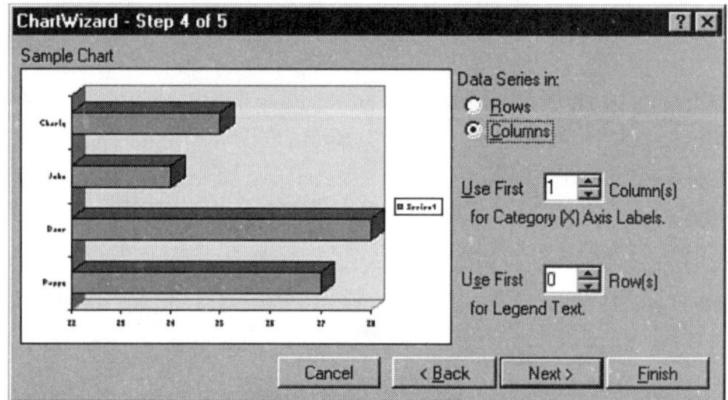

The ChartWizard - Step 4 of 5 dialog box.

Note that the legend and labels change depending on whether you select your data series from rows or columns. Excel automatically uses the data in the first row and column to create its labels and legends. You can change the values in the **Use First** spinner boxes to have Excel use other data for the labels and legends.

Make your selections from the available options. When you finish, select the **Next** button, and the ChartWizard — Step 5 of 5 dialog box appears (see the following figure). Follow the instructions in this dialog box to modify legends and titles.

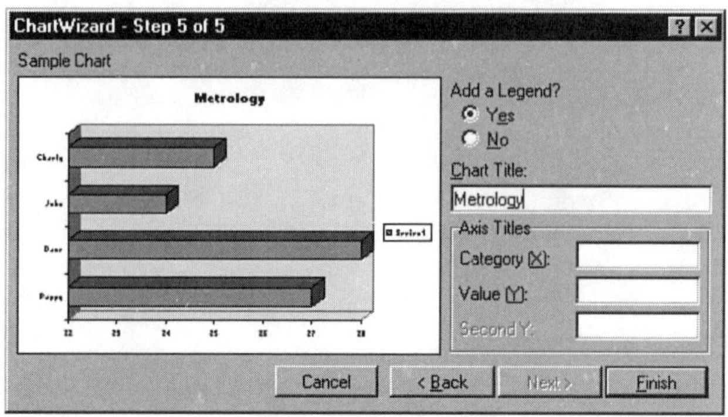

The ChartWizard - Step 5 of 5 dialog box.

Your changes appear as you work. You can modify them from this dialog box. When you're satisfied with the appearance of your entire chart, click the **Finish** button.

When Excel places the chart on your worksheet, it might not look the way you hoped it would. If legends and labels don't show, just resize the chart until they appear. You can resize and reshape by selecting the chart and then dragging the selection handles that appear at the corners across the screen as desired.

Later we'll describe how you can change the components of your chart. But first, we explain Chart Sheets.

Creating a Chart Sheet

A *chart sheet* is nothing more than a worksheet created specifically for a particular chart. A chart on a chart sheet shares all the properties of an embedded chart. Its chief advantage is that it is automatically proportioned to take advantage of as much of the page space as necessary. As with embedded charts, Excel automatically updates the chart with changes you make to your worksheet data.

To create a chart sheet, select the rows and columns (including labels) that you want in your chart. Open the **Insert** menu, select **Chart**, and select **As New Sheet**. Excel opens a new worksheet to the left of the current active sheet and displays the familiar ChartWizard — Step 1 of 5 dialog box. Work through the ChartWizard dialog boxes as you did to create the embedded chart. When you finish, the new chart appears on the chart sheet with the default name Chart1.

Quick and Easy Chart: Excel Knows Best

When time's 'a wastin' and almost any chart will do, just select the data and labels you want included and press the **F11** key. Excel chooses which chart it thinks will best represent the selected data, creates the new chart, and opens it on a new chart sheet automatically. If you don't like it, you can always change it.

In the unlikely event that Excel admits it doesn't know what's best for your data, the ChartWizard begins.

A Chart Sheet with a View

To view a chart sheet later, just click on its worksheet tab as you would to view any other worksheet. But your viewing options don't stop there. By default, the chart is sized to fill the available space on your screen. To see what the chart would look like on the printed page, pull down the **View** menu and deselect the **Sized With Window** command. Excel automatically re-enables the Zoom feature with which you can zoom in or out.

Creating Charts from Noncontiguous Cells

Cells do not have to be adjacent to be included in charts. To create a chart with cells from different areas of your worksheet, select the first group of cells you want to include in the chart. Press and hold the **Ctrl** key and select an additional group of cells from another area of your worksheet. You can do this more than once if necessary. Open the **Insert** menu, select **Chart**, and select either **As New Sheet** to place the chart on a new chart sheet or **On This Sheet** to create an embedded chart. Then proceed as usual.

Facts and Figures to Consider

Besides the fact that throwing too many things on a single chart can render that chart a worthless hodgepodge of colorful blocks, there are some other limitations to consider. Truth is, though, that few worthwhile charts will even come close to these maximum limits:

4	Line weights
8	Line styles
12	Drummers drumming
16	Area patterns (on-screen)
255	Worksheets that a chart can refer to
255	Data series in a chart
255	Fonts in a chart
666	Evil software programmers
4,000	Data points per series
32,000	Data points for all data series
56,448	Pattern and color combinations

And one final finger-pointing number (meaning that no one is willing to accept responsibility): the total number of charts that your worksheet can link is limited by your available memory.

Morning After Modifications

You've made your chart, but it's UGLY! It's INCOMPLETE! Who ya gonna call?

Adding Data to a Chart

You can usually add new data to an existing chart without too many complications. First, enter your new data where it belongs on your worksheet and select the cells you want to add to the chart. Move the pointer toward the edge of the selected cells until it becomes an arrow, and then click the left mouse button and drag the pointer into the chart. Excel automatically updates the chart to include the new group.

If for some reason Excel is unable to add the new data directly to the chart, the Paste Special dialog box appears on-screen. Enter the extra information as required and click **OK**.

What Becomes a Legend?

To create a legend, make up a story about a band of merry men who live in trees, wear pantyhose, rob from the rich, and star in hit movies. To place a legend of a different sort in your Excel chart, read on.

Adding a legend is simple. To place a legend on an embedded chart double-click on the chart; if the chart is on a chart sheet, just select the sheet by clicking its worksheet tab. Then open the **Insert** menu and select **Legend**. Excel inserts a legend box on the right side of the chart. You can adjust the size and shape by dragging the selection handles in the corners.

Data Labels

To add data labels, double-click on the chart, select the data series you want to modify, and then click the right mouse button. From the shortcut menu that appears, select **Insert Data Labels**. The Data Labels dialog box appears (see the following figure). Select from the available options and click **OK**.

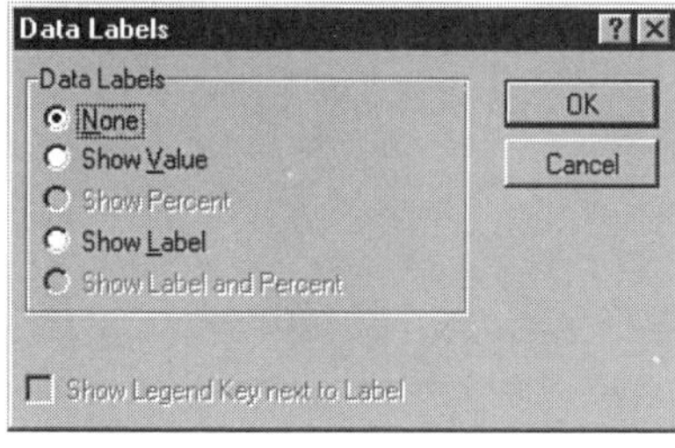

Use the Data Labels dialog box to add data labels.

Tick Marks and You

Tick marks are those small dashes spaced evenly along the axes of your chart that give you a sense of scale. To add or delete those all-important, or cumbersome, tick marks, double-click on the axis you want to change. The Format Axis dialog box (shown below) appears on-screen. Select the **Patterns** tab. In the Tick-Marks Labels section, pick the option you want for your chart.

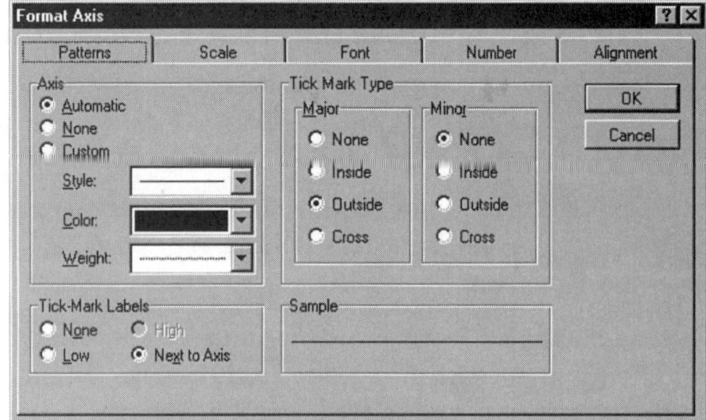

The Patterns tab of the Format Axis dialog box.

From the Patterns tab, you can modify the axis itself with the Axis options (Automatic, which applies default settings to the axis; None, which makes the axis invisible; or Custom, which allows you to choose the line Style, Color, and Weight). You can also choose settings for the major and minor tick marks on the axis. (The minor tick marks are the precision marks.) From this tab, you can also choose where you want the tick-mark labels to appear.

The Format Axis dialog box gives you other choices, as well. From the Scale tab (shown in the following figure), you can change the tick-mark values for either axis. On the Font tab, you can modify your font selection. The Number tab allows you to choose the format of the tick-mark labels. Use the options on the Alignment tab to make any text orientation changes.

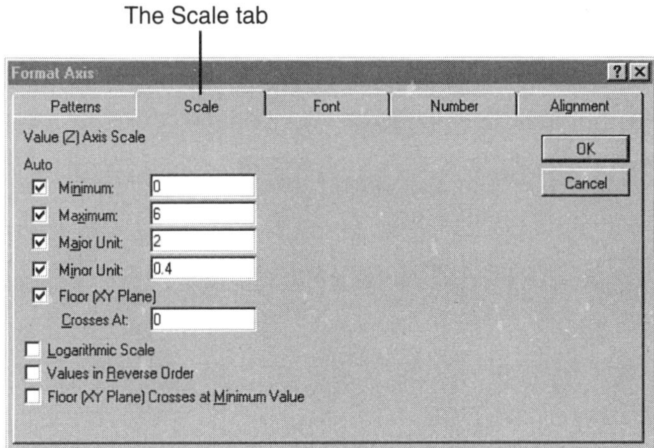

You can change the values for the tick-mark labels.

Gridlines

Like tick marks (which show increments on the axis line), gridlines show the increments across your entire chart. To add gridlines, double-click on an embedded chart or select the tab of a chart on a chart sheet. Click the right mouse button and select **Insert Gridlines** from the shortcut menu. Excel displays the Gridlines dialog box shown in the following figure.

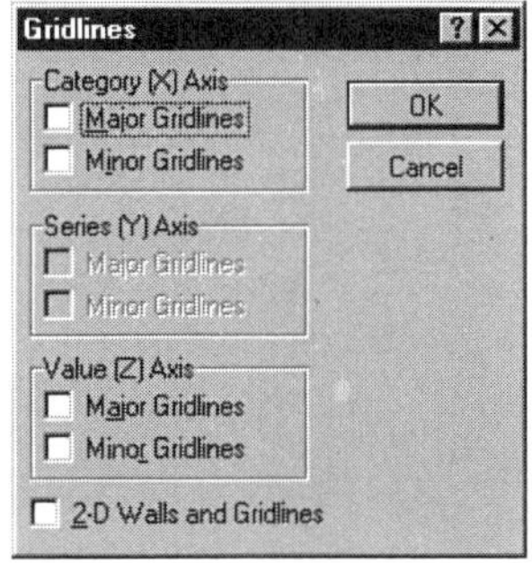

The Gridlines dialog box.

Major gridlines shows just a handful of gridlines. Minor gridlines show more precision. You can select either or both types of gridlines for either or both axes. When you've decided how much gridline you want to display, click **OK**.

Modifying Other Chart Components

You can modify most components of a chart individually when the chart is active. Those components include:

Floors and Walls Floors and walls are the sides and bottoms of 3-D charts, which are displayed as if they're in a three-dimensional room. The Plot Area is any part of the chart that's not an axis, a piece of data, or a gridline.

Axes	Data Series
Data Labels	Data Points
Floors	Gridlines
Legends	Plot Areas
Walls	

Select the chart or any component of the chart by double-clicking on it. The related format box appears, giving you options for changing borders, patterns, colors, names, values, alignments, labels, legends, and many other formatting aspects for each individual component of the chart.

Charts 2-D, 3-D, 4-Matting

Earlier in this chapter you learned to create simple charts. Now we discuss charts that have a bit more body: three-dimensional, combination, radar, scatter, and surface charts.

Width and Depth

Use these complex charts when you're dealing with complicated sets of data. For example, you might use them when you're comparing the costs of various kinds of vegetables with the costs of various kinds of meat; when you're dealing with scores of data points (say, sales volumes) across a period of time and want to see where they group; or when you're trying to prove a correlation (such as the weights of various mammals with their gestation periods).

Let's walk through creating a complex chart. First, enter your complex data sets using as many rows and columns as you need. We advise that you limit yourself to no more than two sets, with seven or eight data points per set. Anything more complicated becomes difficult to read. Label your rows and columns, and then select all (or both) sets of data.

To actually create the chart, you can go through the ChartWizard process as before, or you can take a different approach. This time, press **F11** and watch Excel automatically assign your data to a chart.

You might like Excel's automatic chart, but chances are that you will want to make some changes to it. Double-click anywhere on the chart to make it active. Then pull down the **Format** menu and choose **Chart Type**. The Chart Type dialog box appears (see the following figure).

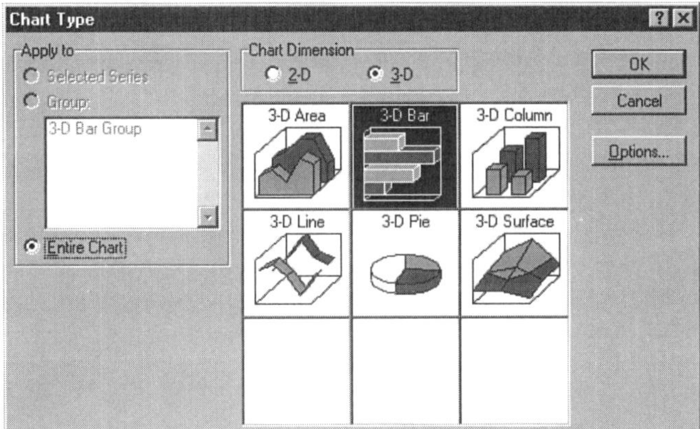

The Chart Type dialog box.

In the Chart Dimension section, select **2-D** or **3-D**, and then select a chart type from the available types shown. Click the **Options** button to continue.

If You Selected a 3-D Chart...

A 3-D chart is a great choice for presentations, and best of all, special glasses are not required! When you choose a 3-D chart type, Excel displays the Format 3-D Group dialog box for the selected chart type. The following figure shows the Format 3-D Group dialog box for a bar chart.

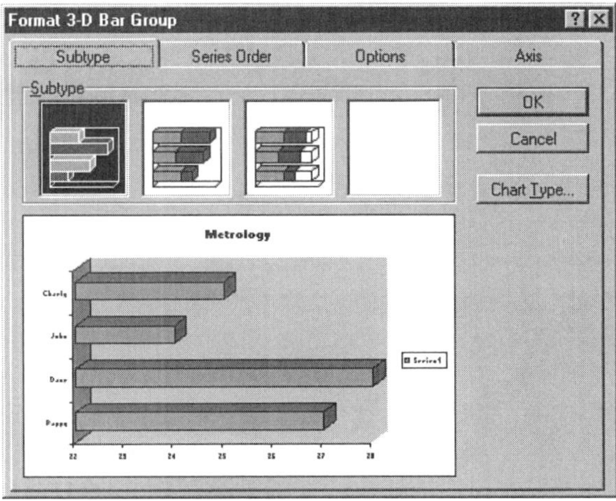

The Format 3-D Bar Group dialog box.

Use the options on the Subtype tab to further refine the appearance of your chart by choosing from the available types. If it exists, use the Series Order tab to change the order in which items are displayed in your chart. The Options tab enables you to adjust the chart depth and the width of the items you've displayed. On the Axis tab, you can choose between primary and secondary axis plotting for the chart. When you're dealing with complex data sets (say, for example, two sets of data), you'll plot on three axes instead of two. In this instance, one of the two X axes becomes primary; the other, secondary. The Y axes are unchanged. This is what a 3-D chart looks like with two X axes:

Graphing a complex data set with primary and secondary axes.

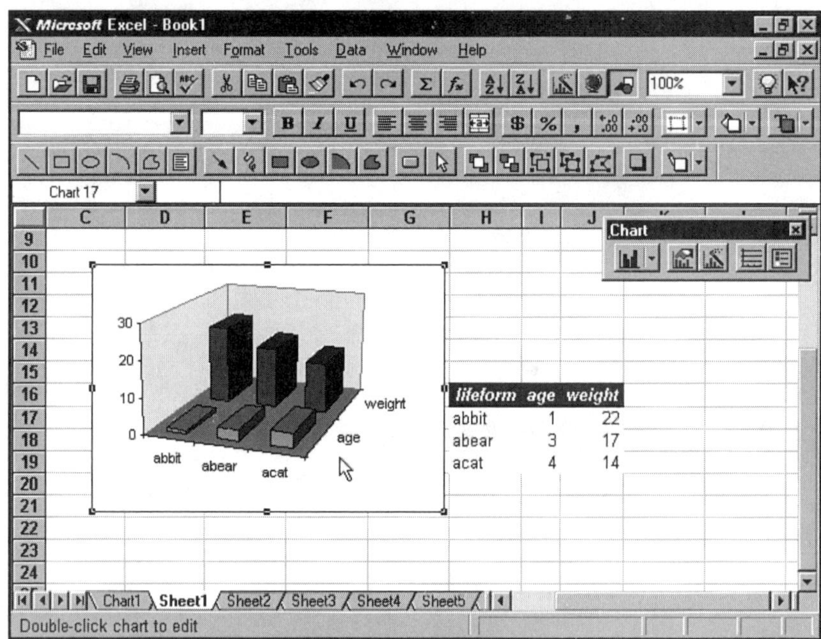

If you can look at a chart from only one angle, it's not 3-D. It's just a 2-D picture trying to look like 3-D. In a genuine Excel 3-D chart, you can turn or twist figures and look over, under, or behind them.

Excel provides two methods for manipulating the 3-D chart. The first is to double-click on the wall of a chart and grab one of the selection handles that appears along the edges of the chart. The mouse pointer changes to a small cross, and as you start to move the chart, it temporarily changes into a line drawing that you can twist and spin by dragging with the mouse within the chart box. The other method is to select the chart, open the **Format** menu, and select **3-D View**. The Format 3-D view dialog box appears (see the following figure). Change the view of the chart using the control buttons in this dialog box.

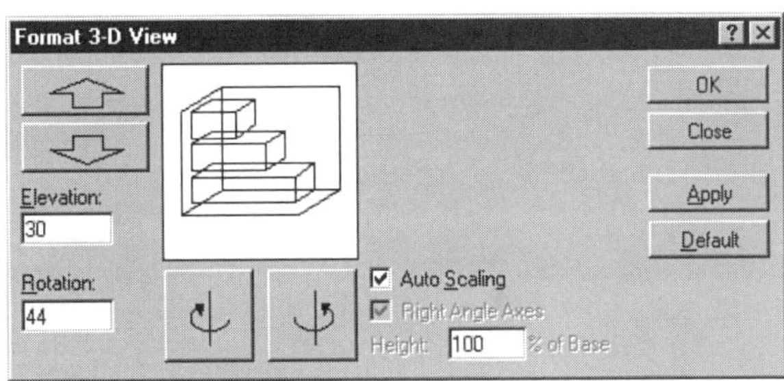

The Format 3-D View dialog box.

If You Selected a 2-D Chart...

The Format Column Group dialog box appears. Other than the title, there is very little to distinguish this from the 3-D selection. As in the 3-D selection, some of the available options will vary, depending on the chart type you chose.

Printing

Printing a chart is no different than printing a worksheet. Pull down the **File** menu and select the **Print Preview** command. Excel shows you the layout of the selected page.

Reshape and resize your embedded charts as necessary before you print. By default, Excel automatically sizes charts in chart sheets so that the chart fills the page. However, you can resize and rescale the chart on the chart sheet if you want.

When you're satisfied with the chart's appearance, click the **Print** button on the Standard toolbar to start printing.

The Least You Need to Know

Thanks to ChartWizard, the complicated process of creating a chart is reduced to following the relatively comprehensive on-screen instructions. This is what you need to remember about charts:

- Charts have immediate impact.
- Charts are linked to cells in a worksheet. When you change the contents of the cells, Excel updates the charts automatically.
- The ChartWizard walks you through the creation of a chart step by step.
- You can modify or add to charts at a later date.

Chapter 19

Mapping Your Future

In This Chapter

- Open the map
- Draw you a map
- Change is everything
- Really radical review

There we were, late for a dinner appointment in the heart of Philadelphia, one of us driving, and the other trying to navigate.

"What does this say? North to Eustice?"

"No, it's one past Ulysses. I think."

"Can we stop to ask directions?"

"Grrrrrr…"

The navigator heaved a sigh and wondered when, exactly, men would learn what women have always known: Quit talking meaningless numbers. Get a map!

Excel's Mapping Function

Where in the world is...?

With Excel's new geographic maps, you can show at a glance where your highest sales or your lowest costs are. Show with graphic symbols the relative staff sizes of your Atlanta, Montreal, and Zaire offices. Graphically compare Hong Kong's export volumes to those of Taipei, Bangkok, and Singapore.

Excel-generated maps enable you to visualize your worksheet results. And with the visual aids, your data, trend, and relationship analyses become easier.

Whatever you want to show on a geographic map, you can do with the new mapping function.

What's Available

The Map feature—or *module*—is based on an extensive database of maps and demographic information. To see the demographics of the Map module, open the workbook called Mapstats.xls. (The location of this file varies, depending on your setup. In our latest incarnation of Excel, it was located in a folder called C:\Program Files\Common Files\Microsoft Shared\Datamap\Data. Say that three times fast without breathing!)

Early releases of Excel 7.0 contain the following maps:

Australia

Canada

Europe

Mexico

North America

UK Standard Regions

US with AK & HI insets

World Countries

Need More Maps?

You can purchase additional maps from the software developer MapInfo Corporation at One Global View, Troy, NY 12180-8399 USA. For telephone orders in the United States, call (800) 488-3552 toll free; for international orders, call (518) 285-7110. Or you can fax MapInfo Corp on (518) 285-6070 or contact them via e-mail at sales@mapinfo.com.

You can find a catalog of other maps in the map Help file, a separate Help file available within the Map module.

Maps As Graphics

Geographic maps become graphic objects on your Excel worksheet. You can place them, move them, and resize them just as you would any of the graphic objects we've described in the last two chapters.

There are a few differences, however:

- **Maps are huge.** The underlying map commands make any worksheet you put them in very large. This means that once you embed a map, your worksheet runs more slowly and takes up a lot more hard disk space than it did before.
- **Maps are complex.** When you update the data underlying a map, you need to execute a separate command to update the actual map. Excel doesn't do this automatically as it does with charts.

Those are the cautions. Here's how to get around them:

- Completely assemble your entire worksheet before you start to deal with maps.
- Make sure that your data is in place and in good tabular format before you even attempt to draw your map.
- Consider putting your map on a separate worksheet to speed up data entry and manipulation on the original sheet.
- Make sure you have lots of free hard disk space before you start creating maps and saving files.

In this chapter, you'll learn how to create and manipulate a map, update it, and change its appearance. Let's get started!

Create the Map

Creating the map involves two procedures: setting up the data and using the Map module.

Data Setup

Your map data works best when it's arranged as a two- or three-column table. Other layouts work, but they're more awkward.

Put labels at the top of each column. Then put your locations (geographic areas, regions, states, countries, postal codes, cities, whatever) in the left column and the corresponding data points (sales figures, profit, expenses, staff size, market size, saturation percentages, or anything else that can be represented numerically) in the second column. If you have a second set of data points, list those in the third column.

Some locations (such as US states, Canadian provinces, European countries, UK regions, and Australian states) can be abbreviated. Look in the Excel workbook Mapstats.xls for the acceptable abbreviations. If you use postal codes, you must format them as text. If you leave them formatted as numbers, the leading zeros will not show.

Select the cells that contain your map data, including the column labels, and get ready to create.

Unfolding the Map: Using the Map Module

With the relevant cells selected, click the **Map** button on the Standard toolbar. Your mouse pointer turns into a cross hair, and Excel displays the following reminder in the Status bar at the bottom of the screen:

Drag in document to create a map

This is your cue to select the area on your worksheet where you want the map to appear. Click at one corner of the desired area and drag your mouse pointer to the opposite corner. A blank rectangle appears on your screen, and the hard disk starts cranking as it looks for the information you need for your map.

If Excel finds an exact match for all of your geographic labels in its map database (found in the workbook Mapstats.xls), you go directly to the next step in map creation. If not, it displays the Multiple Maps Available dialog box shown in the following figure. The box at the bottom lists multiple Excel maps that are available. Select the appropriate map and click **OK**.

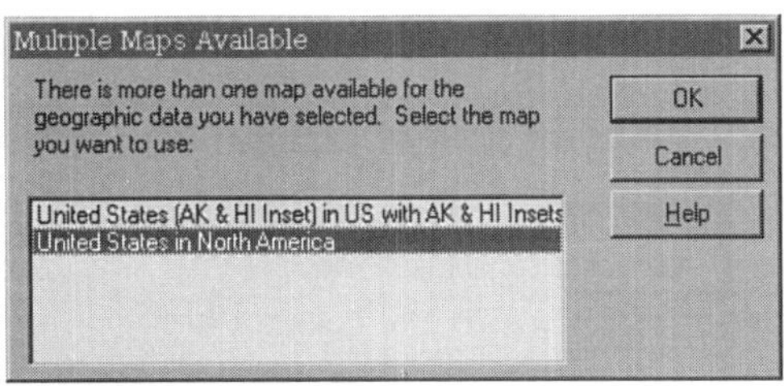

Choose the appropriate map from the Multiple Maps Available dialog box.

A preliminary map appears on-screen, and if your geographic areas were available in the map database (Mapstats.xls or other add-in maps), your data points are graphed. If your geographic areas don't appear on the map, you need to create a custom push-pin map. See the section "Pin Maps" later in this chapter.

Controlling the Damage

After Excel draws your preliminary map, it displays the Data Map Control dialog box (see the following figure).

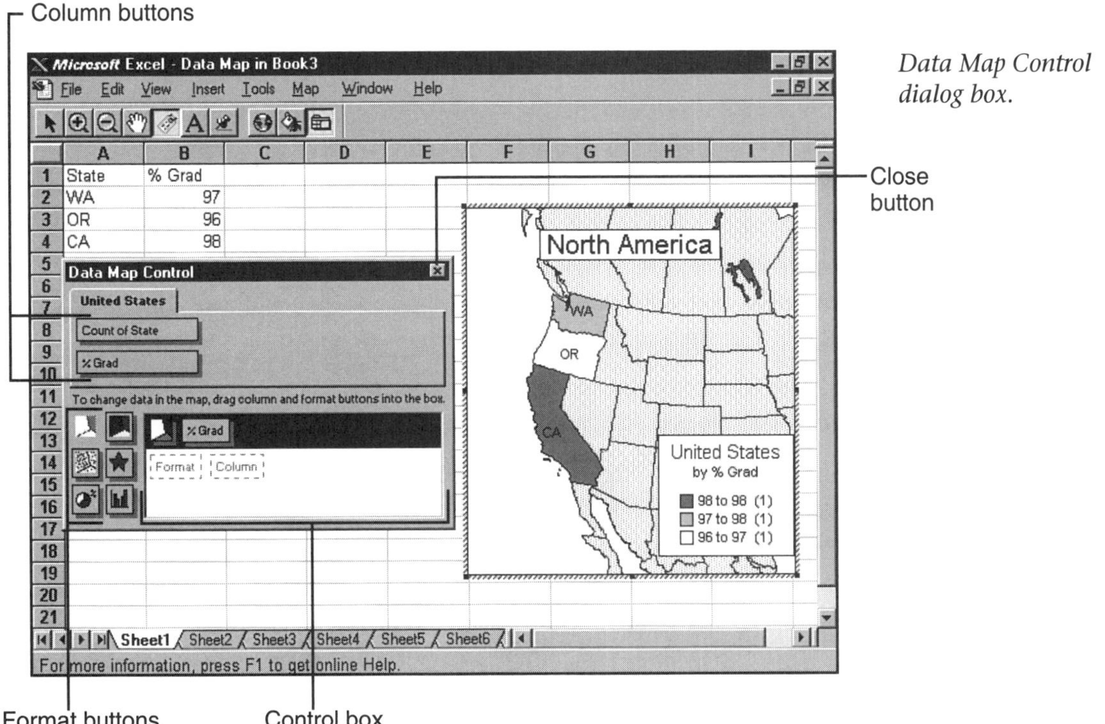

Data Map Control dialog box.

This dialog box contains three items: column buttons at the top that match the column labels you assigned when you set up the data; format buttons on the left that you'll use to lay out your map; and a control box that contains buttons with the labels "Format" and "Column." (These labels are simply place markers; they don't serve any function other than to show you where your buttons belong.) If you used multiple columns of data, you'll see multiple column buttons in the control box.

You can change the way your data is graphed by dragging different format buttons onto the existing format button in the control box. The various format buttons enable you to shade the map areas by value (higher values have higher color intensity), by category (each value receives its own color), dot density (geographically smaller areas get denser data points), graduated symbol (the symbol gets smaller or larger according to value), pie chart, and column chart.

You can also change the column upon which your data is based or add another column. Drag a different column button into the control box, over the existing column button, and Excel changes your map formatting accordingly.

When you finish making changes, click the **Close** button (the X in the upper right corner) to confirm your choices.

Loose Change

Inevitably, at some point you'll want to change something—your underlying data, the features of your map, or your entire presentation. All of that is done quite simply.

But changes may be confusing until you discover that the Map module is virtually a separate piece of software from Excel. When the Map module is operational, it has its own menus, its own toolbar buttons, and its own Help files. What this means is that you will make some changes from within Map, and you'll make others from the worksheet.

When the Map module is active, a wide striped frame surrounds your map. When it's inactive, the worksheet is active, and the map has a regular Excel frame.

The following sections outline the things you can change from outside the map (when the worksheet is active and the map is inactive) and those you can change within the Map module.

Changes from the Outside

From the Excel worksheet, you can change the size and position of the map, delete the map altogether, or change the data within your map.

Size and Position

You can move or resize your map or change its position as you would any graphic object. Select your map by clicking on it once to make it an active Excel object. Do not click twice; that's how you restart the Map module.

You can now grab any of the *sizing handles*—the small squares on the perimeter of the box—to resize the map. Move the map by clicking on a sizing handle and dragging until it's in the proper position.

Another Option
You can also resize maps (but not move them) from within the active Map module. Just click on and drag the sizing handle.

Delete Map

To delete your entire map, click on it once to make it an active Excel object. When the map is selected, press the **Delete** key on your keyboard. The map disappears.

Changing Map Data

You can update the data in your worksheet without harming your map. Simply edit as usual by overwriting the cell or editing in the Formula bar.

Remember that Excel does not update maps automatically as it does charts. So every time you change parts of the worksheet data that underlie the map, you need to refresh the map display. Fortunately, Excel reminds you to refresh by displaying the Refresh button (as shown in following figure).

Click on the **Refresh** button to incorporate the changes into your map. On older computers and computers with limited disk space or memory this process can be quite time-consuming.

While you're waiting, read about the changes you can make from within the Map module.

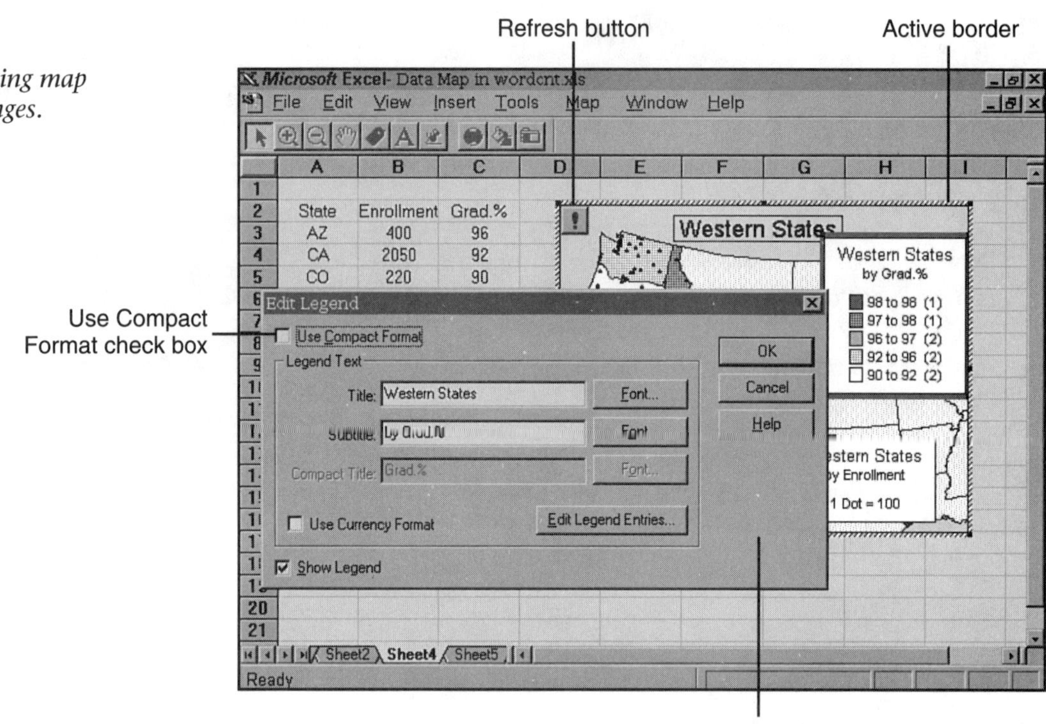

Making map changes.

Active Changes

When the Map module is active, you can make changes to features, text, view, and graphics.

When you activate the Map module by double-clicking on it, you see that it has its own toolbar for making other changes. These toolbar buttons are essential for making changes within the Map module. (If the Map toolbar isn't visible, go to the **View** menu and select **Toolbar**.) The following table shows the Map toolbar and tells you what each button does.

The Map Toolbar Buttons

Button	Name	Description
[arrow button]	Select Objects	Changes your mouse pointer back to an arrow shape, which allows you to select an object for modification.

Button	Name	Description
	Zoom In	Magnifies the selected area. (See the section "A Map with a View" for more information.)
	Zoom Out	Decreases the magnification. (See the section "A Map with a View" for more information.)
	Grabber	Lets you shift the location of your map within its frame. (We explain how to use this tool in the section "A Map with a View.")
	Map Labels	Lets you create text labels. (See the section "Just Words" to learn about adding labels.)
A	Add Text	Prints text directly on the map.
	Custom Pin Map	Enables you to spotlight certain areas of your geographical map.
	Display Entire	Forces the entire map to fit in your designated frame size.
	Redraw Map	Updates the map when you've made changes to the underlying data.
	Show/Hide Data Map Control	Recalls the Data Map Control dialog box.

The following sections explain in more detail some of the changes you can make from within your Excel Map module.

Changing Map Features

When you want to change features on your map (such as lakes, cities, countries, or highways), you need to make the Map module active. Click or double-click on the map until the active border is visible. When your map is active, you can double-click anywhere on the actual map to call up the Map Features dialog box shown in the following figure.

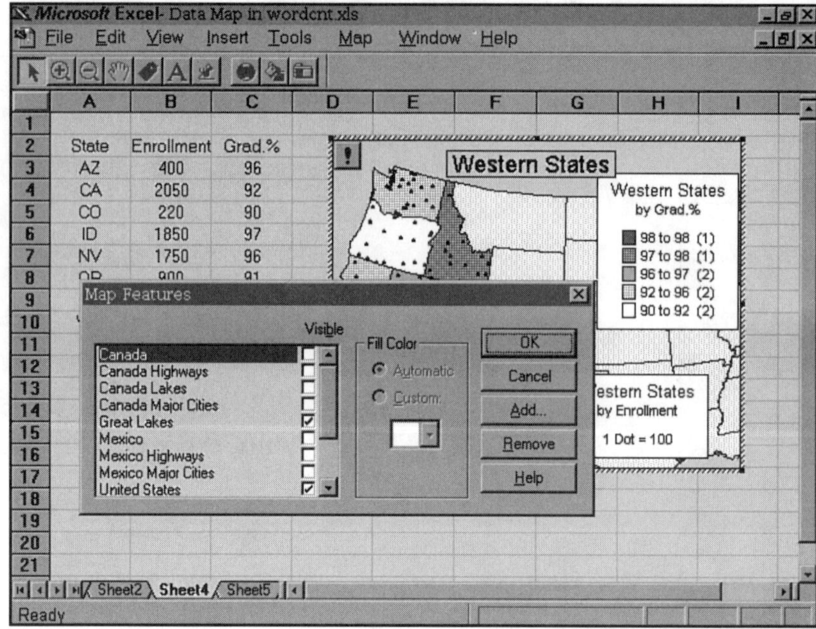

The Map Features dialog box.

The Visible area contains a list of check boxes for available map features. Check the check boxes of the features you want to make visible, and remove the check from the check boxes of the features you want to hide. Choose colors and symbols for your map in the center box. Select the **Custom** option if you want to choose your own color and style. Select the **Automatic** option to let Excel use its best judgment. We predict you'll want to choose your own.

Just Words

You can make several changes to the text features of your map. These include:

- **Modifying legends** By default, Excel displays legends in Compact Format, which shows as little as possible. To change to the expanded format, double-click on the legend box on your map (the area that describes your graphic symbols). The Edit Legends dialog box appears. Uncheck the **Use Compact Format** option, and Excel creates an expanded legend. Other options in this dialog box enable you to edit and format the text of your legends. You can change the default by opening the **Tools** menu, selecting **Options**, and unchecking the **Compact Legends by Default** check box in the **Data Map Options** dialog box.
- **Adding labels** To add labels to the geographic areas on your map, click on the **Map Labels** button on the Map toolbar. The **Map Labels** dialog box appears, asking you to choose which features you want to label. Select from the pull-down list of

map features (items like the Great Lakes) or click on the **Values From** option button to get labels from your worksheet columns. Click **OK** to return to the map. Then the pointer becomes a cross hair, and you're ready to begin. As you move the cross hair over various regions of your map, labels appear under the cross hair. Click the left mouse button when you're satisfied with the placement of one label, and then continue placing others throughout your map. When you finish, choose the **Select Objects** toolbar button to turn off the Map Labels tool.

- ➤ **Adding text** To add other text to your map, select the **Add Text** button and click in the place on your map where you want to add text. Then type in the text. You can change the text formatting by reselecting it, right-clicking, and choosing **Format Font** from the shortcut menu.
- ➤ **Changing the title** You can amend the map's title by selecting the existing title and typing in a new name.

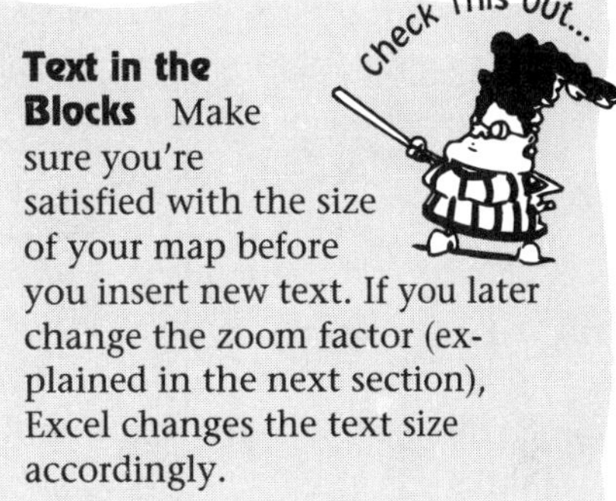

Text in the Blocks Make sure you're satisfied with the size of your map before you insert new text. If you later change the zoom factor (explained in the next section), Excel changes the text size accordingly.

A Map with a View

If you want to see a more detailed view of a certain area, you can zoom in on that specific portion of your map. To do so, click on the **Zoom In** button on the Map toolbar. Your mouse pointer changes to a magnifying glass. Place the magnifying glass over the portion of your map you'd like to magnify, and click the left mouse button. Excel magnifies the selected area.

There is no simple way to fine-tune the degree of magnification. You're pretty much stuck with the automatic percentages the Map feature uses.

When you zoom in on an area, it may not be centered properly in the frame. You can use the Grabber toolbar button to reposition the map within the frame. To do so, click on the **Grabber** button, and the mouse pointer changes to a hand shape. Then position the mouse pointer anywhere on the map, hold down the left mouse button, and drag the map to its new location within the frame. If you want to fit the entire map within your frame, select the **Display Entire** tool.

You can continue magnifying the map, or you can shrink it back down again with the **Zoom Out** tool.

Change to the **Select Objects** tool when you've properly adjusted your view to change your mouse pointer back to an arrow. This change prevents you from accidentally reapplying the effects of the last tool you selected.

If you dislike a view change you've made, you can return to your last view by opening the **View** menu and selecting **Previous**.

Customize the Graphics

To format the dot density, value shading, category shading, or graduated symbols you created originally, pull down the **Map** menu and choose the appropriate option. Depending on the format options you chose for your map, your **Map** menu might display the Category Shading Options command, the Dot Density Options command, or various other choices as the last command on the menu. When you click on the option, a related dialog box appears, asking you for your color, sizing, values, summary, and visibility choices. Make your choices, and click **OK** to make them effective.

Redo the Map

The **Redraw Map** button on the Map toolbar enables you to quickly display minor changes you make to the map. Also use this button whenever you make changes to the underlying data on your Excel worksheet. The **Redraw Map** button is the only mechanism for updating the map to reflect changes.

The **Show/Hide Data Map Control** button gives you access to the Data Map Control dialog box you saw at the beginning of this chapter so you can change your original choices.

Pin Maps

When you need to mark elements on your map (key cities, countries, recreation sites, or target markets, for example), try using the Pin Map function. Just click the **Custom Pin Map** button on the Map toolbar. Your pointer changes to a push-pin shape. Position the pointer in the location you want to mark and click your left mouse button. A pin appears on your map!

When you finish adding pins, reselect the **Select Objects** button. To delete a pin, click on it with the Select Objects pointer and press the **Delete** key on your keyboard.

A Call for Help

Because the Map module runs as a separate piece of software, you'll need to view the related Help files separately from those found in Excel itself. Fortunately, that's easy to do. When the Map module is active, press **F1**. That's it. You get full access to Map's Help files.

The Least You Need to Know

- The Excel Map feature enables you to create geographic representations of your data.
- Set up your map data in columns with labels.
- Go to the Mapstats.xls workbook to see the abbreviations and demographic data available for your maps.
- The Map feature runs as a separate piece of software within Excel, which means that you must make most changes to your map from within the activated Map module.
- The only changes you can make to the map when the Module is not active are resizing, repositioning, and deletion.
- To read the Map Help files, you must first create a map. Then double-click on the map and press **F1** to call up Map Help.

Part 4
Data Manipulation

It's back to the number stuff now.

In this section, you learn how to work with databases and import, manipulate, and analyze data from other applications.

Chapter 20

List Management

In This Chapter

- De base! De base!
- Call the manager
- Filter down
- Sort it out
- Unique uses for uncommon database undertakings

Top Ten Reasons to Read This Chapter

10. Siddhartha traveled thousands of miles to get information this good.
9. What else are you going to do in the smallest room?
8. It's a great resumé builder.
7. You'd feel guilty if you skipped it.
6. It's the only chapter written entirely in the nude.
5. This chapter read backwards is McCartney's biography.

4. It's the only chapter good enough to have a top-ten list.
3. To find small, intentional misspellings.
2. We promise that if we're going to hide a sex scene in this book, it'll be in this chapter.
1. Because you've got to now, or people will think you read this page solely for the sexual content.

This Thing Called List

You can't shop without them; politicians couldn't tell their friends from their enemies if those didn't exist; and you'd be reading the next chapter right now if Excel didn't have them. What are they? They're lists, of course. A bunch of vaguely related items under a common heading.

Most of the time you probably take lists for granted. Oh, yes you do. Lost the 10 pounds yet from your New Year's resolution list?

Excel's different. Excel takes lists seriously. Enter a list in Excel, and it begins to think that it is a powerful database program. It treats columns of data as though they were *fields* in a database and looks at rows as the equivalent of *records*. (If you don't know a thing about databases, don't worry. A field is simply a label at the top of a column, and a record is just a single line of information—like a name, rank, and serial number—listed below the column labels.)

Excel isn't a database program, but it may perform adequately enough to make a separate database program unnecessary for your system. In this section, we'll treat Excel as though it really were a database performer. Nobody ever said that a piece of software couldn't initiate its own wish list.

Why You're Reading This Chapter

Database management programs give you a record of everything about something, and then let you yank out the good bits later on. Famous databases include the phone book, the ugliest pages of the *Wall Street Journal*, the public library's card catalog (remember those?), box scores from baseball games (remember those?), your checkbook, and the TV Guide.

In this chapter, you'll learn how to create a database-like *list* in Excel and how to search your list to compile data based on your own criteria (such as "All TV shows without Tony Danza"). You'll also learn how to make automated additions to your list.

Making a List

You don't have to learn any special tricks, buried commands, passwords, or secret handshakes to create a database, or *list,* in Excel. Simply enter some labels at the tops of your columns and type the entries below them. That's all there is to it—sort of.

There are a few guidelines that you probably ought to follow. Doing so will make life sweeter and easier for both you and the folks manning the telephones at the Excel customer support desk.

- Make sure your list is made up of several columns of data (which we'll call fields of data in this section), with labels at the top of each column—er, field.
- Each field (column) must contain items of related information. In other words, one field may contain names, addresses, figures, percentages, labels, social security numbers, or the fat contents of fast-food meals. But you never want to mix different kinds of information in the same column.
- If you're going to play database games, don't create more than one list on a worksheet. Hey, we don't make up the rules—at least not all of them. Anyway, this is a rule with reason. Some Excel features don't function properly if you have more than one list on a worksheet.

  This is not to be confused with the limit on the number of records or fields you can use. Excel treats contiguous columns as a single list. You can use as many records and fields as your worksheet can hold, which is a mere 16,384 records and 256 fields.
- Leave a buffer zone of at least one blank column and one blank row between your list and other data on the worksheet. Spreadsheeting is not a contact sport; this enables Excel to differentiate between your list and randomly scattered data.
- If you absolutely must have critical data on the same worksheet as your list, avoid putting it to the side or bottom of your list because later, when you attempt to filter, that data may get hidden. Instead, use a practice some refer to as *diamond-backing* (yeah, like the snake). The following figure shows an example of diamond-backing in a worksheet.

To do this, enter blocks of unrelated information in a diamond pattern so that you can later add, delete, and hide columns and rows without disturbing information in other blocks.

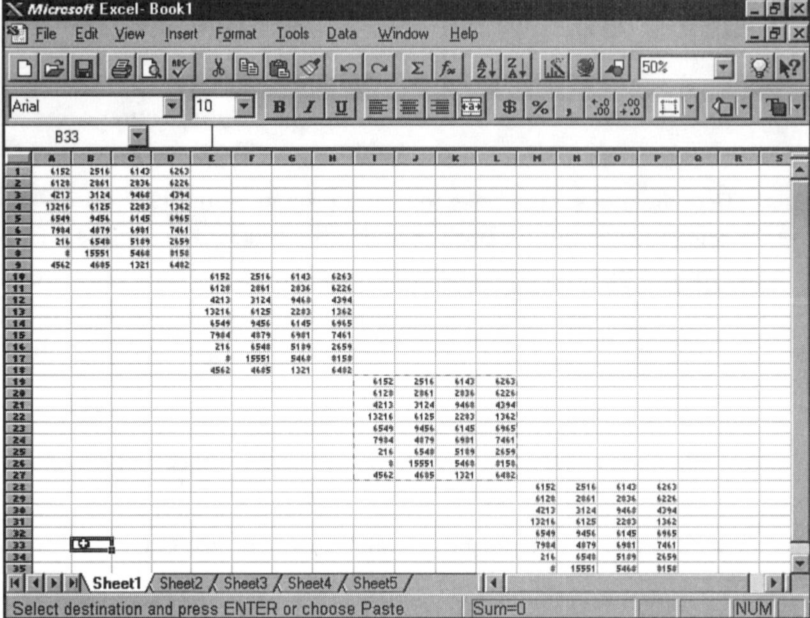

Diamond-backing enables you to add data to your worksheet without fear of it being hidden from view.

- ➤ Make the first row of your list into column labels—also called *field names*. Excel is going to treat that first entry as a label whether you like it or not, so you may as well play along. It becomes important later when sorting data, creating reports, and performing other kinds of automatic manipulation.
- ➤ Choose fancy fonts and crazy colors for your labels. This is not actually a requirement, but setting off the labels from the rest of the data can make a long list a little easier to read.
- ➤ Don't use dashes or blank rows to separate your labels from your data. This is an actual requirement. Excel assumes that blank cells are not a part of the contiguous set. If it were up to Excel, Alaska would be handed over to Canada right now.
- ➤ When entering your data, remember that all characters (even spaces) count when it comes to sorting, filtering, and other kinds of data manipulation.

- If you have protected cells or formulas in your list, you might run into difficulties doing some database work. But they're not fatal.

Copy It!

Because some database features don't get along well with formulas, you might want to change all your formulas to text or numbers. Of course, that would destroy your formulas, so here's a better way.

Select your entire list and click the **Copy** button on the Standard toolbar (or press **Ctrl+C**) to copy it to the Windows Clipboard. Then open a new worksheet, pull down the **Edit** menu, and select **Paste Special**. In the Paste Special dialog box, click the **Values** option button to copy all your formula values as figures. Your original worksheet remains unchanged.

List Management and Other Sleight-of-Hand Tricks

The problem with lists is that nobody has yet found an effective way of stopping them from growing. Before you know it, a small list of a few hundred entries suddenly shoots up towards thousands of entries. By then, there's too little time and not enough paper to handle the list without some sort of help.

Professional help comes at a high cost, though. People actually earn college degrees in this stuff. In fact, if the guy standing next to you in the bookstore is thumbing through a database book, offer him a compassionate smile. Then walk to the counter, buy this book, and be glad you got out of the store safely. This section covers all you really need to know about databases.

Data Forms

Let's say you've already done everything you can do. You entered your list in a worksheet following the rules we described above, you assigned great labels, and it looks good in general. So now is a good time to ask, what can Excel do for you?

One thing it can do is give you a cool, easy way to add even more data to your list. This feature is called the Data Form. The Data Form makes it easier for you to add, change, and delete data. As an added bonus, it enables you to find certain items based on specific criteria. Think of it as a look-up function, and we'll keep the hype to a minimum.

If you haven't already created a list to play around with, do so now. You need fields of related data with labels at the top. Once you've laid out your list correctly, you're ready to try Data Form.

First, click on any cell in your list to make it active. Then open the **Data** menu and select **Form**. A dialog box appears with the name of your current worksheet in the title bar (see the following figure).

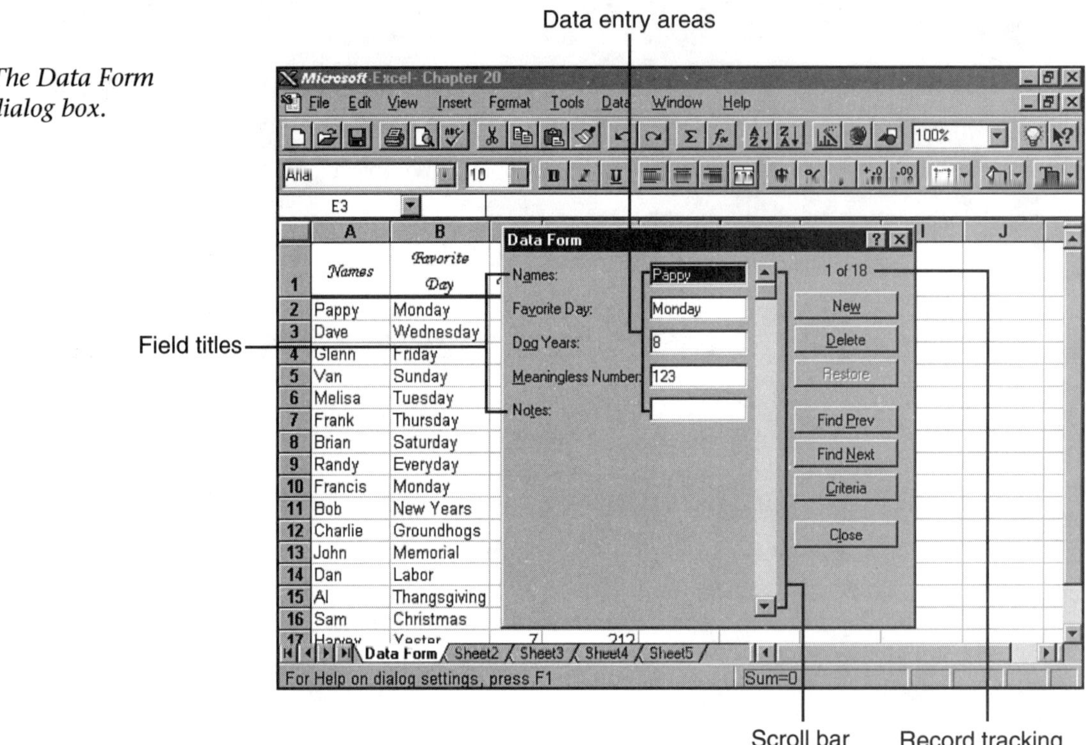

The Data Form dialog box.

Excel creates the data form for you based on your list and field label information. To enter new records, just click on **New** and input the information in the blank data entry areas. To remove a record, click the **Delete** button.

You can edit the text in any field except those that are protected or that contain Excel formulas. Simply find the data you want to edit, click in its data entry area, and edit the text. If you change your mind about an edited change, click the **Restore** button before you leave the record.

To navigate quickly through your entire data list, use the scroll bar or select the **Criteria** button. The Criteria option enables you to search your list for records that match the parameters you assign. For example, if you had a database of telephone numbers, you could search all records that match (801)*, where (801) is the area code and * is a wild card for anything that follows (801). Use the asterisk (*) as a wild card for multiple characters at the end of a string, and the question mark (?) as a wild card for single characters within a string. You can look for records that match your criteria by clicking on the Find Prev and Find Next buttons.

When you finish entering and editing data, click the **Close** button.

AutoTemplates

In the beginning, lists were created by hand. In those days, you took a sharpened number-two pencil, scribbled all pertinent data on yellow legal pads, and scurried back to your desk to enter it in your computer.

Thankfully those days are behind us, in most cases. With Excel, you can keep data from various sources in a master database and create darling little workbooks for other people, so that they can collect your data for you. Then, from time to time, you can gather up those workbook juniors, and let Excel add their data to your master database automatically.

Excel's AutoTemplates are database input forms created for a specific task. The input form, or AutoTemplate, might look like an invoice, a receipt, an order form, or an index card. Certain cells in the form—you'll decide which cells—are linked to your master database. Entries made in the linked cells can then be automatically added to your database list as a new *record* (the data in a single row of an Excel database list).

All that remains now is to create a template. Sounds scary—and the truth is, it probably would be if not for the Template Wizard.

Prep Time

Once again we're off to see a wizard for help and guidance in performing a function the Excel way. The Template Wizard takes you through AutoTemplate construction with a minimum of pain and suffering—but there are a few preliminary steps that you must take.

Begin by creating a brand new workbook that will contain your database *list*. Click the **New Workbook** button on the Standard toolbar to get started. Then put labels at the top of the list columns (or *fields*). The following figure shows a sample database list. The data from the input form will eventually be entered as a new row (or record) into this workbook. Click the **Save** button on the Standard toolbar to save the database workbook.

The database list with field labels.

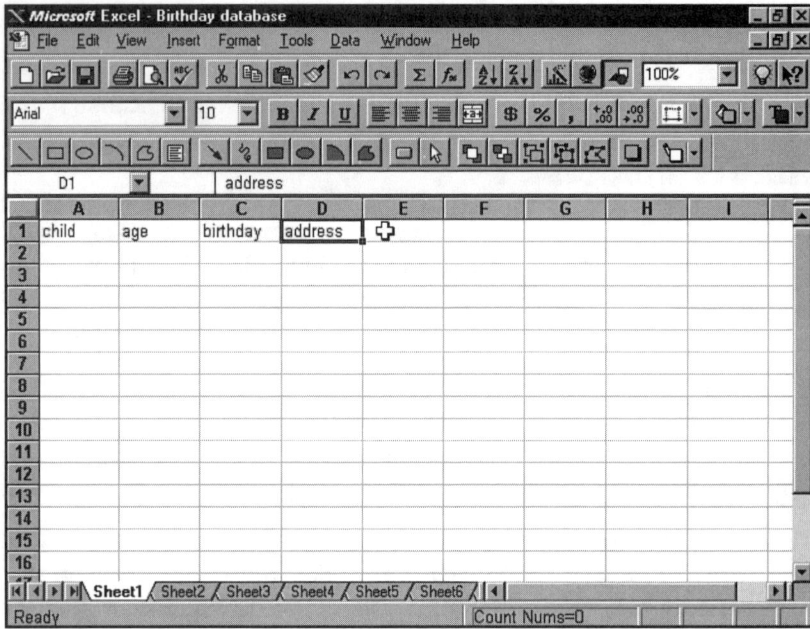

Next, open a whole new workbook and create your input form. Using your database list as a guide, create an input form (such as a sales receipt or an order form) that features places for all of the data you want recorded in your database. Make it look any way you like; you can add pretty pictures, curly letters, and explanatory or audio notes if it suits you, but be sure to label the cells in the input form exactly as they are labeled in your database list. You can create as many additional labels as you like, but, of course, their contents won't be recorded in your database workbook. Once again, save the input form by clicking on the **Save** button.

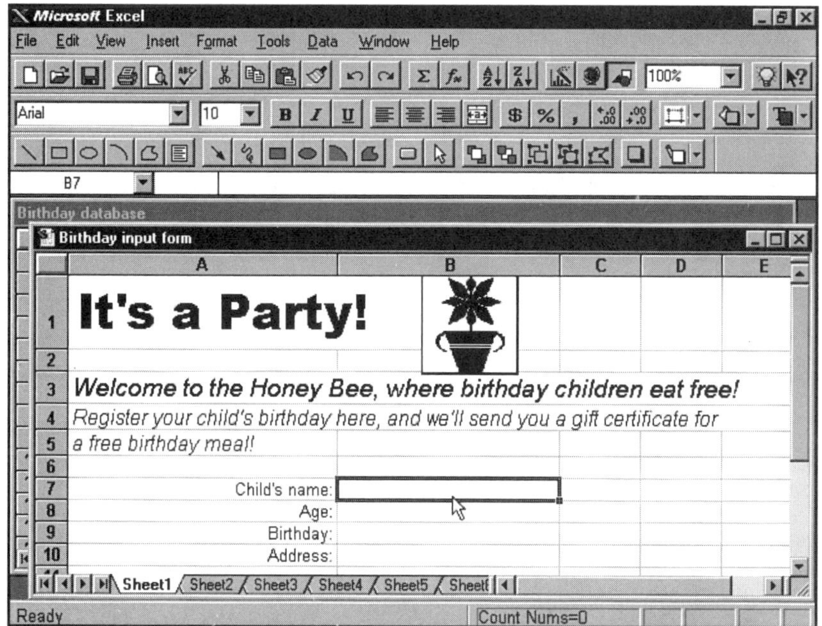

The input form, with labels that correspond to the database.

The Template Wizard: Five Steps to Template Nirvana

So you've created your input form. The layout is beautiful; the instructions are concise; you've included text notes and audio notes. All that's left now is to link this form to your database workbook. Then you can sit back and watch as the data starts marching in.

Now quit your humming and let's get started on this thing. It's time to call the wizard.

Start by opening that template workbook—the input form—you created. Then open the **Data** menu and select **Template Wizard**. The first Template Wizard dialog box (shown in the following figure) appears.

Step 1: Select the name given to the template workbook and click on **Next**. (If the template workbook is not open or does not appear on the selection list, close the Template Wizard by selecting the **Cancel** button, open the template workbook, and start again.) The Template Wizard - Step 2 of 5 dialog box appears.

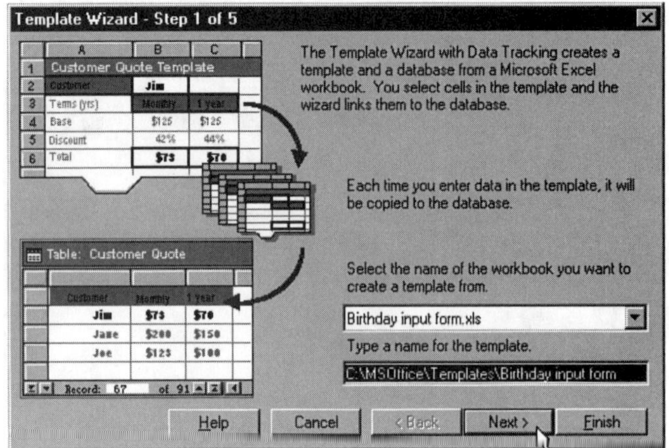

The Template Wizard - Step 1 of 5 dialog box.

Step 2: Confirm that the name and location of the database workbook are correct or type in the correct name and location if necessary. You may need to click on the **Browse** button to open a dialog box that will help you locate your database workbook. Click on **Next** to move on to the dialog box shown in the next figure.

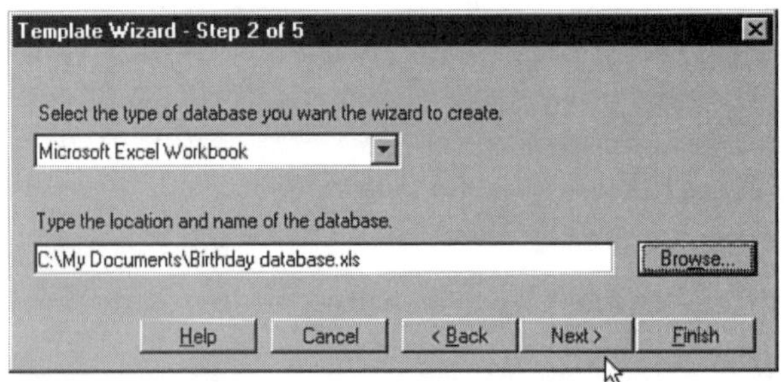

The Template Wizard - Step 2 of 5 dialog box.

Step 3: In this step, you select the cells that will be linked to your database. Only data from the linked cells is recorded in the database workbook. Enter the cell addresses from the input form (either manually or by clicking on them with the mouse pointer) in the cell column. If the selected cell is properly labeled—a label appears in an adjacent cell—the label will automatically appear in the Field Name box. Click **Next.**

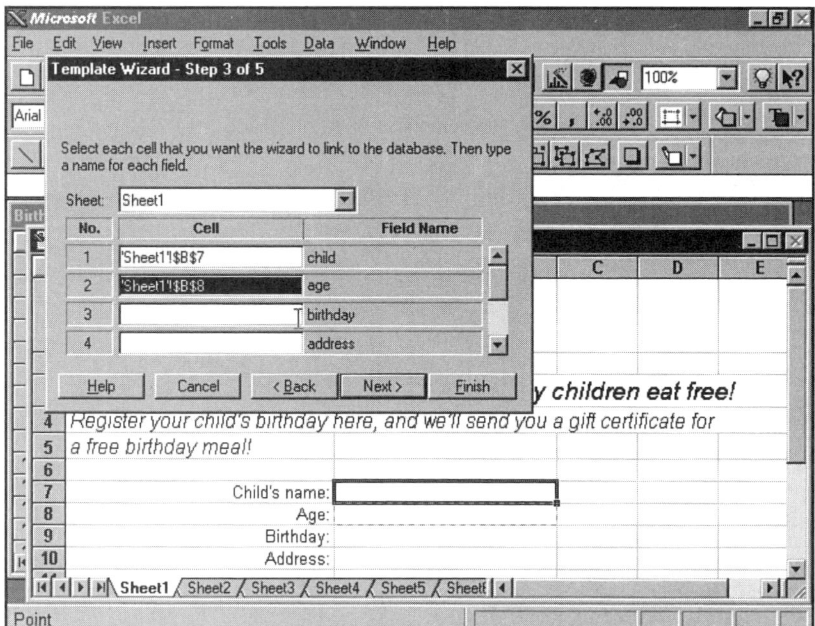

The Template Wizard - Step 3 of 5 dialog box.

Step 4: This step is useful only if you've been doing this stuff for awhile and have a backlog of old input forms. If you do, go ahead and repent for past sins. But be prepared. If you answer yes, you'll be expected to name names… of the workbooks. There is some help. A preview area is available to make sure only correct values are copied. Normally, though, you'll simply click on the **No, skip it** option button and continue. Click **Next.**

Step 5: Template Wizard displays the name and location of the new template. At this point you can select **Finish** to finish the process, **Cancel** to discard your work, or **Back** to modify your original selections.

There. You've finished your AutoTemplate.

Now you can use your AutoTemplate input form to collect one record at a time. The AutoTemplate input form is slightly different from your original input form because it has a new name (which ends in .XLT instead of .XLS, and which is probably located in your Templates folder). Open the input form as you would any other workbook. Input the information into the template. (If you're on a network and want other users to input information into the same template, simply make the template workbook available to them in a common directory.)

The Template Wizard - Step 4 of 5 dialog box.

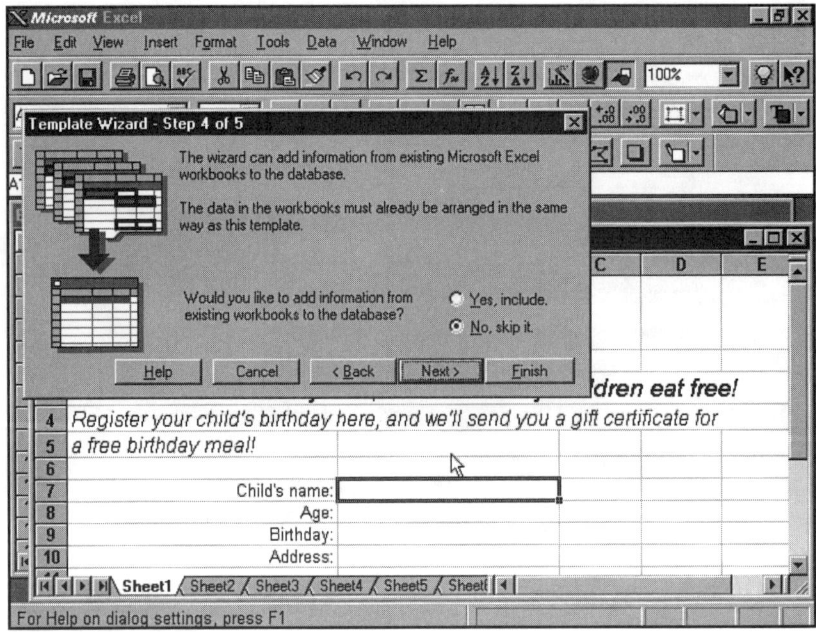

Save the template using either the Save command or the Save As command if you want to assign a unique name to the worksheet. When you save or close the template, Excel asks if you want to add the data to your database as a new record or to replace the last record, or if you simply want to ignore it. Normally you will want to create a new record.

Now you can enter the data for the next record by simply overwriting the one that was saved.

Open the database workbook at any time to check on the progress of your database.

Sorting

A database is a living, vibrant thing with data constantly streaming in from several sources. Without a mechanism to straighten it out, your list represents a slice of time: records appear in the same order in which they arrived. This could be valuable as a time capsule, but it does not always make it convenient when you need to look for a particular entry. Excel enables you to sort data stored in columns or rows, a feature that no long list should be without.

To sort all rows or columns in a database, select any cell from within the group that you want to sort. Select **Sort** from the **Data** menu, and the Sort dialog box appears in the center of the screen. Excel automatically selects all cells that are part of your database (all connecting rows of cells) to be sorted. Select your sorting criteria from among the options in the Sort dialog box, and then click on **OK**.

To sort only a particular row or column, select the row or column headers that you want to sort. Then select **Sort** from the **Data** menu. Excel asks you to confirm that you only want to sort the selected rows or columns. After you make your selection, the Sort dialog box appears in the middle of the screen. Criteria selection options are the same.

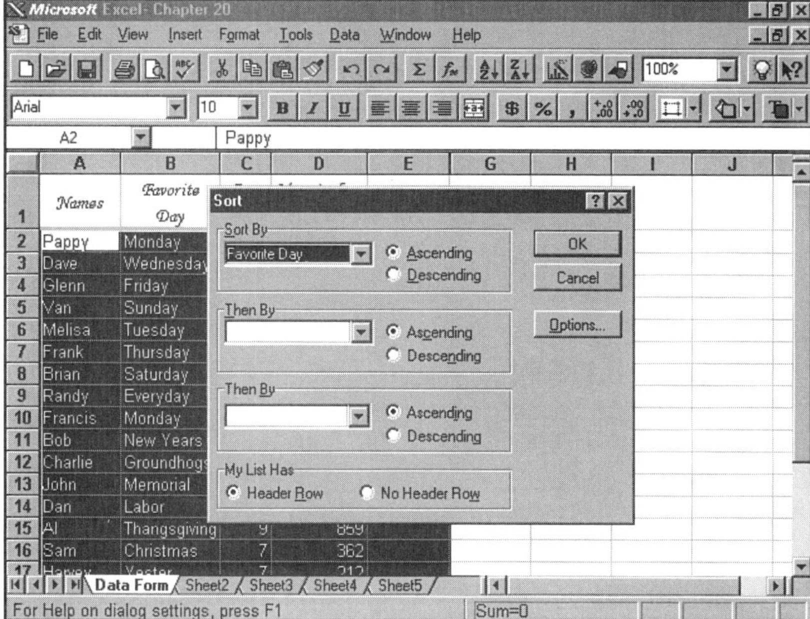

Enter your sorting criteria in the Sort dialog box.

You can sort by as many as three columns at a time, as indicated by the three text boxes in the Sort dialog box. For each column you want to sort by, enter its label in the text box and choose whether you want the results displayed in ascending or descending order. If you choose Ascending, Excel sorts text from A to Z or sorts numbers from smallest to largest; if you choose Descending, Excel sorts text from Z to A or sorts numbers from largest to smallest.

To sort by more than three columns, begin the sorting process by first selecting the three least significant columns. Then repeat the sort function selecting the next least important column each time. Continue this cycle until all columns have been sorted.

Fortunately, Microsoft anticipated those trying times when the header is to the left and the data is to the right, and they're no longer trying. Select any cell from among the group to be sorted, pull down the **Data** menu, and select **Sort**. Click the **Options** button in the Sort dialog box, and the Sort Options dialog box appears. Select the **Sort Left to Right** button in the Orientation box.

Enter your sorting criteria in the Sort dialog box.

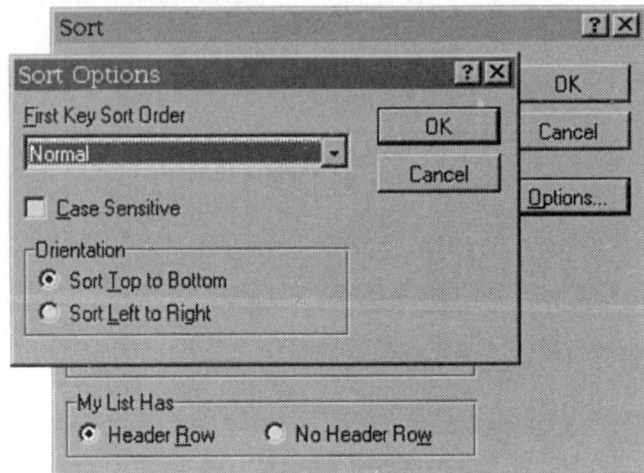

The Least You Need to Know

In this chapter, we had a brief soiree´ with Excel on the dark side, attempting to walk the walk of the database.

- ➤ There are no complicated tricks to creating a database list in Excel. Simply place a label at the top of your columns and fill in the entries below it.
- ➤ Use the Data Form as an easy method of entering or altering data in a list. Select any cell from your list and select **Form** from the **Data** menu.
- ➤ Let Template Wizard create a template from your workbook and link it with your database list.
- ➤ Use AutoFilter to break the on-screen list down into workable chunks.
- ➤ You can sort data by as many as three columns by selecting **Sort** from the **Data** menu.

Chapter 21

Retrieving and Consolidating Data

In This Chapter

- The data day business of imports
- Go get 'em
- Query-vents
- Last ditch imports
- Giving it all away
- Consolidation must-knows
- Very valuable advice for import vexations

Yeah, we've heard dog stories. Heroic stories about dogs who climb mountains to lie on the chests of unsuspecting travelers lost in the snow. Courageous stories of dogs who rescued their owners from burning buildings. Tear-jerking stories of dogs who lay by the sides of their owner's graves for, oh, say, seven or eight years.

Well the authors of this book have owned a dog or two in their respective lives. Smart dogs, dumb dogs, St. Bernard dogs, little dogs… and we're here to tell you now:

Not one of them actually responded when ordered to fetch.

That's why we're getting a cat.

Whole Lotta Data Going On

You might not believe it if you've caught the myopic vision of this book, but not everyone uses Excel. There's a whole world out there of vendors competing for a place in your wallet—er, heart. As a result, you may sometimes find yourself in a position where the data you want already exists in a non-Excel file.

You could reinvent the wheel and enter the data manually into an Excel worksheet. Or you could simply retrieve the data using one of Excel's import tools and convert it to a format you can use.

The choice is yours; but personally, we prefer the path of least typing.

Bringing Home the Data

Just because a file is different doesn't mean it's going to be difficult. Excel can import some files almost as easily as if they were native Excel workbooks.

Doesn't Match Up? This list was a current sampling at the time this book was put together. Your mileage—and list of import filters—may vary.

You can open the following file types very easily in Excel without any special manipulation:

Data Interchange Format

dBase Files

Lotus 1-2-3

Microsoft Excel

Microsoft Excel 4.0 Charts

Microsoft Excel 4.0 Macros

Microsoft Excel 4.0 Workbooks

Microsoft Works 2.0

Quattro Pro DOS

Quattro Pro Windows

To import one of the easy files in the previous list, pull down the **File** menu and select **Open**. The standard Open dialog box appears.

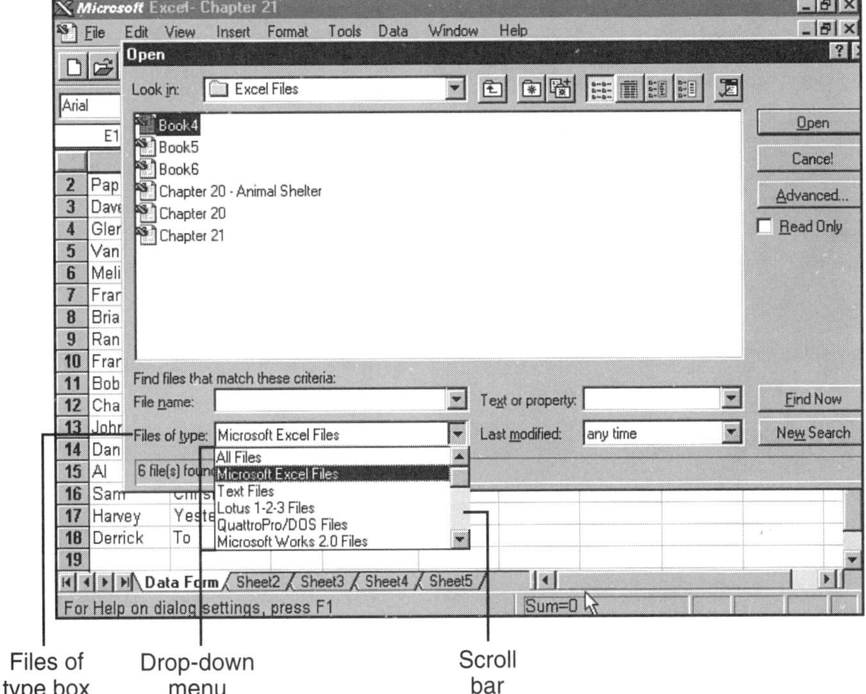

Select the type of file you want to import.

In the lower left corner of the dialog box is the Files of type box. Click on its down arrow, and a drop-down menu appears, listing the names of various file types. If the type of file you are opening appears on the list, simply select it. Excel displays all files of the selected type in the dialog box display area. Select and open the file as you would a regular Excel workbook.

Fit to be Tied—In

Even if a file type doesn't appear in the Files of type list of the Open dialog box, you may still be able to import a usable version. The following procedure works on files that contain straight text, and on some that contain variations of straight text. If the last procedure didn't work, try this.

Choose **Open** from the **File** menu again, and select **All Files** from the Files of type list in the Open dialog box. Select your file. Excel asks if you want to import the file as a text file. Click **OK**, and stand ready to meet the Text Import Wizard.

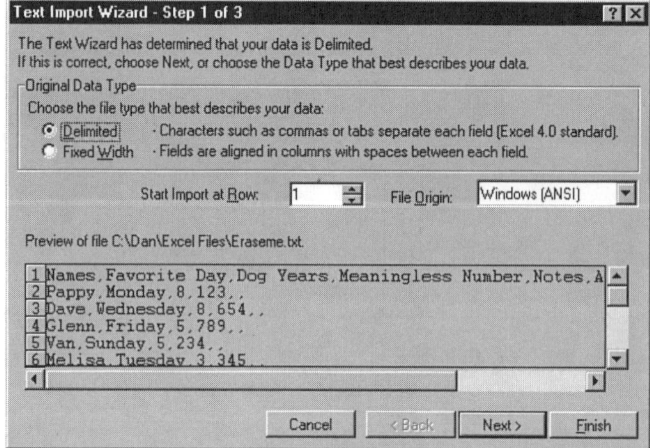

The Text Import Wizard - Step 1 of 3 dialog box.

The Text Import Wizard leads you through a three-step process that ought to import your data to Excel in as near a standard layout as possible. It helps, of course, if your text is already lined up in neat rows and columns. A display window in the Text Import Wizard dialog box gives you a preview of what your imported file will look like in Excel. Follow the wizard's instructions to import the file and get back to Kansas.

Another Source of Data: Microsoft Query

So far we've talked openly about relatively simple methods of importing data, opening a file, and having Excel do the conversion. But there's still a world of data out there waiting to be sucked in, twisted, sorted, filtered, and averaged.

An Introductory Word or Two

You can retrieve data directly from outside sources using Excel either alone or in conjunction with a program called Microsoft Query. Microsoft Query needs no support from Excel. It's a standalone application that can take data from various sources and filter it, mix it, and match it to create something Excel can make good use of.

Sometimes the choice of which method to use is obvious (such as when Excel simply can't import a file). Other times, however, you may have to decide which method to use to retrieve data. Follow these guidelines to help you decide when to use Query to retrieve data.

Retrieve data with Query when:

➤ Excel can't access the files.

➤ You want limited, filtered information from a non-Excel database.

➤ You're using two or more tables to generate your database.

For the record, applications being read by Microsoft Query must support dynamic data exchange (DDE). That's a great line for dropping at nerdy parties, but other than that it's of no real concern. It's one of those square-peg-in-a-round-hole kind of things: it either fits or it doesn't. Here are a few of the programs Query considers square pegs (it can read them):

Btrieve 5.1

dBase 3.0 and 4.0

Microsoft Access 1.0, 1.5, and 2.0

Microsoft Excel (XLS) 3.0, 4.0, 5.0, and 7.0

Microsoft FoxPro 2.0 and 2.5

ODBC ODS gateway

Paradox 3.0, 3.5, and 4.0

SQL Server 1.1, 4.2, NT, and Sybase 4.2

Text

Installing Microsoft Query

Microsoft Query should have been installed when you initially installed Excel. To find out if it was, check your Data menu for a command called Get External Data. If the command doesn't exist, Query's not installed. If Microsoft Query is not on your system now, reinstall Excel. (We tell you all the ins and outs of installing Excel in Appendix A, "Installation and Technical Support.")

In terms of the installation process, Microsoft Query is actually two different programs. One is the Microsoft Query application, and the other is the Microsoft Query add-in, which you install with the **Add-Ins** command from the **Tools** menu. The add-in program provides an orderly pathway from Excel to the Microsoft Query application program, and places the command you use to start Query (Get External Data) in Excel's Data menu.

Let's Go Query

Now's a good time to go out and fetch Excel some data. Of course, to use this function you must have some data to be retrieved in one of the database formats noted above (the square pegs). If you've already got your data, you can go out and fetch it now. The end result will, we hope, be a file that fits seamlessly into Excel.

This is the procedure:

1. Open the **Data** menu and select **Get External Data**. Microsoft Query starts, and the Select Data Source dialog box appears (see the following figure).

Microsoft Query's Select Data Source dialog box.

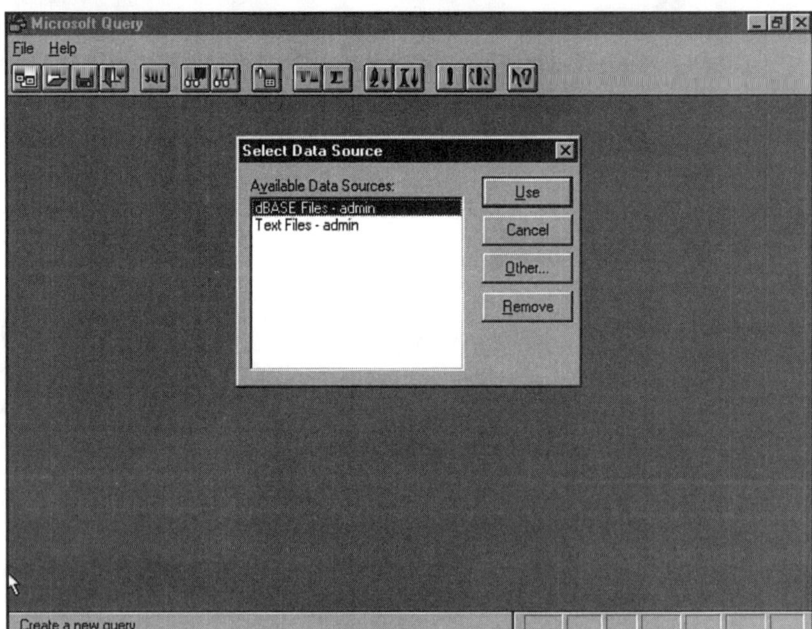

2. Select the file name of the data source you want to access.

Dig Deep

If the data source doesn't initially appear in the dialog box, select the **Other** button. Another dialog box, the ODBC Data Sources dialog box, appears. Choose the data source.

Still no luck? There's still one more layer to travel down before you give up. Select the **New** button in the ODBC Data Sources dialog box. A third dialog box, called Add Data Source, appears. Make your selection from the menu in this box. If you have to install a new driver, Query displays another dialog box to lead you through the process.

3. When you've selected your data source, click **Use** to return to the Query screen. The Add Tables dialog box opens up.
4. Select the tables that contain data you want to include in your spreadsheet. A list box for each table you select appears in the table pane.
5. Drag the fields you want to include in your Excel spreadsheet down to the data pane area.

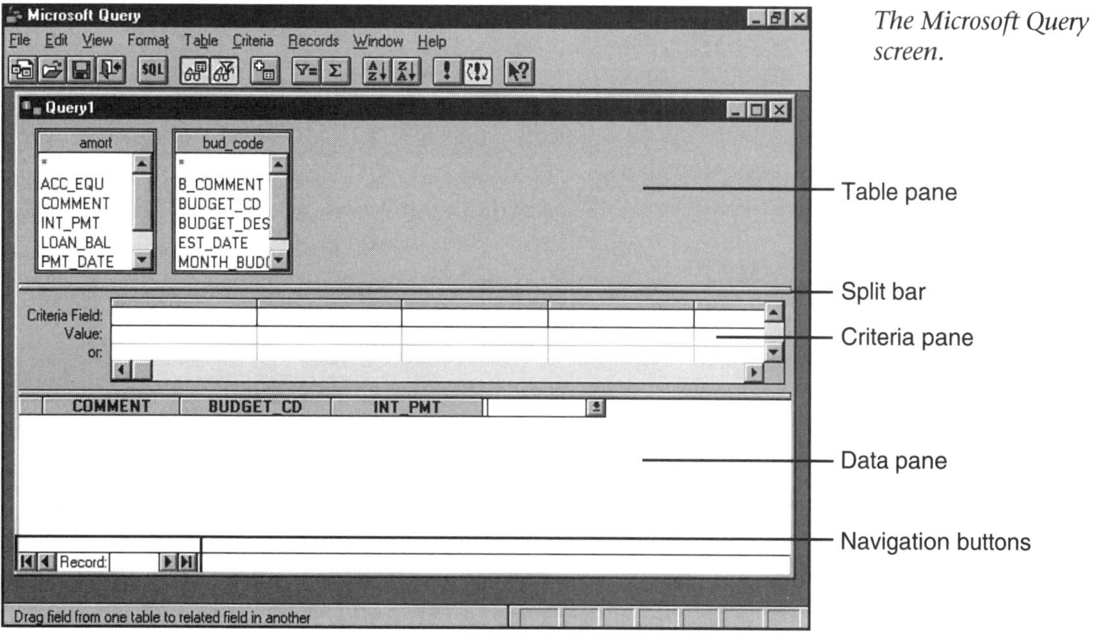

The Microsoft Query screen.

6. When you've selected all the data you want to include, pull down the **File** menu and select **Return Data to Microsoft Excel**. The Excel screen reappears, with the Get External Data dialog box displayed.

The Get External Data dialog box.

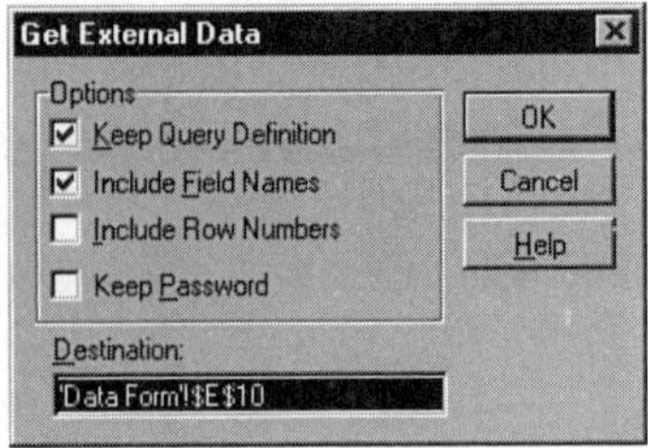

7. In the Destination box, enter the upper-left corner cell of the range where you want to place the Microsoft Query data.
8. Click on any of the following check boxes that are appropriate:

   Keep Query Definition saves the query definition.

   Include Field Names includes the field names as column headers on your worksheet.

   Include Row Numbers includes row numbers in the order they appeared in the original query.

   Keep Password includes a password for updating from the external data source.

9. When you finish making your selections, click **OK**. The data from the outside file appears in your Excel worksheet.

When All Else Fails

No matter how many filtering options you install, you will eventually come across a file type that no one has seen before and Excel cannot possibly import. In those rare cases, search for a common middle ground. Perhaps the mystery application itself can export its files into a format Excel can read, such as a text file.

Export Data from Excel

It's not always the other guy's fault.

You're the kid with the new toy—this latest and greatest version of Excel. If your co-workers need to access your data to perform work on their machines, chances are they won't be able to read your files. After all, your software was still a Beta when theirs were coming of age.

Facilitate them a little—especially if it's the boss you're swapping files with. Excel can save worksheets in formats other than its own.

To save a worksheet in a non-Excel format, pull down the **File** menu and select **Save As**. As you might expect, the Save As dialog box appears.

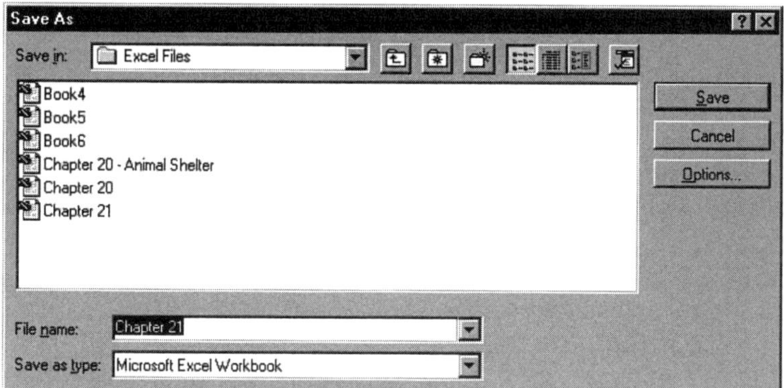

The Save As dialog box.

Near the bottom is a **Save as type** box. Click on its down arrow to see which formats are available. Select the format in which you want to save the file, enter the file name in the **File name** box, and click the **Save** button.

Unfortunately, not all saves are equal. Some formats save the whole workbook, while others save only the active worksheet. This means that in some cases you'll be required to save every worksheet of a workbook as a separate file. C'est la vie. The following table lists which programs save what, and how.

Good Save

Format	File Name Extension
Formats That Save the Entire Workbook	
Excel 4.0 workspace	.xlw
Excel 5.0 template	.xlt
Excel 5.0 workbook	.xls
Excel 5.0 workspace	.xlw
Lotus 1-2-3 Release 3.x (worksheets and chart sheets only)	.fm3, .wk3
Lotus 1-2-3 Release 4.0	.wk4

continues

Good Save Continued

Format	File Name Extension
Formats That Save Only the Active Worksheet	
dBase II, III, and IV	.dbf
DIF (Data Interchange Format)	.dif
Excel 2.x formats	.xlc, .xlm, .xls, .xlw
Excel 3.0 formats	.xla, .xlc, .xlm, .xls, .xlt, .xlw
Excel macro	.xlm
Lotus 1-2-3	.wks, .wk1
Quattro Pro (DOS)	.wq1
Quattro Pro for Windows	.wq*
SYLK (Symbolic link format)	.slk
Text	.txt
Text, Comma-separated values	.csv
Text, Formatted	.prn

Consolidation

Until now, this chapter has focused on retrieving data from the great unknown outside the world of Excel. Consolidation works from the inside out. You use consolidation to summarize data from one worksheet in a single cell on another worksheet.

A Must See

Although consolidation tables are useful for pulling in data from multiple sources, they lack the flexibility of Pivot Tables. Pivot Tables are covered in Chapter 22, coming soon to a chapter near you.

Here's an example of consolidation in practice. "Type A" worksheets contain daily reports. Consolidate all of the "Type A" worksheets into weekly reports. We'll call these new workbooks "Type B." Then consolidate the data from all of the "Type B" workbooks into yearly reports, which we'll call "Type C" workbooks. Carry on this process of consolidation for as long and in as many different directions as you want.

The Work of Consolidation

You can use either of two methods to consolidate data:

- Consolidate by *position* when data and labels are in the same position on both the source and destination documents.
- Consolidate by *category* when labels and data are not in the same position on both the source and destination documents.

To consolidate by position, begin by selecting the upper left cell of the destination worksheet. Open the **Data** menu and select **Consolidate**, and the Consolidate dialog box appears. In the Function drop-down list, select the summary function you want to use for your consolidation.

In the Reference box, enter the areas you want to consolidate. Click **Add** for each additional entry in the Reference box. Check the **Create Links to Source Data** box if you want Excel to update your consolidated data whenever a change is made to the source data. When you finish making your selections, click **OK**.

To consolidate by category, begin by selecting the upper left cell of the destination worksheet. Open the **Data** menu and select **Consolidate**, and the Consolidate dialog box appears (see the following figure).

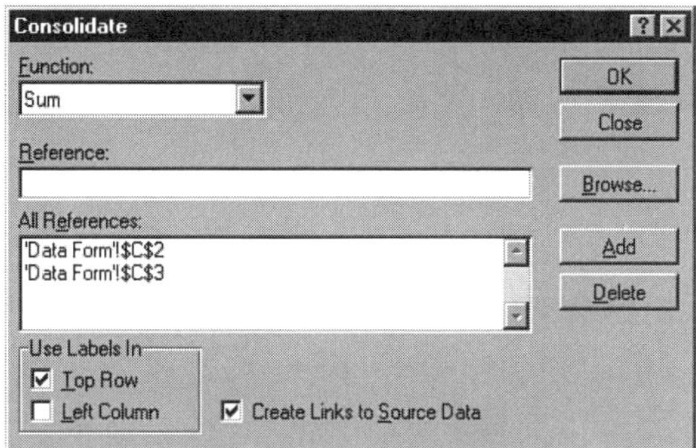

The Consolidate dialog box.

In the Function drop-down list, select the summary function that you want to use for your consolidation. In the Reference box, enter the areas you want to consolidate, including the data labels in the selection. Click **Add** for each additional entry in the Reference box.

In the Use Labels In box, check the box that indicates where the labels are in the source area. (Check both boxes if applicable.) Click on the **Create Links to Source Data** box if you want Excel to update your consolidated data whenever a change is made to the source data. When you finish making your selections, click **OK**.

Now you've got yourself a fine little consolidation table. Enjoy!

The Least You Need to Know

- Excel can import the most common file types without any difficulty. Just select the file type from the Files of type drop-down list in the Open dialog box.
- You can import less common file types, but the procedure is more complicated.
- Obscure file types have to be converted to a common format by the originating software.
- Consolidate data from multiple worksheets to make it more readable.

Chapter 22

Pivot Tables

In This Chapter

- Pivot to heel
- Get it together
- Make it work
- Twist and shout
- Change it all about
- Wacky ways to wiggle your work

"Say that again!" she demands.

"If you marry your stepfather's father, you become the mother of your own parents. And if you are your mother's mother, you are your own grandmother. See?"

She's only six years old, but she's starting to catch on. She screws up her face, looks completely puzzled, and says "Now tell me one more time."

Intro to Pivot Tables

You have masses of data, and somehow it's all related. Somehow. Your job is to find out whether the larger sales staffs are more productive than the smaller ones, and whether paying a high commission gets better results than paying a lower commission. Of course, those answers might vary depending on what country you're operating in and what the product line is.

Pivot tables enable you to view all these relationships in a single place and switch them around to see what factors correspond with which results. Then, once you have your consolidated table in shape, you can create charts and maps that are more effective than they ever could have been with the masses of data on your entire list.

How They Work

Pivot tables work by showing you new relationships between categories: Julia and Keifer vs Julia and Lyle vs Keifer and Lyle vs Julia and Richard... well, you see how it works. Normally, spreadsheets show relationships in two dimensions: Dimension 1 is a budget category, and Dimension 2 is a dollar figure (your budget). But what if you want to add a third dimension, say, a rating for how critical the budget item is. Food and shelter get an A rating, genuine vinyl siding gets a B rating, and ABBA CDs get a C rating.

With a pivot table, you can drag columns to rows and rows to columns, and—like a supermarket tabloid—make otherwise unseen relationships very apparent.

Definitions

Before we get too deeply into this, there are a few terms you'll need to understand:

Pivot Table A table you create to show interactive relationships between many kinds of things. A pivot table enables you to drag columns and rows back and forth.

List The underlying database (arranged in columns, with labels at the top of each column) that is the source of the pivot table's data.

Field Each column of a typical Excel database list.

Record Each row of a typical Excel database list.

Source Data The data in the list or lists upon which a pivot table is based.

Pivot Table Data All the summarized data out in the middle of the table.

Pivot Table Control Your pivot table looks very much like a regular table, except that the row and column labels turn into buttons that you can drag to other locations. These buttons are called controls.

Summary Functions All the calculations Excel performs on the data out in the middle of the pivot table (it's summarized, calculated, subtotaled, and grand-totaled).

Page Field Individual fields of data that you've instructed the pivot table to break out into separate pages and display one at a time.

Group To subdivide categories of data and regroup the subdivisions. If Africa and Europe were categories, for example, all the separate countries in each location could be grouped together.

It's a Setup

Begin your pivot table by setting up a list the same way you did in Chapter 20. Note, however, that pivot tables are particularly adept at using data that can be broken out by category, subcategory, and sub-subcategory. The more ways Excel can group the data in your database list, and the more often the same words or figures appear in different categories, the more interesting your pivot tables will be.

Enter your list data in columns, or fields, with a label at the top of each column. (These labels will appear in your pivot table as button-like controls.) The following figure shows a sample database list that could be used as the source data for a pivot table.

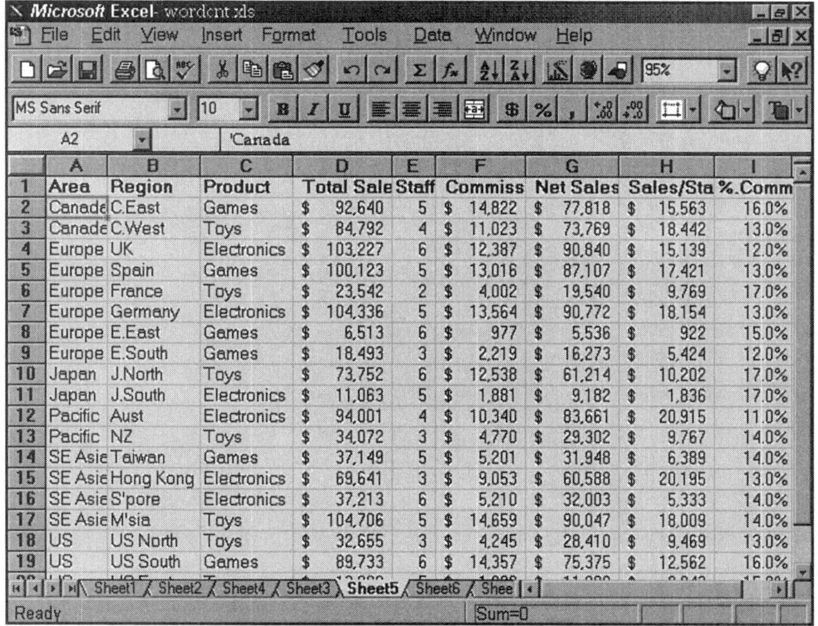

	A	B	C	D	E	F	G	H	I
1	Area	Region	Product	Total Sale	Staff	Commiss	Net Sales	Sales/Sta	%.Comm
2	Canada	C.East	Games	$ 92,640	5	$ 14,822	$ 77,818	$ 15,563	16.0%
3	Canada	C.West	Toys	$ 84,792	4	$ 11,023	$ 73,769	$ 18,442	13.0%
4	Europe	UK	Electronics	$ 103,227	6	$ 12,387	$ 90,840	$ 15,139	12.0%
5	Europe	Spain	Games	$ 100,123	5	$ 13,016	$ 87,107	$ 17,421	13.0%
6	Europe	France	Toys	$ 23,542	2	$ 4,002	$ 19,540	$ 9,769	17.0%
7	Europe	Germany	Electronics	$ 104,336	5	$ 13,564	$ 90,772	$ 18,154	13.0%
8	Europe	E.East	Games	$ 6,513	6	$ 977	$ 5,536	$ 922	15.0%
9	Europe	E.South	Games	$ 18,493	3	$ 2,219	$ 16,273	$ 5,424	12.0%
10	Japan	J.North	Toys	$ 73,752	6	$ 12,538	$ 61,214	$ 10,202	17.0%
11	Japan	J.South	Electronics	$ 11,063	5	$ 1,881	$ 9,182	$ 1,836	17.0%
12	Pacific	Aust	Electronics	$ 94,001	4	$ 10,340	$ 83,661	$ 20,915	11.0%
13	Pacific	NZ	Toys	$ 34,072	3	$ 4,770	$ 29,302	$ 9,767	14.0%
14	SE Asia	Taiwan	Games	$ 37,149	5	$ 5,201	$ 31,948	$ 6,389	14.0%
15	SE Asia	Hong Kong	Electronics	$ 69,641	3	$ 9,053	$ 60,588	$ 20,195	13.0%
16	SE Asia	S'pore	Electronics	$ 37,213	6	$ 5,210	$ 32,003	$ 5,333	14.0%
17	SE Asia	M'sia	Toys	$ 104,706	5	$ 14,659	$ 90,047	$ 18,009	14.0%
18	US	US North	Toys	$ 32,655	3	$ 4,245	$ 28,410	$ 9,469	13.0%
19	US	US South	Games	$ 89,733	6	$ 14,357	$ 75,375	$ 12,562	16.0%

Create a database list.

Heed these additional rules when creating lists for your pivot tables:

- ➤ Column labels are not optional. Without them, your pivot table won't work.
- ➤ Avoid including totals and subtotals in the portions of your database that you will include in the pivot table. (You don't have to use the entire worksheet in your pivot table, and calculations off to the side probably won't cause any problems.)
- ➤ Formulas work better in pivot tables than they did in the Data Forms you saw in Chapter 20. The whole point of the pivot table is to change the relationships between data. Formulas can handle the stress.
- ➤ If you've used filters in your list, the pivot table ignores them and uses all the data.

Now you know the ground rules. Let's make a pivot table!

The Creation Story

To create a pivot table from a database list, first make the worksheet containing your list the active sheet. Then select the entire list or the segment that contains the information you want to review in pivot table form. Be sure to include the column labels when you make your selection. Open the **Data** menu and choose the **PivotTable** command. The PivotTable Wizard - Step 1 of 4 dialog box appears (see the following figure).

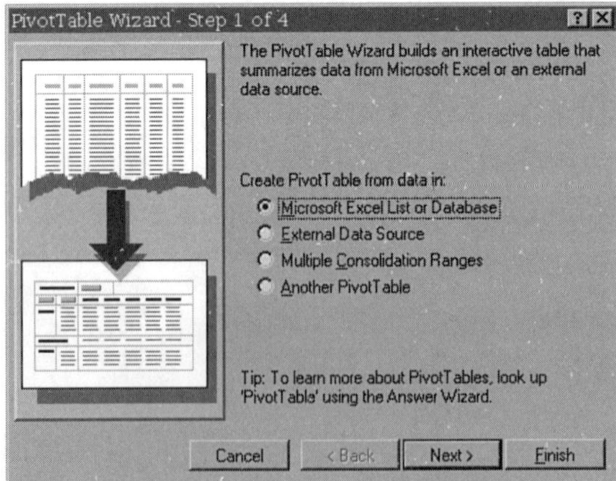

The PivotTable Wizard - Step 1 of 4 dialog box.

The Microsoft Excel List or Database option is automatically selected. You also have the option of importing data from an external data source (see Chapter 21), from multiple consolidation ranges (Chapter 21), or from another pivot table. For now, we'll use only the Excel list as a data source. Click the **Next** button to proceed to the next step.

In the PivotTable Wizard - Step 2 of 4 dialog box (shown in the following figure), Excel asks for the range of the data you're using. The range address of the selected cells appears in the Range text box with absolute references, as indicated by the dollar signs attached to each of the references.

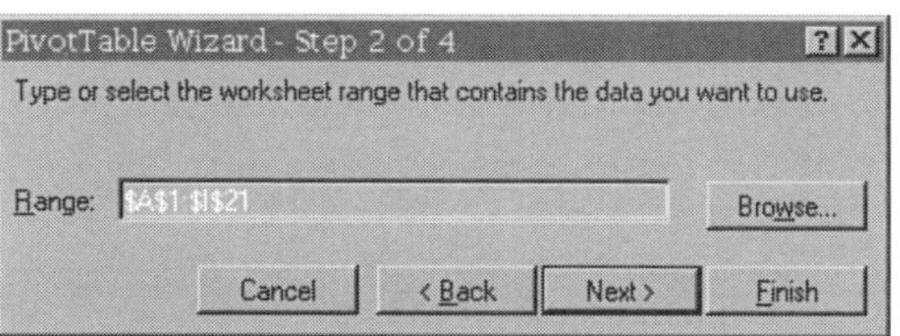

Enter the range address of the list in the Step 2 of 4 dialog box.

You can change the selection by entering a new reference or address, by dragging over a new range directly in the worksheet, or by using the Browse dialog box. To access the Browse dialog box (which looks exactly like the Open dialog box you use to open a workbook), select the **Browse** button. If you choose another Excel file from the Browse dialog box, Excel creates your pivot table from that data instead of the information on your current worksheet.

We'll continue with the current worksheet. With your range selected, click the **Next** button. Predictably, the Step 3 of 4 dialog box (shown here) appears.

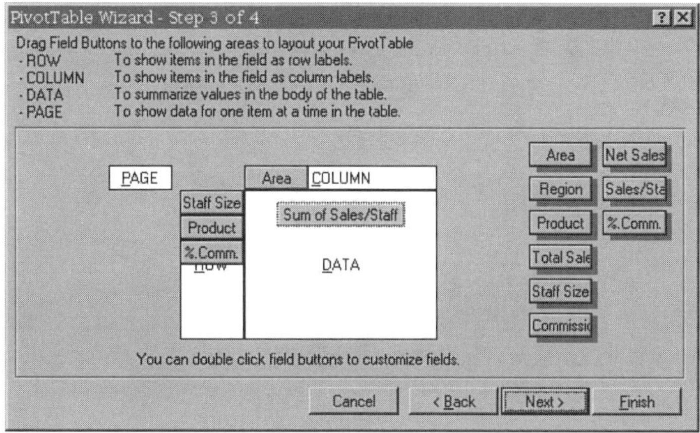

The PivotTable Wizard - Step 3 of 4 dialog box.

This is where you do all the hard work of creating the pivot table. Decide whether you want your original column labels—which are now called *field buttons*—to appear in your pivot table as row labels, as column labels, as data to be summed or counted, or as separate pages called *page fields*. You can change these assignments later if you want, so it's okay to be a little haphazard for the time being.

Do You Use All of Them? No, you don't need to use all of the field buttons. If you're well acquainted with your data, you'll understand immediately which items you want to see the relationships for.

When you drag field buttons into the page, row, and column areas, nothing changes. But when you drag them into the data area—and you must put at least one button in the data area—the pivot table wants to perform some calculations on it. After you've done the drag, double-click on the button you dragged to the data area to call up the PivotTable Field dialog box (shown in the following figure).

In the **Summarize by** area, you see a list of 11 ways the pivot table can perform mathematical and statistical calculations. Pick any of them and click **OK**; you can change it later if necessary.

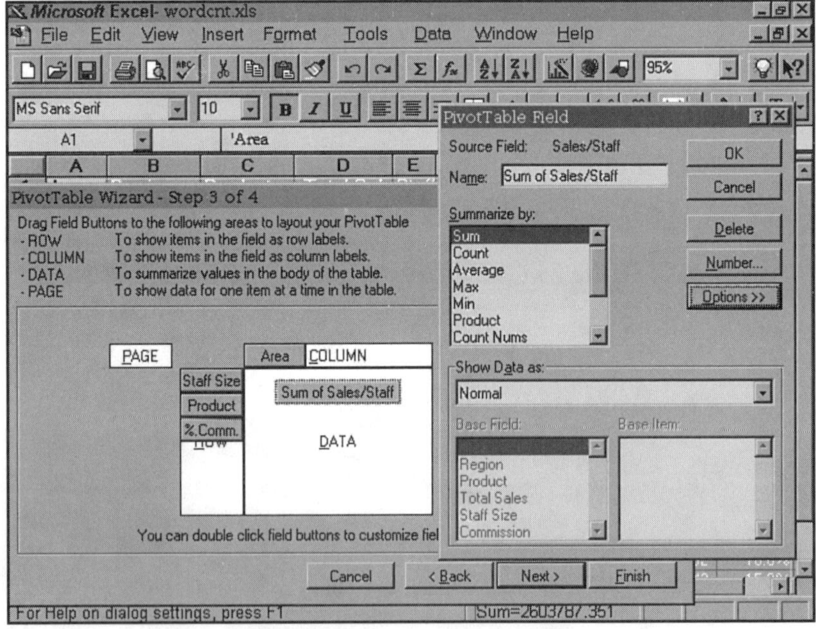

PivotTable Field dialog box with options selected.

Techno Talk

blah blah blah bla

Those Amazing Calculations

Here are some quick descriptions of each of the 11 mathematical and statistical calculations available in the pivot table:

Sum Sum of values in underlying data. The default function for numeric data fields.

Count Number of records or rows in underlying data. The default summary function for data fields that contain something other than numbers.

Average Average of values in underlying data.

Max Largest value in underlying data.

Min Smallest value in underlying data.

Product Product of underlying data.

Count Nums Number of records or rows in underlying data that contain numeric data.

StdDev Estimate of standard deviation of a population, based on a sample of underlying data.

StdDevp Standard deviation of a population, based on an entire population of underlying data.

Var An estimate of variance of a population, based on a sample of underlying data.

Varp Variance of a population of data, based on an entire population of underlying data.

Click on the **Options** button to choose from the nine options in the Show Data as box. These options enable you to customize your data display in the following ways:

Difference From Shows all data in the data area as the difference between Base Field and Base Item you select. (You choose the Base Field and Base Item in the corresponding boxes in this dialog box.)

% Of Shows all data in data area as a percentage of Base Field and Base Item.

% Difference From Same as Difference From, but shows difference as a percentage of Base data.

Running Total In Shows data for consecutive items as a running total. Select field with items you want shown in a running total.

% Of Row Shows data in each row as percentage of total of the row.

% Of Column Shows all data in each column as percentage of the total of the column.

% Of Total Shows data in data area as percentage of grand total of all data in pivot table.

Index Shows data by using following equation:
((value in cell) x (Grand Total)) / ((Grand Row Total) x (Grand Column Total))

Click on the **Next** button, and ta-da! It's Step 4 of 4! In this dialog box (see the following figure), you can set formatting options that control how your final pivot table will look. Make your choices and click on **Finish**, and you're ready to start pivoting.

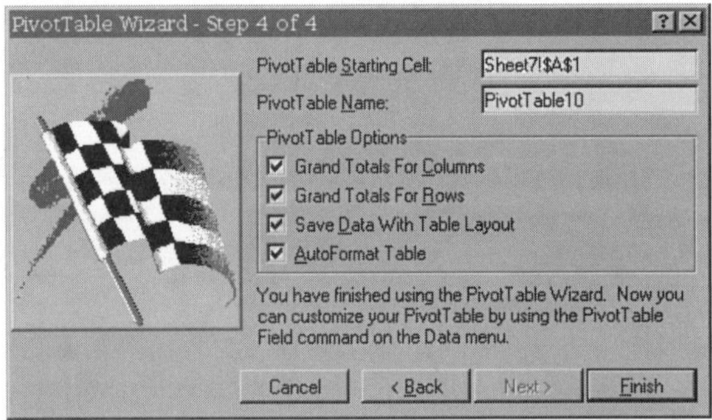

Format your pivot table with the options in the Step 4 of 4 dialog box.

The Hokey Pokey

Your new pivot table looks something like the following figure. The information in the pivot table is grouped by category (in this case, by area). Within each category are secondary groupings.

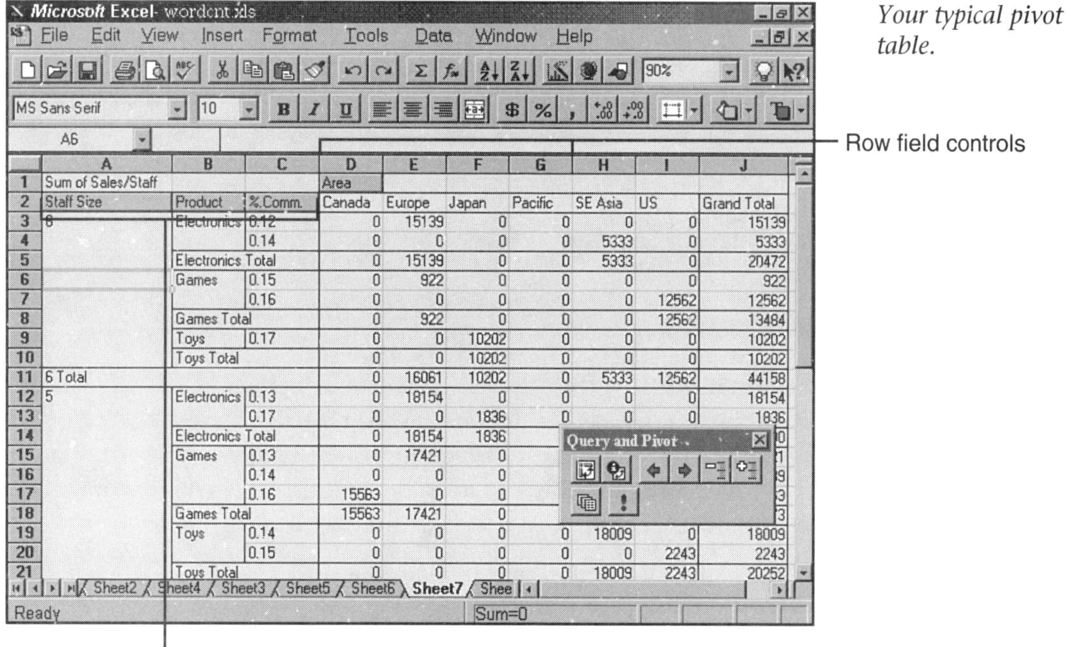

Your typical pivot table.

Now let's see how to make some changes.

The Toolbar

When Excel displays your new pivot table, it also displays the Query and Pivot toolbar shown in the following figure. If the Query and Pivot toolbar doesn't appear automatically, force an appearance by opening the **View** menu, selecting **Toolbars**, and choosing **Query and Pivot**. We'll consider each of the buttons on the Query and Pivot toolbar as we discuss ways to change the pivot table.

For now, dock your toolbar by dragging it off the work area of your worksheet. The toolbar changes shape. Stay calm. None of the buttons are lost.

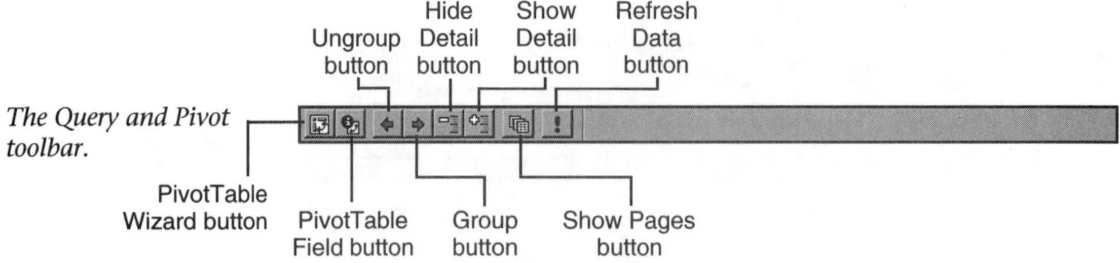

The Query and Pivot toolbar.

Make It Pivot

Now that you've got your table ready, the fun begins. You can change the layout of your pivot table simply by grabbing any field control and moving it to a different row or column or to a different place on its current row or column. As you do so, the shape of your pointer changes to reflect column or row shapes, depending on where you drag. You may also see some other pointer shapes, which we explain later in this chapter.

This figure shows the same pivot table after we moved some controls around. Notice that the data is simply reorganized into new views to show different relationships. You can make changes as often as necessary to see every possible relationship of your data.

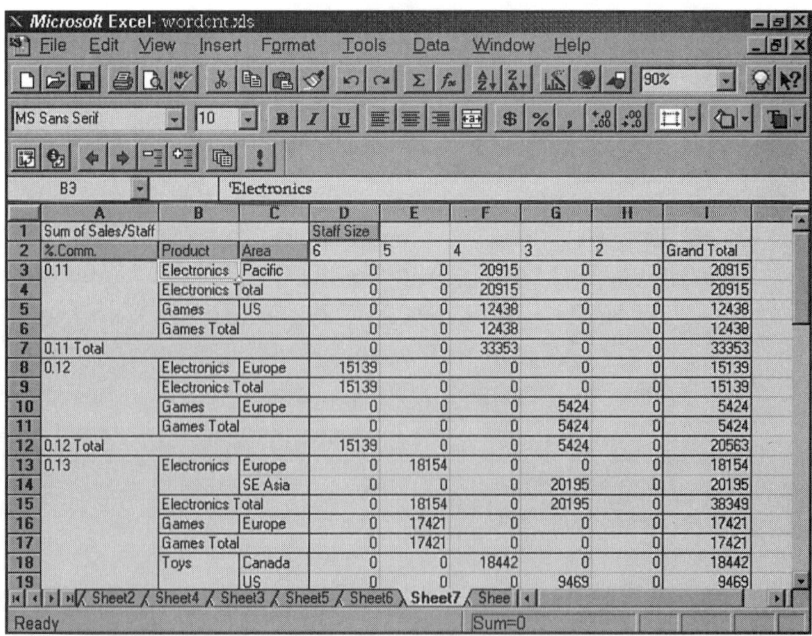

	A	B	C	D	E	F	G	H	I
1	Sum of Sales/Staff			Staff Size					
2	%.Comm.	Product	Area	6	5	4	3	2	Grand Total
3	0.11	Electronics	Pacific	0	0	20915	0	0	20915
4		Electronics Total		0	0	20915	0	0	20915
5		Games	US	0	0	12438	0	0	12438
6		Games Total		0	0	12438	0	0	12438
7	0.11 Total			0	0	33353	0	0	33353
8	0.12	Electronics	Europe	15139	0	0	0	0	15139
9		Electronics Total		15139	0	0	0	0	15139
10		Games	Europe	0	0	0	5424	0	5424
11		Games Total		0	0	0	5424	0	5424
12	0.12 Total			15139	0	0	5424	0	20563
13	0.13	Electronics	Europe	0	18154	0	0	0	18154
14			SE Asia	0	0	0	20195	0	20195
15		Electronics Total		0	18154	0	20195	0	38349
16		Games	Europe	0	17421	0	0	0	17421
17		Games Total		0	17421	0	0	0	17421
18		Toys	Canada	0	0	18442	0	0	18442
19			US	0	0	0	9469	0	9469

The modified pivot table.

You can make changes to the setup of any field by selecting the field control button and double-clicking on the **PivotTable Field** button on the Query and Pivot toolbar. When you do, the PivotTable Field dialog box appears (see the following figure).

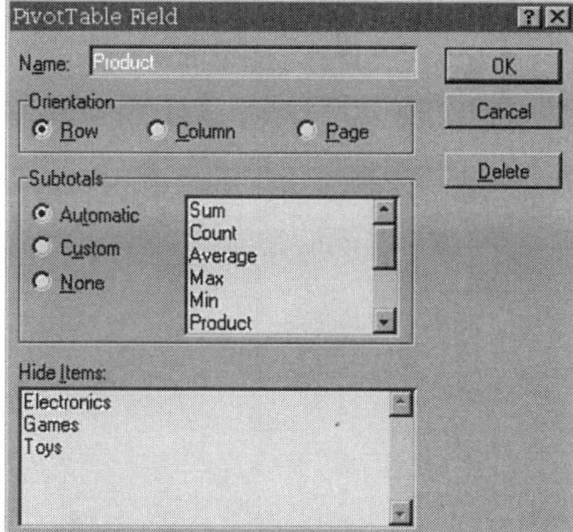

The PivotTable Field dialog box.

In this box you can change the location—the *orientation*—of your field control, change the way the summaries are calculated, select items in your field you want to hide, or delete the field altogether.

Page Fields

Sometimes, when the data gets just too complicated, you'll want to break your data out even further and view separate pivot tables for each record in your field. That's what page fields are for. Page fields simply add one more dimension to your pivot table analysis. Here's how they work.

In the PivotTable Wizard - Step 3 of 4 dialog box, you had the option to drag fields into the page field box. Now that your table is in place, you can recall the wizard by clicking the **PivotTable Wizard** button on the toolbar. Then simply drag your field labels into the page field box and click **Finish**.

Alternatively, instead of recalling the wizard, you can just drag existing field controls up to the northwest corner of your pivot table. The pointer shape changes from a row or a column to a series of steps. Release the pointer, and you've got yourself a page field control.

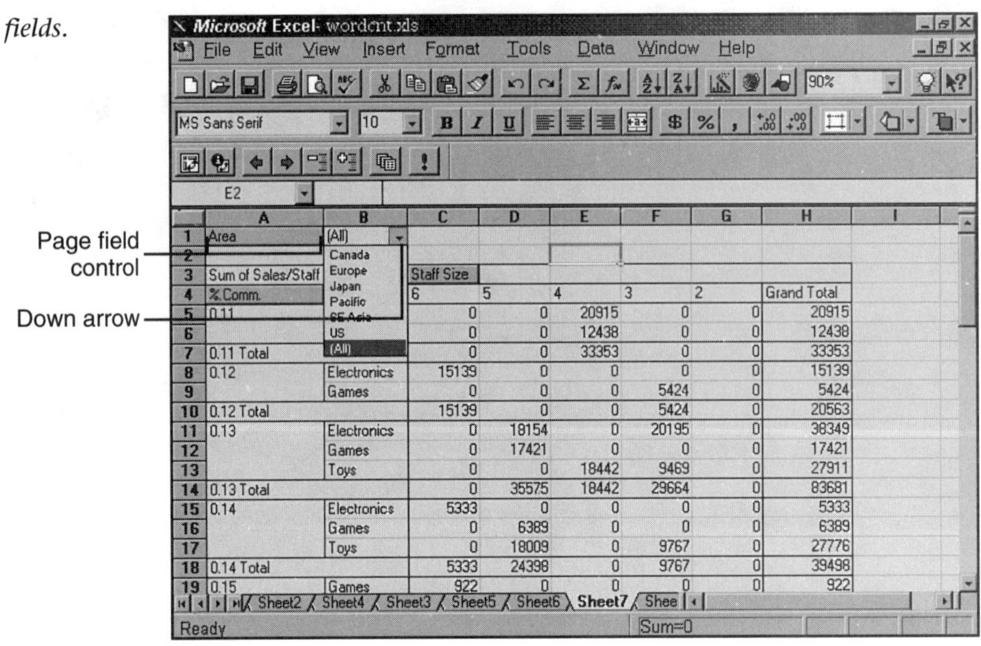

Using page fields.

Page fields are always located two full rows above the main body of the pivot table. To use the page fields, click the down arrow of the page field control on your pivot table. A drop-down list appears, and you can select a view. At the bottom of the list is the All option, which gives you a consolidated view.

You can click the **Show Pages** button on the Query and Pivot toolbar to copy each page field to its own separate worksheet. Click **OK** to see worksheet tabs at the bottom of your screen for the new worksheets.

Refining the View

The pivot table is supposed to simplify the way you view your data. Often, though, the pivot table introduces so much new information that you get confused all over again. The next three sections tell you about options that can make your life easier.

Delete Fields

Maybe you've just tried too hard. Drive the irrelevant fields out of your life forever (or until you change your mind, whichever comes first) by dragging the field control off the main body of your pivot table. When the pointer changes to a large X over a bar, release the mouse button, and the field disappears.

You can get it back by recalling the PivotTable Wizard (click on the leftmost button on your Query and Pivot toolbar) and dragging the field control back in. Then click on **Next** and click **Finish**.

Group and Ungroup Fields

You can consolidate items in a category with the grouping command. To do so, select two or more items in a column or a row that can be grouped together. For example, if you have a column of items numbered 1 through 4, you might want to combine 1 with 2 to create the first group, and combine 3 with 4 to create the second group.

You needn't select every cell in the column from the group; a representative sample from each column will do. To select noncontiguous cells, click the first cell, press and hold down **Ctrl**, and click on additional cells. With at least two cells selected, choose the right-arrow **Group** button from the Query and Pivot toolbar. The following figure shows the sample pivot table after grouping fields.

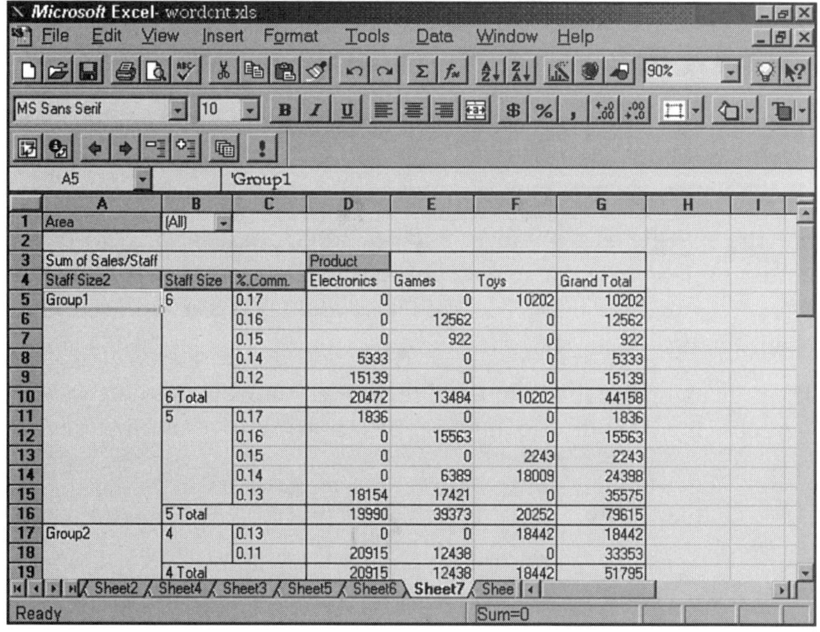

	A	B	C	D	E	F	G
1	Area	(All)					
2							
3	Sum of Sales/Staff			Product			
4	Staff Size2	Staff Size	%.Comm.	Electronics	Games	Toys	Grand Total
5	Group1	6	0.17	0	0	10202	10202
6			0.16	0	12562	0	12562
7			0.15	0	922	0	922
8			0.14	5333	0	0	5333
9			0.12	15139	0	0	15139
10		6 Total		20472	13484	10202	44158
11		5	0.17	1836	0	0	1836
12			0.16	0	15563	0	15563
13			0.15	0	0	2243	2243
14			0.14	0	6389	18009	24398
15			0.13	18154	17421	0	35575
16		5 Total		19990	39373	20252	79615
17	Group2	4	0.13	0	0	18442	18442
18			0.11	20915	12438	0	33353
19		4 Total		20915	12438	18442	51795

A grouped field.

A new field, with the new groupings, appears to the left of your original field with the new groupings. You can drag this field around the table as you would any other.

To remove the new groupings, select a representative cell in the field and click the left-arrow **Ungroup** button. When you've ungrouped every grouping, the entire field disappears.

Hide 'Em

You can collapse your pivot table into manageable views by hiding the details. To hide the details of a particular field (including its subtotals and subcategories), select the field control and click the **Hide Detail** button on the Query and Pivot toolbar.

Reverse the process by reselecting the field control and pressing the **Show Detail** button.

Making Changes

You've changed the format, changed the options, even swapped the columns and rows. Can there be any more?

Sure! Believe it or not, there are still more changes you can make to your new pivot table.

Changing the Source Data

If you add new information to your original database list, you'll want to update the pivot table to reflect those changes. There's a simple way to do this and a more complicated way, but which method you use depends on what kinds of changes you make.

If you're changing only the existing data numbers, and not adding or deleting rows or columns, you can do the simple update. Make your changes to the database, return to the pivot table, and click the **Refresh Data** button on the Query and Pivot toolbar. Excel updates your changes automatically.

On the other hand, if you're changing the number of rows or columns in the database list, changing the pivot table is a little more complex. The following steps outline the procedure.

1. Make your database changes, return to the pivot table, and select any cell in the pivot table to make it active.
2. Then pull down the **Data** menu and choose **PivotTable**. The Step 3 dialog box reappears.
3. Click the **Back** button to return to Step 2. In the Step 2 dialog box, amend the database range to include the new rows or columns.
4. Then finish the steps in the dialog boxes as you did originally, and your changes appear in the revised pivot table.

Retrieving More Fields

In the unlikely event that your pivot table isn't complicated enough, you can add fields for further analysis.

Just click the **PivotTable Wizard** button on the Query and Pivot toolbar. Excel returns you to Step 3 of the wizard, where you can add, subtract, and customize your fields to your heart's content. Click the **Finish** button in the dialog box to return to the pivot table.

Changing Number Format

Formatting numbers in a pivot table is an unwieldy process. You can change only the numbers in the data area; numbers in the other fields are unchangeable. Here's the procedure for changing number formats in the data area.

First, click on a cell in the data area to make it active. Then open the **Data** menu and select **PivotTable Field/Number**. The Format Cells dialog box appears. Select your number format from the Category list, and click **OK** to return to the pivot table.

The Road Less Traveled
Although you normally access the Format Cells dialog box by choosing the Cells command from the Format menu, you can't do that when you're working with a pivot table. If you do, you lose the formats each time you rearrange the pivot table.

Sorting Fields

Excel can sort your pivot table fields alphabetically or numerically or by a combination of the two, and it can sort from top to bottom or bottom to top.

To sort a field, click the button for the field you want to sort. Then select one of these sort buttons from the Standard toolbar at the top of your Excel screen:

 Sort Ascending

 Sort Descending

When you select Sort Ascending, Excel sorts the text fields in alphabetical order (A to Z) and sorts numbers from lowest to highest. The Sort Descending button reverses these orders (Z to A and highest to lowest). Within a field, Excel sorts items in this order: numbers, text, logical values, error values, and blank cells.

The Name Game: Renaming Fields

You can rename a pivot table field in one of two ways:

- Make the change in the original database list. Then return to the pivot table, click on an active cell, and click the **PivotTable Wizard** toolbar button. The Step 3 dialog box appears. Click on **Back** to go back to Step 2. Then recapture the cell range, click **Next**, and drag the field labels back into position. Click **Finish** to exit the dialog box. The field is renamed when you return to the pivot table.
- Make the change in the pivot table, without changing the underlying database list. Just click on the field name to make it active, and edit the name in the Formula bar above the column headers or in the cell itself. Then return to the pivot table and click the **Refresh Data** button on the Query and Pivot toolbar.

Deleting the Table

You can delete the entire table without affecting the underlying source data. To do so, select the entire pivot table. Then open the **Edit** menu and select **Clear/All.**

What? You didn't really want to delete it? Press **Ctrl+Z** to bring it back—but you have to act fast. Once you go on to another task, it's lost forever.

The Least You Need to Know

- Pivot tables let you look at data in multiple dimensions.
- Pivot tables work best with data that has multiple layers and identical subcategories repeated throughout.
- Build your database list first, and then create the pivot table using the **Data, PivotTable** command.
- You can drag field labels to other places on the rows or columns to see new relationships.
- Pivot tables can be formatted to perform a variety of mathematical and statistical calculations.

Chapter 23

The What-If Conundrum

In This Chapter

- First and goal
- Final solution
- Making a scene
- Zounds, Batman! A zinger at the problem-solving zenith!

By the time you read this, our "The Book's Finished and Now We Can Sleep" party will have been long past. That much we know. But as we write, we still haven't decided how many guests, how many bottles of 7-Up, or how many bags of charcoal briquettes we're going to need. Guess it's time to pull out a worksheet and figure it out, right?

What Is What-If?

This chapter is for people who like to read magazines—and books—from back to front. Throughout this book, we've been teaching you how to get from a set of variables to a result. In this, the last real chapter of the book, we tell you how to turn it around: how to go from a result to a whole bunch of variables.

This chapter introduces you to some advanced Excel features that you will use when you want to do some planning. In other words, when you still have time to influence the variables.

Go ahead and ask Excel all those burning questions in your life. What if I could earn a little more money? What if I made a few more charitable donations? How would that affect my taxes? What if my worthless son-in-law repaid the $8,000 I loaned him last year? Excel lets you do your planning with a set of "what-if" features that'll have you on the phone calling in your IOUs in no time flat.

Each of the assumptions you make (about future interest rates, commission rates, sales figures, tax rates, or your income level, for example) is called a *variable*. In this chapter, we discuss Excel's Goal Seek feature, which you use when you want Excel to adjust a single *variable* to help you achieve a predetermined result; the Solver feature, which you use when you can adjust multiple variables; and the Scenario Manager, which gives you the power to save lots of different *scenarios* (suppositions about future events).

Working Backwards: The Excel Goal Seek Function

Theoretically, when you shop for refrigerators or used cars, you're out there comparing prices. "We have enough money to buy a 1983 Hyundai," you tell your spouse. Your spouse nods in assent as you pull into the lot. Three hours later, you leave with a late-model Miata and five years of payments. Why?

You fell for *goal-seeking*, a mechanism whereby you twist the facts to fit a predetermined ending—in this case, the old "The monthly payment is just a little higher, and we've got this trade-in, and even though we have to make payments well into the next millennium, well, we'd probably have to pay for repairs on the older car, so it all works out the same" routine.

Excel's Goal Seek function works backwards from the usual formula routine. Normally, you input a formula and read the results. With Goal Seek, you choose the result, and the formula adjusts the factors to make the result come out the way you say.

This is how it works. Suppose you're working on commission, and you write a formula in cell A3 that calculates your expected income for next year, based on your sales figures and commission rate. The income figure is a little on the low side. You can keep playing with the sales figures and commission rates until the income figure looks right, or you can use Goal Seek.

To use Goal Seek, click on the cell that shows your income, open the **Tools** menu and select **Goal Seek**. The Goal Seek dialog box appears (see the following figure).

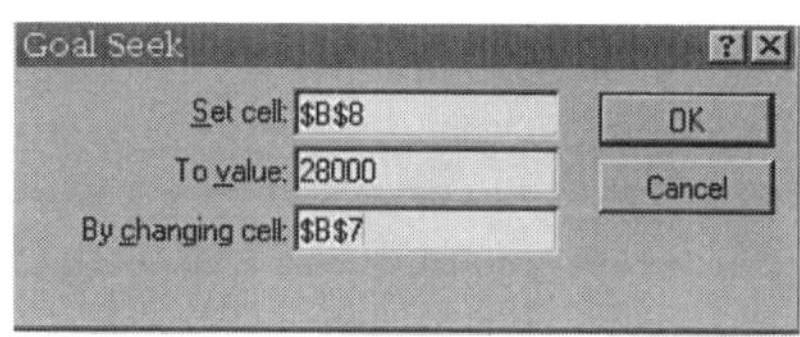

The Goal Seek dialog box.

In the Set cell box, you enter the cell reference address for which you want to set a value. Because you already selected a cell, its address appears automatically. In the To value box, enter your dream number. Then enter the address of the cell you are willing to adjust in the By changing cell box. (In our example, because your sales figure is calculated from other figures, you can change only the commission rate.) When you finish entering the necessary data, click **OK**. Goal Seek makes the required adjustment. If only your boss would change your commission rate that easily.

Solving Problems

Okay, Goal Seek works for simple problems—but yours are more complex, right? When you've got multiple variables to consider, you need something stronger. To find the ideal solution within parameters you define, use Solver.

Using Solver

With Solver, you set up your "what-if" situation by actually changing a few variables in an existing worksheet. Therefore, you need to have your worksheet already set up.

Add Solver

Before you try to use Solver, make sure it's installed on your system. To determine whether Solver has already been installed, see if the Tools menu contains the Solver command. If it doesn't, you have to install it. Open the **Tools** menu and select **Add-Ins**. Select **Solver** from the list in the Add-Ins dialog box. If Solver isn't listed in the dialog box, you'll have to re-run the Excel Setup altogether.

To use Solver, select the cell in which you'll do your solving work. Then choose **Solver** from the **Tools** menu. The Solver Parameters dialog box (shown in the following figure) appears.

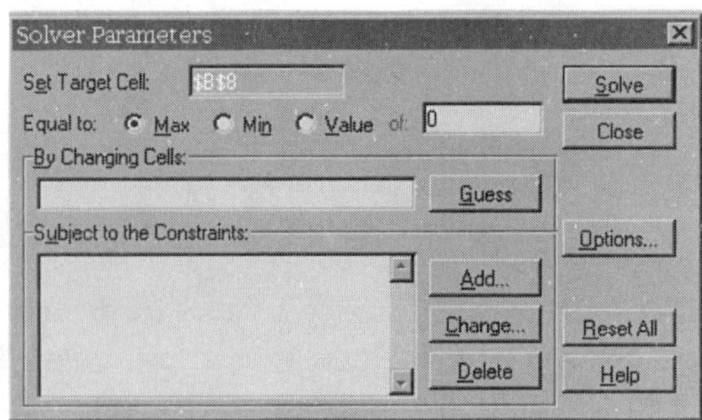

The Solver Parameters dialog box.

Your selected cell address appears in the Set Target Cell box. To select the smallest possible value for the target cell, click on the **Min** option button. To select the largest possible value for the target cell, select the **Max** option button. To set your own value for the target cell, click the **Value** option button and enter a value in the box provided.

In the By Changing Cells text box, enter the reference addresses of all the cells you will allow Solver to change in order to achieve your target value. If you want Solver to determine which cells to change, click on the **Guess** button instead. Then enter any constraints (you have four choices: greater than, less than, equal to, or integer) in the Subject to the Constraints box and click the **Solve** button. Solver calculates the solution and displays the Solver Results dialog box.

Now you've got some decisions to make. To retain the solution values, select the **Keep Solver Solution** option button in the Solver Results dialog box (as shown in the following figure). Alternatively, you can select Restore Original Values to replace the solution values with the original values.

Free Sample

Excel comes with some sample workbooks that illustrate Solver's problem solving capabilities. You can find the workbooks Solverex.xls and Solvsamp.xls in the Examples\ Solver folder under Excel.

Solvsamp.xls contains six worksheets. Each worksheet includes a brief description of the problem, shows the target cell, and indicates which cells and constraints are changing.

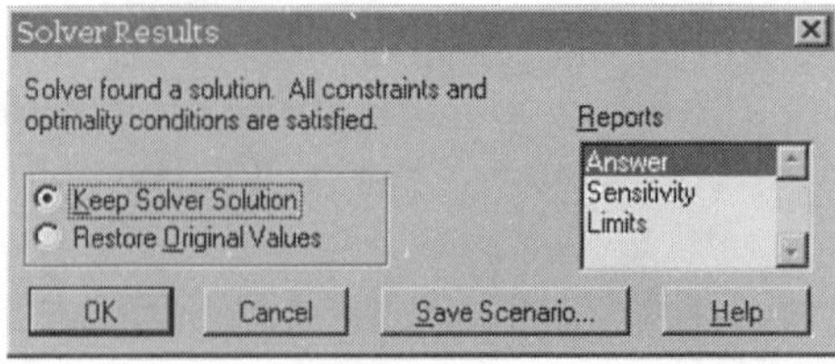

Tell Solver what you want to do with the results of the calculation.

If you think you might need the solution values later, click on the **Save Scenario** button to save the Solver settings. The Save Scenario dialog box appears, prompting you to enter a name for the saved scenario.

Scenario Management

Excel enables you to define and save different *scenarios* (the set of suppositions you make about your data). Once you save a scenario, you can easily recall it and play the what-if game a thousand different times, a thousand different ways. Excel's Scenario Manager makes the storing and recalling of scenarios an orderly process.

You can create a scenario in either of two ways:

- You can save the results of a Solver calculation as a scenario by selecting the Save Scenario button in the Solver Results dialog box.
- You can create a scenario manually. This is the more flexible method, and the one you'll be using most often.

To create a scenario manually, you must first access the WorkGroup toolbar (shown here) by opening the **View** menu and selecting **WorkGroup** from the **Toolbars** submenu. You can drag it to a side of the screen if necessary.

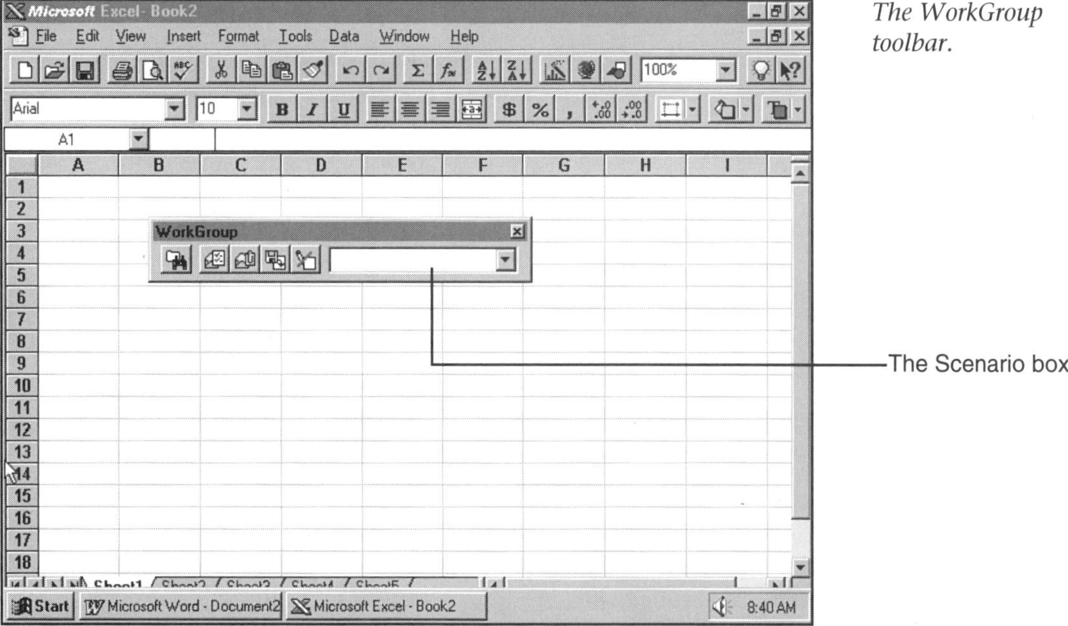

The WorkGroup toolbar.

Enter the values in the cells you want to use in your scenario. Then select those variable cells—up to 32 of them—for inclusion in the scenario. To select non-adjacent cells, hold down the **Ctrl** key while you click on the cells. When you have selected all of the cells whose values can change, click in the Scenario box on the toolbar. Then enter a name for your scenario and press **Enter**. The Scenario Manager saves your scenario.

To recall a scenario, just click on the Scenario box down arrow and choose from the list of scenarios.

That's it! Now you've mastered Excel!

The Least You Need to Know

- Use the Goal Seek feature to solve simple problems involving only one variable.
- Use Solver when you have more than one variable to change or when you want to set other limits on cell modifications.
- You can save your Solver scenarios with Scenario Manager so you can retrieve them at a later time.
- Each scenario can have as many as 32 different cell changes.

Part 5
Stuff at the Back of the Book

This section contains the usual back-of-the-book appendix-type information. You know, stuff like technical support, reference guides, and a glossary.

Please note that this book read backwards provides absolutely no clues as to the whereabouts of Paul McCartney.

Installation and Technical Support

To install Microsoft Excel for Windows 95, you need to have the following on your computer:

- Windows 95 or Windows NT version 3.51
- At least 20MB of available hard disk space

Installation from CD

To install Excel from a CD-ROM, follow these steps:

1. Insert the CD in your CD-ROM drive. Close the door.
2. Click on the Windows 95 **Start** button and select **Run** from the Start menu. The Run dialog box will appear. The Open option in the Run dialog box should automatically display the correct information for running Setup—disk, folder (if applicable) and program name. If this information is correct click on the **OK** button. If the information is not correct or if you are uncertain, click on the Browse button. Select the drive letter assigned to your CD-ROM (usually, D:\) and search for the Setup program for Excel (or Microsoft Office, if you're running Excel from Office). After you click on the **Setup** program Windows will return to the first Run dialog box. Click on the **OK** button.
3. The Excel (or Office) installation routine begins. Select the **Typical** installation to have Excel perform the installation automatically.

Installation from Floppy Disk

To install Microsoft Excel for Windows 95 from floppy disks, follow these steps:

1. Insert Disk #1 in your drive.
2. Click on the Windows 95 **Start** button and select **Run** from the Start menu. The Run dialog box will appear. The Open option in the Run dialog box should contain the correct information for running setup—disk, folder (if applicable) and program name. If this information is correct, click on the **OK** button. If the information is not correct or if you are uncertain, click on the Browse button. Select the drive that you inserted floppy disk #1 into (usually, A:\) and select the **Setup** program. Windows will return to the first Run dialog box. Click on the **OK** button.
3. The Excel (or Office) installation routine begins. Select the **Typical** installation to have Excel perform the installation automatically.

Technical Support

The Microsoft Corporation provides standard technical support between the hours of 6:00 am and 6:00 pm Pacific Time. The number to call for technical support is (206) 635-7110.

This is not a toll-free call, so prepare yourself before you call. You should have these things handy before you start running up telephone charges:

- Software version numbers
- Operating system version numbers
- Hardware types and model numbers
- The exact text of any on-screen messages
- Prepare to describe what you were attempting to do when the problem occurred

Online Support

Online support is available for Microsoft products from the major commercial online providers. Contact your online provider for details.

Appendix B

The Function Guide

Here, in living color, is a complete reference guide to every Excel function in the known universe.

Excel's Functions in All Their Glory

Function Name	Syntax	Task
ABS	ABS(number)	List absolute value of a number
ACCRINT	ACCRINT(issue, first_interest, settlement, rate, par, frequency, basis)	List accrued interest for a security that pays periodic interest
ACCRINTM	ACCRINTM(issue, maturity, rate, par, basis)	List accrued interest for a security that pays interest at maturity
ACOS	ACOS(number)	List arccosine of a number
ACOSH	ACOSH(number)	List inverse hyperbolic cosine of a number
ADDRESS	ADDRESS(row_num, cell in a column_num, abs_num, a1, sheet_text)	List a reference as text to a single worksheet

continues

Excel's Functions in All Their Glory Continued

Function Name	Syntax	Task
AMORDEGRC	AMORDEGRC(cost, rate, date_purchased, first_period, salvage, period, basis)	List depreciation for each accounting period
AMORLINC	AMORLINC(cost, date_purchased, first_period, salvage, period, rate, basis)	List depreciation for each accounting period
AND	AND(logical1, logical2, ...)	List TRUE if all arguments are TRUE
AREAS	AREAS(reference)	List number of areas in a reference
ASIN	ASIN(number)	List arcsine of a number
ASINH	ASINH(number)	List inverse hyperbolic sine of a number
ATAN	ATAN(number)	List arctangent of a number
ATAN2	ATAN2(x_num, y_num)	List arctangent from x- and y-coordinates
ATANH	ATANH(number)	List inverse hyperbolic tangent of a number
AVEDEV	AVEDEV(number1, number2, ...)	List average of absolute deviations of data points from their mean
AVERAGE	AVERAGE(number1, number2, ...)	List average of all arguments
BESSELI	BESSELI(x, n)	List modified Bessel function In(x)
BESSELJ	BESSELJ(x, n)	List Bessel function Jn(x)
BESSELK	BESSELK(x, n)	List modified Bessel function Kn(x)
BESSELY	BESSELY(x, n)	List Bessel function Yn(x)
BETADIST	BETADIST(x, alpha, beta, A, B)	List cumulative beta probability density function
BETAINV	BETAINV(probability, alpha, beta, A, B)	List inverse of cumulative beta probability density function

Function Name	Syntax	Task
BIN2DEC	BIN2DEC(number)	Change a binary number to decimal
BIN2HEX	BIN2HEX(number, places)	Change a binary number to hexadecimal
BIN2OCT	BIN2OCT(number, places)	Change a binary number to octal
BINOMDIST	BINOMDIST(number_s, trials, probability_s, cumulative)	List individual term binomial distribution probability
CALL	CALL(register_id, argument1, ...)	Call a procedure in a dynamic link library or code resource
CEILING	CEILING(number, significance)	Round a number to nearest integer or to nearest multiple of significance
CELL	CELL(info_type, reference)	List information about formatting, location, or contents of a cell
CHAR	CHAR(number)	List character specified by code number
CHIDIST	CHIDIST(x, degrees_freedom)	List one-tailed probability of chi-squared distribution
CHIINV	CHIINV(probability, degrees_freedom)	List inverse of one-tailed probability of chi-squared distribution
CHITEST	CHITEST(actual_range, expected_range)	List test for independence
CHOOSE	CHOOSE(index_num, value1, value2, 1/4)	Choose a value from a list of values
CLEAN	CLEAN(text)	Remove all nonprintable characters from text
CODE	CODE(text)	List a numeric code for first character in a text string
COLUMN	COLUMN(reference)	List column number of a reference
COLUMNS	COLUMNS(array)	List number of columns in a reference

continues

Excel's Functions in All Their Glory Continued

Function Name	Syntax	Task
COMBIN	COMBIN(number, number_chosen)	List number of combinations for a given number of objects
COMPLEX	COMPLEX(real_num, i_num, suffix)	Change real and imaginary coefficients into a complex number
CONCATENATE	CONCATENATE (text1, text2, ...)	Join several text items into one text item
CONFIDENCE	CONFIDENCE(alpha, standard_dev, size)	List confidence interval for a population mean
CONVERT	CONVERT(number, from_unit, to_unit)	Change a number from one measurement system to another
CORREL	CORREL(array1, array2)	List correlation coefficient between two data sets
COS	COS(number)	List cosine of a number
COSH	COSH(number)	List hyperbolic cosine of a number
COUNT	COUNT(value1, value2, ...)	Count how many numbers are in list of arguments
COUNTA	COUNTA(value1, value2, ...)	Count how many non-blank values are in list of arguments
COUNTBLANK	COUNTBLANK(range)	Count number of blank cells within a range
COUNTIF	COUNTIF(range, criteria)	Count number of non-blank cells within a range that meet given criteria
COUPDAYBS	COUPDAYBS(settlement, maturity, frequency, basis)	List number of days from beginning of coupon period to settlement date
COUPDAYS	COUPDAYSNC(settlement, maturity, frequency, basis)	List number of days in coupon period that contains settlement date
COUPDAYSNC	COUPDAYSNC(settlement, maturity, frequency, basis)	List number of days from settlement date to next coupon date

Function Name	Syntax	Task
COUPNCD	COUPNCD(settlement, maturity, frequency, basis)	List next coupon date after settlement date
COUPNUM	COUPNUM(settlement, maturity, frequency, basis)	List number of coupons payable between settlement date and maturity date
COUPPCD	COUPPCD(settlement, maturity, frequency, basis)	List previous coupon date before settlement date
COVAR	COVAR(array1, array2)	List covariance, average of products of paired deviations
CRITBINOM	CRITBINOM(trials, probability_s, alpha)	List smallest value for which cumulative binomial distribution is less than or equal to a criterion value
CUMIPMT	CUMIPMT(rate, nper, pv, start_period, end_period, type)	List cumulative interest paid between two periods
CUMPRINC	CUMPRINC(rate, nper, pv, start_period, end_period, type)	List cumulative principal paid on a loan between two periods
DATE	DATE(year, month, day)	List serial number of a particular date
DATEVALUE	DATEVALUE(date_text)	Change a date in form of text to a serial number
DAVERAGE	DAVERAGE(database, field, criteria)	List average of selected database entries
DAY	DAY(serial_number)	Change a serial number to a day of month
DAYS360	DAYS360(start_date, end_date, method)	Calculate number of days between two dates based on a 360-day year
DB	DB(cost, salvage, life, period, month)	List depreciation of an asset for a specified period using fixed-declining balance method
DCOUNT	DCOUNT(database, field, criteria)	Count cells containing numbers from a specified database and criteria

continues

Excel's Functions in All Their Glory Continued

Function Name	Syntax	Task
DCOUNTA	DCOUNTA(database, field, criteria)	Count nonblank cells from a specified database and criteria
DDB	DDB(cost, salvage, life, period, factor)	List depreciation of an asset for a specified period using double-declining balance method or some other method you specify
DEC2BIN	DEC2BIN(number, places)	Change a decimal number to binary
DEC2HEX	DEC2HEX(number, places)	Change a decimal number to hexadecimal
DEC2OCT	DEC2OCT(number, places)	Change a decimal number to octal
DEGREES	DEGREES(angle)	Change radians to degrees
DELTA	DELTA(number1, number2)	Test whether two values are equal
DEVSQ	DEVSQ(number1, number2, ...)	List sum of squares of deviations
DGET	DGET(database, field, criteria)	Extract from a database a single record that matches specified criteria
DISC	DISC(settlement, maturity, pr, redemption, basis)	List discount rate for a security
DMAX	DMAX(database, field, criteria)	List maximum value from selected database entries
DMIN	DMIN(database, field, criteria)	List minimum value from selected database entries
DOLLAR	DOLLAR(number, decimals)	Change a number to text, using currency format
DOLLARDE	DOLLARDE(fractional_dollar, fraction)	Change a dollar price expressed as a fraction into a dollar price expressed as a decimal number
DOLLARFR	DOLLARFR(decimal_dollar, fraction)	Change a dollar price expressed as a decimal number into a dollar price expressed as a fraction

Function Name	Syntax	Task
DPRODUCT	DPRODUCT(database, field, criteria)	Multiply values in a particular field of records that match criteria in a database
DSTDEV	DSTDEVP(database, field, criteria)	Estimate standard deviation based on a sample of selected database entries
DSTDEVP	DSTDEVP(database, field, criteria)	Calculate standard deviation based on entire population of selected database entries
DSUM	DSUM(database,field,criteria)	Sum numbers in field column of records in database that match criteria
DURATION	DURATION(settlement, maturity, coupon, yld, frequency, basis)	List annual duration of a security with periodic interest payments`
DVAR	DVAR(database, field, criteria)	Estimate variance based on a sample from selected database entries
DVARP	DVARP(database, field, criteria)	Calculate variance based on entire population of selected database entries
EDATE	EDATE(start_date, months)	List serial number of date that is indicated number of months before or after start date
EFFECT	EFFECT(nominal_rate, npery)	List effective annual interest rate
EOMONTH	EOMONTH(start_date, months)	List serial number of last day of month before or after a specified number of months
ERF	ERF(lower_limit, upper_limit)	List error function
ERFC	ERFC(x)	List complementary error function
ERROR.TYPE	ERROR.TYPE(error_val)	List a number corresponding to an error type
EVEN	EVEN(number)	Round a number up to nearest even integer

continues

Excel's Functions in All Their Glory Continued

Function Name	Syntax	Task
EXACT	EXACT(text1, text2)	Check to see if two text values are identical
EXP	EXP(number)	List e raised to power of a given number
EXPONDIST	EXPONDIST(x, lambda, cumulative)	List exponential distribution
FACT	FACT(number)	List factorial of a number
FACTDOUBLE	FACTDOUBLE(number)	List double factorial of a number
FALSE	FALSE( )	List logical value FALSE
FDIST	FDIST(x, degrees_freedom1, degrees_freedom2)	List F probability distribution
FIND	FIND(find_text, within_text, start_num)	Search one text value within another (case-sensitive)
FINV	FINV(probability, degrees_freedom1, degrees_freedom2)	List inverse of F probability distribution
FISHER	FISHER(x)	List Fisher transformation
FISHERINV	FISHERINV(y)	List inverse of Fisher transformation
FIXED	FIXED(number, decimals, no_commas)	Format a number as text with a fixed number of decimals
FLOOR	FLOOR(number, significance)	Round a number down, toward zero
FORECAST	FORECAST(x, known_y's, known_x's)	List a value along a linear trend
FREQUENCY	FREQUENCY(data_array, bins_array)	List a frequency distribution as a vertical array
FTEST	FTEST(array1, array2)	List result of an F-test
FV	FV(rate, nper, pmt, pv, type)	List future value of an investment
FVSCHEDULE	FVSCHEDULE(principal, schedule)	List future value of an initial principal after applying a series of compound interest rates

Function Name	Syntax	Task
GAMMADIST	GAMMADIST(x, alpha, beta, cumulative)	List gamma distribution
GAMMAINV	GAMMAINV(probability, alpha, beta)	List inverse of gamma cumulative distribution
GAMMALN	GAMMALN(x)	List natural logarithm of gamma function, G(x)
GCD	GCD(number1, number2, ...)	List greatest common divisor
GEOMEAN	GEOMEAN(number1, number2, ...)	List geometric mean
GESTEP	GESTEP(number, step)	Test whether a number is greater than a threshold value
GROWTH	GROWTH(known_y's, known_x's, new_x's, const)	List values along an exponential trend
HARMEAN	HARMEAN(number1, number2, ...)	List harmonic mean
HEX2BIN	HEX2BIN(number, places)	Change a hexadecimal number to binary
HEX2DEC	HEX2DEC(number)	Change a hexadecimal number to decimal
HEX2OCT	HEX2OCT(number, places)	Change a hexadecimal number to octal
HLOOKUP	HLOOKUP(lookup_value, table_array, row_index_num, range_lookup)	Look in top row of an array and return value of indicated cell
HOUR	HOUR(serial_number)	Change a serial number to an hour
HYPGEOMDIST	HYPGEOMDIST(sample_s, number_sample, population_s, number_population)	List hypergeometric distribution
IF	IF(logical_test, value_if_true, value_if_false)	Specify a logical test to perform
IMABS	IMABS(inumber)	List absolute value (modulus) of a complex number

continues

Excel's Functions in All Their Glory Continued

Function Name	Syntax	Task
IMAGINARY	IMAGINARY(inumber)	List imaginary coefficient of a complex number
IMARGUMENT	IMARGUMENT(inumber)	List argument theta, an angle expressed in radians
IMCONJUGATE	IMCONJUGATE(inumber)	List complex conjugate of a complex number
IMCOS	IMCOS(inumber)	List cosine of a complex number
IMDIV	IMDIV(inumber1, inumber2)	List quotient of two complex numbers
IMEXP	IMEXP(inumber)	List exponential of a complex number
IMLN	IMLN(inumber)	List natural logarithm of a complex number
IMLOG10	IMLOG10(inumber)	List base-10 logarithm of a complex number
IMLOG2	IMLOG2(inumber)	List base-2 logarithm of a complex number
IMPOWER	IMPOWER(inumber, number)	List a complex number raised to an integer power
IMPRODUCT	IMPRODUCT(inumber1, inumber2, ...)	List product of two to 29 complex numbers
IMREAL	IMREAL(inumber)	List real coefficient of a complex number
IMSIN	IMSIN(inumber)	List sine of a complex number
IMSQRT	IMSQRT(inumber)	List square root of a complex number
IMSUB	IMSUB(inumber1, inumber2)	List difference of two complex numbers
IMSUM	IMSUM(inumber1, inumber2, ...)	List sum of complex numbers
INDEX	INDEX(array, row_num, column_num) or INDEX (reference, row_num, column_num, area_num)	Use an index to choose a value from a reference or array

Function Name	Syntax	Task
INDIRECT	INDIRECT(ref_text, a1)	List a reference indicated by a text value
INFO	INFO(type_text)	List information about current operating environment
INT	INT(number)	Round a number down to nearest integer
INTERCEPT	INTERCEPT(known_y's, known_x's)	List intercept of linear regression line
INTRATE	INTRATE(settlement, maturity, investment, redemption, basis)	List interest rate for a fully invested security
IPMT	IPMT(rate, per, nper, pv, fv, type)	List interest payment for an investment for a given period
IRR	IRR(values, guess)	List internal rate of return for a series of cash flows
ISBLANK	ISBLANK(value)	List TRUE if value is blank
ISERR	ISERR(value)	List TRUE if value is any error value except #N/A
ISERROR	ISERROR(value)	List TRUE if value is any error value
ISEVEN	ISEVEN(value)	List TRUE if number is even
ISLOGICAL	ISLOGICAL(value)	List TRUE if value is a logical value
ISNA	ISNA(value)	List TRUE if value is #N/A error value
ISNONTEXT	ISNONTEXT(value)	List TRUE if value is not text
ISNUMBER	ISNUMBER(value)	List TRUE if value is a number
ISODD	ISODD(value)	List TRUE if number is odd
ISREF	ISREF(value)	List TRUE if value is a reference
ISTEXT	ISTEXT(value)	List TRUE if value is text
KURT	KURT(number1, number2, ...)	List kurtosis of a data set
LARGE	LARGE(array, k)	List k-th largest value in a data set

continues

Excel's Functions in All Their Glory Continued

Function Name	Syntax	Task
LCM	LCM(number1, number2, ...)	List least common multiple
LEFT	LEFT(text, num_chars)	List leftmost characters from a text value
LEN	LEN(text)	List number of characters in a text string
LINEST	LINEST(known_y's, known_x's, const, stats)	List parameters of a linear trend
LN	LN(number)	List natural logarithm of a number
LOG	LOG(number, base)	List logarithm of a number to a specified base
LOG10	LOG10(number)	List base-10 logarithm of a number
LOGEST	LOGEST(known_y's, known_x's, const, stats)	List parameters of an exponential trend
LOGINV	LOGINV(probability, mean, standard_dev)	List inverse of lognormal distribution
LOGNORMDIST	LOGNORMDIST(x, mean, standard_dev)	List cumulative lognormal distribution
LOOKUP	LOOKUP(lookup_value, lookup_vector, result_vector) or LOOKUP(lookup_value, array)	Look up values in a vector or array
LOWER	LOWER(text)	Change text to lowercase
MATCH	MATCH(lookup_value, lookup_array, match_type)	Look up values in a reference or array
MAX	MAX(number1, number2, ...)	List maximum value in a list of arguments
MDETERM	MDETERM(array)	List matrix determinant of an array
MDURATION	MDURATION(settlement, maturity, coupon, yld, frequency, basis)	List Macauley modified duration for a security with an assumed par value of $100
MEDIAN	MEDIAN(number1, number2, ...)	List median of given numbers

Function Name	Syntax	Task
MID	MID(text, start_num, num_chars)	List a specific number of characters from a text string starting at position you specify
MIN	MIN(number1, number2, ...)	List minimum value in a list of arguments
MINUTE	MINUTE(serial_number)	Change a serial number to a minute
MINVERSE	MINVERSE(array)	List matrix inverse of an array
MIRR	MIRR(values, finance_rate, reinvest_rate)	List internal rate of return where positive and negative cash flows are financed at different rates
MMULT	MMULT(array1, array2)	List matrix product of two arrays
MOD	MOD(number, divisor)	List remainder from division
MODE	MODE(number1, number2, ...)	List most common value in a data set
MONTH	MONTH(serial_number)	Change a serial number to a month
MROUND	MROUND(number, multiple)	List a number rounded to desired multiple
MULTINOMIAL	MULTINOMIAL(number1, number2, ...)	List multinomial of a set of numbers
N	N(value)	List a value converted to a number
NA	NA( )	List error value #N/A
NEGBINOM-DIST	NEGBINOMDIST(number_f, number_s, probability_s)	List negative binomial distribution
NETWORK-DAYS	NETWORKDAYS(start_date, end_date, holidays)	List number of whole workdays between two dates
NOMINAL	NOMINAL(effect_rate, npery)	List annual nominal interest rate
NORMDIST	NORMDIST(x, mean, standard_dev, cumulative)	List normal cumulative distribution
NORMINV	NORMINV(probability, mean, standard_dev)	List inverse of normal cumulative distribution

continues

Excel's Functions in All Their Glory Continued

Function Name	Syntax	Task
NORMSDIST	NORMSDIST(z)	List standard normal cumulative distribution
NORMSINV	NORMSINV(probability)	List inverse of standard normal cumulative distribution
NOT	NOT(logical)	Reverse logic of argument
NOW	NOW( )	List serial number of current date and time
NPER	NPER(rate, pmt, pv, fv, type)	List number of periods for an investment
NPV	NPV(rate, value1, value2, ...)	List net present value of an investment based on a series of periodic cash flows and a discount rate
OCT2BIN	OCT2BIN(number, places)	Change an octal number to binary
OCT2DEC	OCT2DEC(number)	Change an octal number to decimal
OCT2HEX	OCT2HEX(number, places)	Change an octal number to hexadecimal
ODD	ODD(number)	Round a number up to nearest odd integer
ODDFPRICE	ODDFPRICE(settlement, maturity, issue, first_coupon, rate, yld, redemption, frequency, basis)	List price per $100 face value of a security with an odd first period
ODDFYIELD	ODDFYIELD(settlement, maturity, issue, first_coupon, rate, pr, redemption, frequency, basis)	List yield of a security with an odd first period
ODDLPRICE	ODDLPRICE(settlement, maturity, last_interest, rate, yld, redemption, frequency, basis)	List price per $100 face value of a security with an odd last period
ODDLYIELD	ODDLYIELD(settlement, maturity, last_interest, rate, pr, redemption, frequency, basis)	List yield of a security with an odd last period

Function Name	Syntax	Task
OFFSET	OFFSET(reference, rows, cols, height, width)	List a reference offset from a given reference
OR	OR(logical1, logical2, ...)	List TRUE if any argument is TRUE
PEARSON	PEARSON(array1, array2)	List Pearson product moment correlation coefficient
PERCENTILE	PERCENTILE(array, k)	List k-th percentile of values in a range
PERCENTRANK	PERCENTRANK(array, x, significance)	List percentage rank of a value in a data set
PERMUT	PERMUT(number, number_chosen)	List number of permutations for a given number of objects
PI	PI( )	List value of Pi (3.14159)
PMT	PMT(rate, nper, pv, fv, type)	List periodic payment for an annuity
POISSON	POISSON(x, mean, cumulative)	List Poisson distribution
POWER	POWER(number, power)	List result of a number raised to a power
PPMT	PPMT(rate, per, nper, pv, fv, type)	List payment on principal for an investment for a given period
PRICE	PRICE(settlement, maturity, rate, yld, redemption, frequency, basis)	List price per $100 face value of a security that pays periodic interest
PRICEDISC	PRICEDISC(settlement, maturity, discount, redemption, basis)	List price per $100 face value of a discounted security
PRICEMAT	PRICEMAT(settlement, maturity, issue, rate, yld, basis)	List price per $100 face value of a security that pays interest at maturity
PROB	PROB(x_range, prob_range, lower_limit, upper_limit)	List probability that values in a range are between two limits
PRODUCT	PRODUCT(number1, number2, ...)	Multiply all arguments

continues

Excel's Functions in All Their Glory Continued

Function Name	Syntax	Task
PROPER	PROPER(text)	Capitalize first letter in each word of a text value
PV	PV(rate, nper, pmt, fv, type)	List present value of an investment
QUARTILE	QUARTILE(array, quart)	List quartile of a data set
QUOTIENT	QUOTIENT(numerator, denominator)	List integer portion of a division
RADIANS	RADIANS(angle)	Change degrees to radians
RAND	RAND( )	List a random number between 0 and 1
RAND-BETWEEN	RANDBETWEEN(bottom, top)	List a random number between numbers you specify
RANK	RANK(number, ref, order)	List rank of a number in a list of numbers
RATE	RATE(nper, pmt, pv, fv, type, guess)	List interest rate per period of an annuity
RECEIVED	RECEIVED(settlement, maturity, investment, discount, basis)	List amount received at maturity for a fully invested security
REGISTER.ID	REGISTER.ID(module_text, procedure, type_text)	List register ID of specified dynamic link library (DLL) or code resource that has been previously registered
REPLACE	REPLACE(old_text, start_num, num_chars, new_text)	Replaces characters within text
REPT	REPT(text, number_times)	Repeat text a given number of times
RIGHT	RIGHT(text, num_chars)	List rightmost characters from a text value
ROMAN	ROMAN(number, form)	Change an Arabic numeral to Roman, as text
ROUND	ROUND(number, num_digits)	Round a number to a specified number of digits
ROUNDDOWN	ROUNDDOWN(number, num_digits)	Round a number down, toward zero

Function Name	Syntax	Task
ROUNDUP	ROUNDUP(number, num_digits)	Round a number up, away from zero
ROW	ROW(reference)	List row number of a reference
ROWS	ROWS(array)	List number of rows in a reference
RSQ	RSQ(known_y's, known_x's)	List square of Pearson product moment correlation coefficient
SEARCH	SEARCH(find_text, within_text, start_num)	Search one text value within another (not case-sensitive)
SECOND	SECOND(serial_number)	Change a serial number to a second
SERIESSUM	SERIESSUM(x, n, m, coefficients)	List sum of a power series based on formula
SIGN	SIGN(number)	List sign of a number
SIN	SIN(number)	List sine of given angle
SINH	SINH(number)	List hyperbolic sine of a number
SKEW	SKEW(number1, number2, ...)	List skewness of a distribution
SLN	SLN(cost, salvage, life)	List straight-line depreciation of an asset for one period
SLOPE	SLOPE(known_y's, known_x's)	List slope of linear regression line
SMALL	SMALL(array, k)	List k-th smallest value in a data set
SQL.REQUEST	SQL.REQUEST (connection_string, output_ref, driver_prompt, query_text, col_names_logical)	Connect to external data source and run query from worksheet
SQLREQUEST	SQL.REQUEST (connection_string, output_ref, driver_prompt, query_text, col_names_logical)	Connect with an external data source and run a query from a worksheet, then return result as an array without need for macro programming
SQRT	SQRT(number)	List a positive square root

continues

Excel's Functions in All Their Glory Continued

Function Name	Syntax	Task
SQRTPI	SQRTPI(number)	List square root of (number * PI)
STANDARDIZE	STANDARDIZE(x, mean, standard_dev)	List a normalized value
STDEV	STDEV(number1,number2,...)	Estimate standard deviation based on a sample
STDEVP	STDEVP(number1,number2,...)	Calculate standard deviation based on entire population
STEYX	STEYX(known_y's, known_x's)	List standard error of predicted y-value for each x in regression
SUBSTITUTE	SUBSTITUTE(text, old_text, new_text, instance_num)	Substitutes new text for old text in a text string
SUBTOTAL	SUBTOTAL(function_num, ref)	List a subtotal in a list or database
SUM	SUM(number1, number2, ...)	Sum all arguments
SUMIF	SUMIF(range, criteria, sum_range)	Sum cells specified by a given criteria
SUMPRODUCT	SUMPRODUCT(array1, array2, array3, ...)	List sum of products of corresponding array components
SUMSQ	SUMSQ(number1, number2, ...)	List sum of squares of arguments
SUMX2MY2	SUMX2MY2(array_x, array_y)	List sum of difference of squares of corresponding values in two arrays
SUMX2PY2	SUMX2PY2(array_x, array_y)	List sum of sum of squares of corresponding values in two arrays
SUMXMY2	SUMXMY2(array_x, array_y)	List sum of squares of differences of corresponding values in two arrays
SYD	SYD(cost, salvage, life, per)	List sum-of-years' digits depreciation of an asset for a specified period
T	T(value)	Change arguments to text
TAN	TAN(number)	List tangent of a given angle
TANH	TANH(number)	List hyperbolic tangent of a number

Function Name	Syntax	Task
TBILLEQ	TBILLEQ(settlement, maturity, discount)	List bond-equivalent yield for a Treasury bill
TBILLPRICE	TBILLPRICE(settlement, maturity, discount)	List price per $100 face value for a Treasury bill
TBILLYIELD	TBILLYIELD(settlement, maturity, pr)	List yield for a Treasury bill
TDIST	TDIST(x, degrees_freedom, tails)	List Student's t-distribution
TEXT	TEXT(value, format_text)	Format a number and convert it to text
TIME	TIME(hour, minute, second)	List serial number of a particular time
TIMEVALUE	TIMEVALUE(time_text)	Change a time in form of text to a serial number
TINV	TINV(probability, degrees_freedom)	List inverse of Student's t-distribution
TODAY	TODAY( )	List serial number of today's date
TRANSPOSE	TRANSPOSE(array)	List transpose of an array
TREND	TREND(known_y's, known_x's, new_x's, const)	List values along a linear trend
TRIM	TRIM(text)	Remove spaces from text
TRIMMEAN	TRIMMEAN(array, percent)	List mean of interior of a data set
TRUE	TRUE( )	List logical value TRUE
TRUNC	TRUNC(number, num_digits)	Truncate a number to an integer
TTEST	TTEST(array1, array2, tails, type)	List probability associated with a Student's t-Test
TYPE	TYPE(value)	List a number indicating data type of a value
UPPER	UPPER(text)	Change text to uppercase
VALUE	VALUE(text)	Change a text argument to a number
VAR	VAR(number1, number2, ...)	Estimate variance based on a sample

continues

Excel's Functions in All Their Glory Continued

Function Name	Syntax	Task
VARP	VARP(number1, number2, ...)	Calculate variance based on entire population
VDB	VDB(cost, salvage, life, start_period, end_period, factor, no_switch)	List depreciation of an asset for a specified or partial period using a declining balance method
VLOOKUP	VLOOKUP(lookup_value, table_array, col_index_num, range_lookup)	Look in first column of an array and move across row to return value of a cell
WEEKDAY	WEEKDAY(serial_number, return_type)	Change a serial number to a day of week
WEIBULL	WEIBULL(x, alpha, beta, cumulative)	List Weibull distribution
WORKDAY	WORKDAY(start_date, days, holidays)	List serial number of date before or after a specified number of workdays
XIRR	XIRR(values, dates, guess)	List internal rate of return for a schedule of cash flows that is not necessarily periodic
XNPV	XNPV(rate, values, dates)	List net present value for a schedule of cash flows that is not necessarily periodic
YEAR	YEAR(serial_number)	Change a serial number to a year
YEARFRAC	YEARFRAC(start_date, end_date, basis)	List year fraction representing number of whole days between start_date and end_date
YIELD	YIELD(settlement, maturity, rate, pr, redemption, frequency, basis)	List yield on a security that pays periodic interest
YIELDDISC	YIELDDISC(settlement, maturity, pr,redemption, basis)	List annual yield for a discounted security such as a treasury bill
YIELDMAT	YIELDMAT(settlement, maturity, issue, rate, pr, basis)	List annual yield of a security that pays interest at maturity
ZTEST	ZTEST(array, x, sigma)	List two-tailed P-value of a z-test

Excel Shortcut Keys

Shortcut Keys (By Key Combination and Feature)

Key Combination	Result
F1	Access Help system
F2	Activate a cell
F3	Issue Paste command
F4	Repeat most recent action
F5	Issue Go To command
F6	Move to next pane
F7	Start spelling checker
F8	Extend a selection
F9	Calculate all formulas
F10	Move cursor to Main Menu bar
F11	Create automatic chart
F12	Open Save As dialog box or save named file
Shift+Ins	Insert (Paste) item that was copied or cut
Shift+Home	Select cells from active cell to left edge of current row

continues

Shortcut Keys (By Key Combination and Feature) Continued

Key Combination	Result
Shift+PgUp	Select cells from active cell to top of current column
Shift+Delete	Move selected cells
Shift+PgDn	Select cells from active cell down one screen page
Shift+F1	Get Help on a screen item
Shift+F2	Edit a cell
Shift+F3	Start Function Wizard
Shift+F4	Repeat most recent Find or Go To
Shift+F5	Issue Find command
Shift+F8	Select multiple cells
Shift+F9	Calculate active sheet
Shift+F10	Open shortcut menu related to active cell or object
Shift+F12	Open Save As dialog box or save named file
Ctrl+B	Bold selected text
Ctrl+C	Copy selected item
Ctrl+D	AutoFill down
Ctrl+F	Open Find dialog box
Ctrl+G	Open Go To dialog box
Ctrl+H	Open Replace (and Find) dialog box
Ctrl+I	Italicize selected text
Ctrl+N	Open New worksheet dialog box
Ctrl+O	Open Open worksheet dialog box
Ctrl+P	Open Print dialog box
Ctrl+R	AutoFill right
Ctrl+S	Open Save As dialog box or save existing file
Ctrl+U	Underline selected text
Ctrl+V	Insert (paste) item that was copied or cut
Ctrl+W	Close worksheet
Ctrl+X	Cut selected item
Ctrl+Y	Repeat AutoFill

Key Combination	Result
Ctrl+1	Open Format Cells dialog box
Ctrl+2	Toggle bold on and off
Ctrl+3	Toggle italic on and off
Ctrl+4	Toggle underline on and off
Ctrl+5	Toggle strikethrough on and off
Ctrl+7	Toggle Standard toolbar display on and off
Ctrl+8	Display Outline symbols or create outline
Ctrl+0	Hide Columns
Ctrl+–	Open Delete dialog box to delete rows or columns
Ctrl+' (apostrophe)	Copy information from cell above active cell
Ctrl+' (single open quotation mark)	Resize Columns
Ctrl+;	Show serial number corresponding to current date
Ctrl+Ins	Copy selected item
Ctrl+Home	Move cursor to cell A1
Ctrl+PgUp	Move forward through worksheets
Ctrl+Del	Move active cell to another location
Ctrl+End	Move cursor to end of sheet
Ctrl+PgDn	Move backward through worksheets
Ctrl+up arrow	Move cursor up column, skipping blank cells
Ctrl+down arrow	Move cursor down column, skipping blank cells
Ctrl+left arrow	Move cursor to left, skipping blank cells
Ctrl+right arrow	Move cursor to right, skipping blank cells
Ctrl+F2	Open Info window
Ctrl+F3	Define name
Ctrl+F4	Close window
Ctrl+F5	Restore window
Ctrl+F9	Minimize window
Ctrl+F10	Maximize window

continues

Shortcut Keys (By Key Combination and Feature) Continued

Key Combination	Result
Ctrl+F11	Start Macro sheet
Ctrl+F12	Open Open worksheet dialog box
Alt+D	Open Data menu
Alt+E	Open Edit menu
Alt+F	Open File menu
Alt+H	Open Help menu
Alt+I	Open Insert menu
Alt+O	Open Format menu
Alt+T	Open Tools menu
Alt+V	Open View menu
Alt+W	Open Windows menu
Alt+–	Open File menu
Alt+=	Sum the cells immediately above
Alt+\	Move cursor to left side of current row
Alt+;	Make cells visible
Alt+down arrow	Open AutoComplete dialog box
Alt+PgDn	Move one page to the right
Alt+PgUp	Move one page to the left
Ctrl+Shift+F	Access Font list
Ctrl+Shift+P	Access Font Size list
Ctrl+Shift+2	Format cell as time
Ctrl+Shift+3	Format cell as date
Ctrl+Shift+4	Format cell as currency
Ctrl+Shift+5	Format cell as percentage
Ctrl+Shift+6	Format cell as scientific
Ctrl+Shift+7	Outline selected cells
Ctrl+Shift+8	Select block that includes all cells with data
Ctrl+Shift+'	Copy from above
Ctrl+Shift+;	Display serial number corresponding to current time

Key Combination	Result
Ctrl+Shift+=	Open Insert dialog box
Ctrl+Shift+–	Delete Line selection
Ctrl+Shift+down arrow	Select entire column
Ctrl+Shift+right arrow	Select an entire row
Ctrl+Shift+F3	Open Create Names dialog box
Ctrl+Shift+F4	Repeat Find
Ctrl+Shift+F12	Open Print dialog box

Shortcut Keys (By Feature and Key Combination)

Feature	Key Combination
Activate a cell	F2
AutoFill down	Ctrl+D
AutoFill right	Ctrl+R
Bold selected text	Ctrl+B
Calculate active sheet	Shift+F9
Calculate all formulas	F9
Call up Help on a screen item	Shift+F1
Close window	Ctrl+F4
Close worksheet	Ctrl+W
Copy from above	Ctrl+Shift+'
Copy information from cell above active cell	Ctrl+' (apostrophe)
Copy selected item	Ctrl+C or Ctrl+Ins
Create automatic chart	F11
Cut selected item	Ctrl+X
Define name	Ctrl+F3
Delete Line selection	Ctrl+Shift+–
Display Outline symbols or create outline	Ctrl+8

continues

Shortcut Keys (By Feature and Key Combination) Continued

Feature	Key Combination
Display serial number corresponding to current time	Ctrl+Shift+;
Edit a cell	Shift+F2
Extend a selection	F8
Find command	Shift+F5
Font list	Ctrl+Shift+F
Font size list	Ctrl+Shift+P
Format cell as currency	Ctrl+Shift+4
Format cell as date	Ctrl+Shift+3
Format cell as percentage	Ctrl+Shift+5
Format cell as scientific	Ctrl+Shift+6
Format cell as time	Ctrl+Shift+2
Go To command	F5
Help system	F1
Hide Columns	Ctrl+0
Insert (paste) item that was copied or cut	Shift+Ins
Insert (paste) item that was copied or cut	Ctrl+V
Italicize selected text	Ctrl+I
Make cells visible	Alt+;
Maximize window	Ctrl+F10
Minimize window	Ctrl+F9
Move active cell to another location	Ctrl+Del
Move backward through worksheets	Ctrl+PgDn
Move cursor down column, skipping blank cells	Ctrl+down arrow
Move cursor to cell A1	Ctrl+Home
Move cursor to end of sheet	Ctrl+End
Move cursor to left side of current row	Alt+\
Move cursor to left, skipping blank cells	Ctrl+left arrow

Feature	Key Combination
Move cursor to Main Menu bar	F10
Move cursor to right, skipping blank cells	Ctrl+right arrow
Move cursor up column, skipping blank cells	Ctrl+up arrow
Move forward through worksheets	Ctrl+PgUp
Move one page to the left	Alt+PgUp
Move one page to the right	Alt+PgDn
Move selected cells	Shift+Delete
Open AutoComplete dialog box	Alt+down arrow
Open Create Names dialog box	Ctrl+Shift+F3
Open Data menu	Alt+D
Open Delete dialog box to delete rows, columns	Ctrl+–
Open Edit menu	Alt+E
Open File menu	Alt+– or Alt+F
Open Find dialog box	Ctrl+F
Open Format Cells dialog box	Ctrl+1
Open Format menu	Alt+O
Open Go To dialog box	Ctrl+G
Open Help menu	Alt+H
Open Info window	Ctrl+F2
Open Insert dialog box	Ctrl+Shift+=
Open Insert menu	Alt+I
Open New worksheet dialog box	Ctrl+N
Open Open worksheet dialog box	Ctrl+F12 or Ctrl+O
Open Print dialog box	Ctrl+Shift+F12 or Ctrl+P
Open Replace (and Find) dialog box	Ctrl+H
Open Save As dialog box or save existing file	Ctrl+S
Open Save As dialog box or save named file	F12 or Shift+F12

continues

Shortcut Keys (By Feature and Key Combination) Continued

Feature	Key Combination
Open shortcut menu related to active cell or object	Shift+F10
Open Tools menu	Alt+T
Open View menu	Alt+V
Open Windows menu	Alt+W
Outline selected cells	Ctrl+Shift+7
Paste command	F3
Repeat AutoFill	Ctrl+Y
Repeat Find	Ctrl+Shift+F4
Repeat most recent action	F4
Repeat most recent Find or Go To	Shift+F4
Resize Columns	Ctrl+' (single open quotation mark)
Restore window	Ctrl+F5
Select an entire row	Ctrl+Shift+right arrow
Select block that includes all cells with data	Ctrl+Shift+8
Select cells from active cell down one screen page	Shift+PgDn
Select cells from active cell to left edge of current row	Shift+Home
Select cells from active cell to top of current column	Shift+PgUp
Select entire column	Ctrl+Shift+down arrow
Select multiple cells	Shift+F8
Show serial number corresponding to current date	Ctrl+;
Start Function Wizard	Shift+F3
Start Macro sheet	Ctrl+F11
Start spelling checker	F7
Sum the cells immediately above	Alt+=
Toggle bold on and off	Ctrl+2

Feature	Key Combination
Toggle italics on and off	Ctrl+3
Toggle Standard toolbar display on and off	Ctrl+7
Toggle strikethrough on and off	Ctrl+5
Toggle underline on and off	Ctrl+4
Underline selected text	Ctrl+U

Appendix D

Ten Great Ideas for Things to Do with Your Spreadsheet

1. The Expected: Create a workbook for your checkbook.

It's hard to say whether this is way cool or just a fad, but practically everyone who has ever owned a spreadsheet has done it at one time or another. Either way, it comes in awfully handy when tax time rolls around, and you want to track down all those charitable donations.

2. Track all income and all real expenses.

How many times have you tried to put together a budget, only to have it fall apart because of some unforeseen expenses? This has never happened to us personally, of course, because we're perfect (and because we've never had to deal with income).

Before you create your budget, track all your expenses and all your income for a few months. You'll have a clearer picture of where your money truly goes, and you can make real adjustments to a real budget. Who knows? Maybe a trip to EuroDisney looms in your not-too-distant future. (Hey, *somebody's* got to go!)

3. Volunteer to keep track of all the scores and handicaps for your golf league.

Here's one sure way to reserve yourself a spot at all league banquets and become unpopular at the same time. Eliminate the fudge factor and watch the veins pop out of the necks of the Arnold Palmer wannabes in your home town. Present nothing but the cold hard facts, but do so in warm, wonderful 3-D color charts.

4. Create a list of the greatest movies, books, or songs of all time.

There's no practical purpose here; it's just a diversion for when the numbers you're crunching threaten to crunch you. Ran off your 600th inventory page today? Switch to the other screen. We notice you've placed "Plan 9 from Outer Space" above "E.T." as the greatest movie ever made. Show that to your boss as proof you really do need a vacation.

5. Create your own tax forms; play the ultimate what-if game.

Recreate the infamous 1040 sheet on your screen. Thrill as it appears the tax man owes you a big refund. Feel the chills run down your spine as you anticipate spending your big refund on the dream vacation you've finally convinced your boss you need. Feel the sweat trickle down your forehead as several weeks later you realize you entered 40 in the Dependents box. Would they re-open Alcatraz just for you?

6. Buy low, sell high. Play the stock market game.

Track your stocks as you go. No cash? Play the what-if game here. Imagine you're investing real money, and see what would happen. One word of caution, however. Should your pretend money suddenly become worth pretend millions, you may end up having a pretend heart attack. This could result in a visit to a real doctor, who will then send you a real bill.

7. Make a cool chart tracking your weight and blood pressure.

Make a cool chart showing the progress you make in keeping your weight and blood pressure under control. Prove the nay-sayers wrong when they tell you you're fatter than you were six months ago. No you're not, and you've got the charts to prove it.

What was that? The chart's upside down? Sorry.

8. Create a list of Excel features you love and respect.

Display your favorite shortcut keys, functions, icon definitions. Keep it handy, where you can easily flip back and forth to it.

Yes, we've tried to cover all the bases with the tear-out card in the front of this book, but we can't possibly anticipate your every possible need. There are, after all, literally millions of you out there reading this book. (We can say millions because one of us comes from a very large family.)

9. Create a list of your children and make a colorful graph showing who's been naughty and who's been nice.

Be sure to hang this one up by the chimney with care. If you're intent on playing Scrooge, you should at least have the figures to back you up.

10. Take the time Excel is going to save you, grab up the kids, and go fishing.

In the beginning, the idea behind clever software was to free you from mundane tasks and let you follow more ethereal pursuits. Excel is a powerful package and should free up enough time for that fishing trip you promised the family.

Speak Like a Geek: The Complete Archive

A sure-fire way to sound good at cocktail parties in Redmond, Washington.

absolute reference A reference that doesn't change when you move or copy it. You make a reference absolute by preceding it with a dollar sign ($) as in C3.

active cell area The area of cells that will be affected by your commands or changes. A heavy border surrounds the cell or group of cells.

active cell marker The bold outline that shows where you are on the worksheet. It marks which cell will be affected by your commands or changes.

address The location of a cell or a group of cells. Takes the form B3, where B is the second column and 3 is the third row, or R3C2. Also called a reference.

argument The part of the equation that's not an operator. How's that for a bum definition? Okay, it can be a constant, function, name, cell reference, or value.

Auditing toolbar A group of buttons that simplifies the auditing process.

block Any group of cells. Usually a block gets a name because it's a place you go to again and again. A simple "group of cells" is too fleeting to get a name.

cell A block on the worksheet grid; the intersection of a column and row.

cell reference The address that describes the location of a cell.

click What you do with a mouse to an object. Click is that satisfying sound made by the button on your mouse when you press it. To click on a word or a cell or anything else, position the mouse pointer (which is usually shaped like an arrow) over the object of your affections and press the left mouse button. Sometimes you'll double-click, and sometimes you'll right-click (click on the right mouse button instead of the usual left mouse button).

Close button The third button (the X) in the upper right corner of your screen. It closes the application, but it won't put the toilet seat down.

constant A number or text entry that you type directly into the formula (as opposed to something like a cell reference, with which you tell Excel where to find its own numbers or text).

cursor The blinking line or square that shows where you are on the spreadsheet. Sometimes it happens to be in the same place as the active cell indicator, but that's only a coincidence.

data points Sales figures, profit numbers, expenses, staff size, market size, saturation percentages, or anything else that can be represented numerically on a chart or database.

database A list of data arranged in columns. It's basically any table to which you can assign a name.

database workbook The workbook that contains your database list; used in the AutoTemplate feature.

dependent Any cell that descends in whole or part from a specified cell; used in the Auditing feature.

dialog box A box Excel displays to ask you for more information; usually contains options related to the current function.

direct dependent Any cell that descends in whole or in part from the active cell; used in auditing.

direct precedent The first ancestral line of the formula in the active cell; used in auditing.

equation You learned this in the third grade, right? Something equals something else. Except that in Excel, you don't know what it equals until you hit the Enter key. You might also call it a formula.

external reference A reference to a cell or cells in another workbook; used in formulas.

factor One of the elements of a formula; a value, reference, name, operator, or function. Yeah, you're right. It's the same thing as an argument.

field In a typical Excel database list, each column of the list is a new field.

field buttons When you create a pivot table, the column labels in your data list become field buttons.

folder A section of your hard drive in which you store your files. (Folders were called subdirectories in older versions of Windows and in DOS.)

format The display characteristics you assign to an item, or the thing you put your feet on when you drive. We forget which.

formula A mathematical computation that involves multiple factors and results in a new value. Pretty much the same thing as an equation.

Formula bar The line just above the column headers; Excel displays the contents of the active cell here, so you can edit them.

frame The box that appears around an object or a cell when it's active.

function A prebuilt formula; functions are what give Excel all its power.

graphic A chart, graph, map, drawing, or picture.

graphic report A chart, graph, or table.

group You can subdivide categories of data and group the subdivisions together. Africa or Europe might be a category, for example, and all the separate countries in each location can be grouped together.

icon A picture symbol used by Windows to represent an application or task.

indirect dependent Any cell that descends in any way from a direct descendent of the active cell; used in auditing.

indirect precedent A cell that is any part of the entire ancestral line of the formula in the active cell; used in auditing.

internal reference A reference to another cell on the same worksheet; used in formulas.

keyboard shortcut A combination of keypresses you can use to avoid using the mouse. For example, Ctrl+V is the keyboard shortcut for pasting an object into your spreadsheet.

label Text. Not numbers. Okay, maybe numbers and text together. The word **label** also refers to the heading at the top of a column, when you're working with databases.

legend box The box on a map or chart that describes the graphic symbols being used.

link The process that connects one or more workbooks with shared data. Linking is better than copying because when you change the source cells in one document, Excel automatically updates them in the second document.

list The information in a database, arranged in columns with a label at the top of each column. Pivot tables use database lists as the source for their data.

macro A series of keystrokes Excel records so that you can replay them at will.

Main Menu bar The second line from the top of your Excel screen. It displays the names of menus, which contain groups of related commands. When you click on a word on the menu bar, a pull-down menu appears.

Maximize button The second button in the upper right corner of your screen. It toggles between full-screen and window view.

Minimize button The button in the upper right corner that looks like an underscore character. It reduces the program to a button on the Windows taskbar at the bottom of your screen.

Name Box The box at the left end of the Formula bar where you name your ranges.

object Any graphic you place in your worksheet. This can be a drawing, an imported picture, a map, or a chart.

operator Any of the mathematical symbols that tell a formula what to do. The operators are + (add), – (subtract), / (divide), * (multiply), % (percents), ^ (exponents), and the equivalencies: = (equal), <> (not equal), > (greater than), and < (less than).

page field A separate worksheet page that contains some fields of a pivot table's data. You can direct the pivot table to break certain fields out onto page fields so that they can be displayed one at a time.

pivot table A table you create to show interactive relationships between many kinds of things. A pivot table enables you to drag columns and rows back and forth.

pivot table control The buttons you use to click and drag columns or rows to other locations. Excel creates these buttons from the row and column labels in your data.

pivot table data All the summarized data out in the middle of the table.

pointer The on-screen mouse indicator. It changes shape according to your task and the phase of the moon. Normally, though, it's shaped like an arrow.

precedent The first ancestral line of a formula. Used in auditing.

pull-down menu A menu that drops down when you select a word on the Main Menu.

range A cell or a block of cells identified by either a name or an address.

range name The English-language name that identifies a particular range. (French and Spanish names work, too, but no Chinese names unless you know how to Romanize them, like this: Hau Bu Hau?)

record In a typical Excel list, each row of the list is a new record.

reference The name or address of a cell or a range.

relative reference A reference that doesn't change when you move or copy it. By default, any reference that you copy is a relative reference.

result The answer that Excel calculates when you finish entering a formula.

Select All button The unlabeled square in the upper left corner of your work area (at the intersection of the row and column headers).

selection handles The small black boxes that appear on the periphery of the frame when you select an object. Click between the selection handles to move or copy an object.

scenario A set of suppositions you make about your data

scroll bars The bars at the right side and bottom of your worksheet with which you move around the worksheet.

shortcut key A combination of keyboard keys you can use if you dislike using the mouse or menus.

shortcut menu A quick menu that appears when you right-click on an object.

sizing handles Same thing as a selection handle. Use one to change the size of an object or frame.

source data Each pivot table is created from an existing database list or from a whole bunch of lists. These lists are the source data for the pivot table.

spreadsheet A collection of cells arranged in columns and rows.

summary functions The calculations (summarized, calculated, subtotaled, and grand-totaled) that Excel uses to create a pivot table

syntax The rules about where to put the parentheses, commas, asterisks, and operators in an Excel formula.

taskbar A bar at the bottom of the Windows 95 screen that's visible in all applications. It contains the Start button, buttons that show the other applications you have open, and the current time.

template A blank workbook that you can use as the basis for a useful document for a specific application.

template workbook An input form you design.

Title bar The bar across the top of every page that tells you the name of your application.

toolbars Ribbons of buttons and controls that you can use to circumvent menus, commands, and certain dialog boxes.

value Numbers. Not text.

vertex The small square boxes that appear on a free-form object when it's ready for reshaping.

wizard One of several features in Excel that automates a process, such as creating a chart or a map.

workbook Multiple worksheets combined in a single file.

worksheet A spreadsheet full of cells—blank or otherwise.

Index

Symbols

B

D

E

L

N

O

P-Q

R

S

T

U

V